Comparing Environmental Policies in 16 Countries

Comparing Environmental Policies in 16 Countries

David Howard Davis

CRC Press
Taylor & Francis Group
Boca Raton   London   New York

CRC Press is an imprint of the
Taylor & Francis Group, an **informa** business

CRC Press
Taylor & Francis Group
6000 Broken Sound Parkway NW, Suite 300
Boca Raton, FL 33487-2742

© 2014 by Taylor & Francis Group, LLC
CRC Press is an imprint of Taylor & Francis Group, an Informa business

No claim to original U.S. Government works

Printed on acid-free paper
Version Date: 20131023

International Standard Book Number-13: 978-1-4822-1458-1 (Hardback)

Visit the Taylor & Francis Web site at
http://www.taylorandfrancis.com

and the CRC Press Web site at
http://www.crcpress.com

Dedicated to

David S. Wilson, PhD

Contents

Preface

Teaching at Nanjing University in China as a Fulbright professor shaped this book into its final form. I spent the spring semester of 2009 there at the School of the Environment. My manuscript was half done, and I used those chapters as a textbook. At the time I had not written a chapter on China because I was waiting to learn about it firsthand.

Having published *American Environmental Politics* in 1998 and *Ignoring the Apocalypse* in 2007, the next step for me seemed to be to look at other countries. I was aware, of course, that many countries had policies similar to the American ones. I was interested in their common features and their differences. Furthermore, I was interested in how the United States learned from others, and how the United States sent its ideas abroad. Soon I learned that the interchange has been extensive. All around the globe, democratic countries had had an "Environmental Decade" in the 1970s, and had emulated one another. They had copied laws on water pollution control, sometimes word for word, and had copied techniques like popular mass demonstrations. This was less true for the Communist world, yet even there, the ideas spread, if not as fast.

The worldwide diffusion of ideas could be fast. After Rachel Carson published *Silent Spring* in 1962, her book was soon translated into German and other languages. A decade before that books and films by Jacques Cousteau like *Eighteen Meters Deep* and *Silent World* had won an international audience. Back in the 19th century, the idea of a national park like Yellowstone had spread to Canada and Australia. The technique of mass public demonstrations, with roots in India for its independence movement and in the United States for its civil rights movement, was adapted against nuclear power plants in Denmark in 1962. Indeed, the roots are even deeper in that Gandhi and the Indian leaders were inspired by the nonviolent techniques advocated by 19th-century American environmentalist Henry David Thoreau. Interest groups like the Sierra Club and Greenpeace, originating in the United States and Canada, respectively, first grew in their home countries and then spread internationally. Some groups like World Wildlife Fund (WWF) were international from their inception, founded in Switzerland to protect tigers and lions in India and Africa.

The purpose of comparing policies in different countries is both practical and theoretical. Learning about successes and failures can guide best practices. Comparing various countries can enlighten knowledge of political science. All industrial countries face similar pollution problems and can learn from one another. Laws may be copied word for word, as with the national parks in Canada and Australia or with water quality regulations. From the theoretical perspective, examining how different countries address environmental issues can help us understand their politics and government.

The chapters follow five themes: citizen participation, interest groups, political parties, governmental structure, and the diplomatic agenda. Voting is the standard form of participation in a democracy, but participation can also be less conventional. Mass demonstrations are a common technique, especially against nuclear plants and weapons. Individuals can literally be "tree huggers," like the Chipko protest pioneered in India. Environmentalists have organized interest groups, many now very large. Friends of the Earth has over two million members, and Greenpeace has nearly three million members. Of course, these began with only a few people and grew. Others remain small. Alternatively called nonstate actors, these groups often play important roles. A few countries like Germany have successful green political parties, while in other countries regular parties, such as the Socialists or the Democrats, have adopted environmental platforms. Political scientists often posit that government structure makes a difference, so they examine parliamentary versus presidential systems or federations versus unitary governments. Finally, the diplomatic agenda often pushes environmental policies. Countries that were not paying much attention to the issue suddenly find they have risen to the top due to a big international conference. When in 1972 Sweden convened the first Earth Summit, all of Europe paid attention. The Swedes accused the British and the Dutch of emitting acid falling on them as rain, which led to the Long-Range Transboundary Air Pollution Treaty. Regarding local air pollution, the European Community recognized that automobile emission standards needed to be uniform for purposes of commerce. When the Brazilians hosted the 1992 Earth Summit, local interest groups were energized to address deforestation in the Amazon Basin and air pollution in the cities.

Each chapter concludes with some highlights of what that country received from others, such as the popularity of Rachel Carson's book or Cousteau's films. Then they suggest a few items that that country gave to other countries, such as the idea of the national park or the model of a green political party. One must bear in mind that the global movement dating from the 1970s was not the first time such concepts had spread internationally. In the 18th century, landscape gardening was influenced by the introduction of the Chinese garden to England, which then spread to Germany and France. Starting about 1790, the Romantic Movement promoted love of nature in poetry, song, and painting, extending from Russia to the United States.

I have been to every one of the sixteen countries covered in this book. In some I have interviewed government officials and nonprofit leaders, while in others I have traveled as a tourist to see the parks, wildlife, and natural wonders. While actually visiting a country is not strictly necessary for scholarly analysis, I hope it gives a firsthand flavor. Moreover, it has given me an excuse to see spectacular parks and fascinating cities.

Acknowledgments

Many colleagues have helped in writing this book: Ralph Menning, Johan Gottgens, Chris Weisfelder, Timothy G. Fisher, S. Rina Majumdar, Neusa Hidalgo-Monroy McWilliams, Richard F. Weisfelder, Michael Jakobson, Richard A. Arnold, Gerald McBeath, George Jan, Bi Jun, Liu Beibei, Liu Heng, Lisa Li, and Kelsey Emory.

1

Introduction

Since 1970 virtually every country in the world has grown concerned about the natural environment. From the United States to China and from Sweden to Kenya, citizens and governments have acted to protect air, water, and land. Of nearly 200 independent nations, only a few like North Korea do not at least claim to have programs. Indeed, among democracies, environmental programs are extensive. Moreover they are quite similar, with laws and agencies that are nearly interchangeable (which is not to say they are equally effective). The reasons for similar programs range from parallel histories to direct borrowing. Governments copy laws and protest groups copy demonstrations in other countries. Interest groups imitate one another across national borders, and those such as Greenpeace and Friends of the Earth are worldwide with branches in many countries.

The purpose of comparing policies in different countries is both practical and theoretical. Learning about successes and failures can guide best practices. Comparing how various countries decide can enlighten political science. All industrial countries face similar environmental problems and have often addressed them in similar ways. For example, clean water laws in the United States and Europe are parallel, and indeed often are copied word for word. An older example is the national park movement. The first was Yellowstone National Park in the United States in 1872, followed by Australia and Canada soon after. Later Britain and France established large national parks in the Lake District and the Pyrénées.

Environmental ideas, concepts, and solutions diffuse from one country to another. In 1962 Rachel Carson published *Silent Spring* about the dangers of pesticides, which gained immediate attention in the United States. It also gained popular attention in Europe. Within months, the League for Bird Protection in Germany was distributing thousands of free copies of its guides. The club leaders decided this was the best thing they could do to protect the local birds. Soon it was read everywhere. The biggest example of worldwide diffusion was the Environmental Decade of the 1970s. This phenomenon was simultaneous in North America, Western Europe, and other democracies. It even affected China, albeit 10 years later. Another case was the concern with global warming, which spread rapidly. United Nations scientists reached a consensus in 1985, and only three years later scientists and government officials met in Toronto to organize action. In 1992 nearly 200 countries assembled in Rio de Janeiro to sign a framework treaty, and in another 5 years they approved the Kyoto Protocol to limit greenhouse gases. However, speedy action did not guarantee success, and cooperation stalled.

Although the environmental movement first swept the Western industrial democracies, it soon diffused to developing countries and to Communist ones. Nations like India and Brazil joined the effort. They recognized that while they may have been less industrialized, they were beginning to suffer polluted air and water from the factories they did have. Moreover, such countries often had priceless natural treasures in their remote mountains and river basins that deserved preservation as parks. Some developing countries like Kenya and Costa Rica were natural Edens with mountains, seacoasts, spectacular big game, and exotic birds.

Communist countries like the Soviet Union and the People's Republic of China felt the impact of the environmental movement differently. Because the major tenet of Marxism is materialism, protecting against pollution is contrary to its ideology. The goal was production of steel, concrete, and heavy machinery. Nevertheless, by the 1970s some knowledge of the environmental movement in the West filtered into the USSR and Eastern Europe. People opposed to the government adopted these aspects as a safe form of protest. Citizens spoke out in favor of protecting a pristine lake from pollution, which seemed politically innocent. Others joined the Socio-Ecological Union. In Czechoslovakia young people joined the Brontosaurus Club to enjoy hiking and camping. China was the last country for the environmental movement to penetrate, but now it has a few groups. In the Communist countries, people joined nature groups because it was a safe outlet. Their true opposition was often to lack of civil rights or to religious suppression.

A paradox in environmental policy is that the problems are often global, but the solutions must come from within individual countries. Global warming is an example. As more greenhouse gases are pumped into the atmosphere, the entire world is heating up from the North Pole to the

South Pole and everywhere in between. It cannot be reduced for one country without reducing it for all. China, which produces 24 percent of the gases, declines to cooperate, hence gets a free ride. Consequently, other industrial countries like the United States and Canada do not participate, either. Even Britain, France, and Germany, which had pledged to cooperate and had ratified the Kyoto Protocol, have backed away. Since there is no world government at present, global warming cannot be ended.

Other problems are not quite global, but are international, in that pollution from one country blows or flows into another. Acid rain from the United States falls on Canada, and acid rain from Britain falls on Sweden. The North Americans have signed the Air Quality Agreement and the Europeans have signed the Convention on Long-Range Transboundary Air Pollution. Pollution in the Rhine River flows from Switzerland to Germany and France, and to the Netherlands. The Rhine River Central Commission is the oldest in the world, dating back to 1816.

Finally, many environmental problems, perhaps most, are confined within the boundaries of a single nation, especially if it is a big one. Water pollution is found in the Mississippi River, the Ganges River, and the Loire River. Dirty air afflicts Los Angeles, London, and Paris. The worst air is found in Beijing, Shanghai, and New Delhi. These problems are not international but are nearly identical in many big rivers and big cities. Learning how one city reduces pollution can demonstrate useful techniques to others.

In the absence of world government, environmental policy is dealt with by individual nations. Political scientists approach the topic by examining the form of government, such as a parliamentary as opposed to a presidential system, or the role of courts, or the number and features of political parties. They examine whether a nation is unitary or federated with autonomous provinces or states. They look at the number and role of interest groups like the Sierra Club, Friends of the Earth, or WWF. They may examine the role of the free market as opposed to a command market such as communism or socialism. But political scientists are less likely to study strictly economic factors such as per capita income. Certainly, it is a truism that more prosperous nations devote more efforts to cleaning up the air and water, but political scientists tend to pay less attention to this.

The environmental movement is, of course, a product of its history. Prior to the Industrial Revolution of the 19th century, pollution was slight, but factories and coal mines changed that. Into the 20th century, governments did little. Cities built water mains for drinking and sewers to carry waste to a nearby river. A few cities enacted smoke ordinances. With the Great Depression of the 1930s in America and in Europe, unemployed people longed for the good old days when factories belched smoke into the air. Then came World War II that was so horrible that environmental protection was not possible during the fighting.

After the devastation of the war, Europe spent the next two or three decades rebuilding its industry, and inevitably this recovery increased air and water pollution. On December 4–8, 1952, 4000 people died in London from a "killer smog." The smog was so thick that drivers of autos and buses could not see, and the only transport was the Underground train system. Victims succumbed to heart attacks, asphyxiation, and asthma. The invention of the atomic bomb unleashed the dangers of radiation. When the first atomic bomb was dropped on Hiroshima in 1945, the scientists were surprised that 70,000 died of radiation sickness, equally as many as died from the blast itself. The development of civilian nuclear reactors to generate electricity brought its own risks. In 1957 the Windscale plant in England exploded, sending clouds of radioactive gases into the atmosphere, thus causing people downwind to suffer from cancer in the following years. World War II also sparked the Chemical Revolution with scientists inventing thousands of new compounds, many of them dangerous. All over the world, particularly in the tropics, public health workers sprayed DDT to kill the mosquitoes that transmitted malaria. Unfortunately, the insecticide also killed birds, especially eagles. An ironic consequence of spraying DDT to control malaria, and other improvements in human health, was a population explosion. In turn this led to demand for agricultural land and strain on water and air. In all countries, gasoline refineries added tetraethyl lead to their product, unaware that it caused brain damage.

The picture was not entirely negative, however. Scientific understanding of the dangers of pollution grew. With economic prosperity, people had the money and leisure time to visit parks and enjoy nature. With more education, they could better understand the science and geography of the environment. Jacques Cousteau, the inventor of the aqualung, sold more than five million copies of his book *The Silent World*, about life undersea. He soon produced a film that won an Academy Award. From July 1957 to December 1958 scientists from 67 nations cooperated in the International Geophysical Year to study the polar regions, the oceans, and the atmosphere.

Five Themes: From 1970 on virtually all democracies addressed environmental problems by passing laws and establishing agencies to implement them. In doing so they displayed many similarities. Much of the similarity was due to common challenges and government structures. For example, virtually all found the number of automobiles increasing, hence more air pollution, and virtually all had government bureaucracies with expertise in engineering and chemistry. Other times, they self-consciously copied each other. For example, in 1971 the Japanese prime minister visited Washington where he was quite impressed with the popular approval President Nixon was enjoying by establishing the Environmental Protection Agency, so he established the Japanese Environmental Agency. In all countries the citizens expected government to solve problems. If pollution was a problem, the answer was governmental: pass a law regulating it, and create an agency to enforce the law. It was still a command and control mentality, and the idea that market techniques could be enlisted was not accepted in that era.

Participation: Widespread citizen participation has been a hallmark of the environmental movement. In 1961 thousands of Scots demonstrated against the presence of nuclear submarines in Holy Loch—one of the first citizen protests. In turn, that inspired 30,000 Danes to march in Copenhagen in 1962 to protest nuclear weapons and power plants. In the United States, the very first Earth Day in 1970 brought out 20 million citizens from coast to coast. Popular demonstrations have an even longer genesis. The American civil rights movement used the technique of mass marches, and in turn these were inspired by the movement for Indian independence during the 1930s and 1940s. Still farther back, the Indian leaders found inspiration in the nonviolent demonstration of Henry David Thoreau, often credited as an early environmentalist.

Political scientists maintain that citizen protest groups operate according to a set repertoire. Environmental groups use marches, rallies, street theater, picketing, boycotts, petitions, and letters. They trace modern protests back to the late 18th century when the expansion of newspapers coincided with the emergence of associations outside the control of the government. By the late 20th century, protest movements could exchange information quickly and operate across national boundaries. An example was the collapse of communism in Eastern Europe in 1989 where in the Baltic republics citizens formed a human chain, and in Poland they organized "round tables," thereby copying tactics of the Western European peace movement a few years earlier. Second, television, fax machines, and photocopiers sped up communication. Now e-mail, the Internet, and Twitter speed contact. And third, greater movement of people across boundaries has accelerated information and techniques. Airplanes speeded up decolonization of

Africa and Asia. More convenient travel in Western Europe hastened the spread of the New Left after 1968, environmental movement in the 1970s, and the anti-nuclear movement in the 1980s.

Political scientists often classify participation as conventional or non-conventional. Voting is the prime instance of conventional means; others are writing to a legislator, writing to a newspaper, attending a public meeting, speaking at a hearing, or signing a petition. Nonconventional means are taking part in a demonstration, boycotting a product, joining a strike, or illegal activities like occupying a building, sabotaging a sawmill, or planting a bomb. Voting turnout varies among the democracies. Australians are highest with a 95% rate, the Europeans range from 86% percent and up, and Americans are notoriously low with 54%.

Nonconventional participation like demonstrations has long been a feature of the environmental movement. In Eastern Europe during the last decade of Communism, citizens found the government would tolerate public marches and demonstrations for environmental protection (but not against the government in general), so the movement gained adherents who really wanted an outlet to protest in general. On the individual level, environmentalists have held sit-ins, such as a woman in California who sat in a tree for 738 days. Tree sitting originated in New Zealand in 1978 and remains popular there and in Australia. The radical group Earth First! engaged in sabotage, or as its members called it, ecotage. They hammered spikes into trees cut for delivery to a sawmill. At the mill, the saw would hit the spike, breaking the blade and perhaps injuring a worker. The group planted explosives on electric transmission towers in remote forests, toppling them to the ground. In 1979 the crew of the Canadian ship *Sea Shepherd* scuttled an illegal whaling trawler in a harbor in Portugal.

Interest groups have been another hallmark of the environmental movement. Alternatively called non-state actors, they have grown tremendously. In the United States the Sierra Club went from 70,000 members to a million members in two decades. Since its founding in 1969, Friends of the Earth has spread to affiliates in 70 countries with two million members. Since 1971, when a few opponents of nuclear bomb testing sailed a small boat from British Columbia to Amchitka Island in Alaska, Greenpeace has grown to have affiliates in 40 countries, with a total of nearly three million members.

Typically, groups favoring the environment originate from protest movements. First comes the disturbance, which causes citizens to band together to air their grievances and seek redress. Assuming the group is successful, it organizes a structure, at first informal, but increasingly formal. Industry forms groups, also. These groups are not inherently antienvironmental. They just do not want to increase their costs by cleaning up the air or protecting the land. Often they already exist for other reasons, such as lobbying or representation before regulatory agencies. For example, the Edison Electric Institute in the United States was founded in 1933 to coordinate opposition to New Deal financial policies unfriendly to private companies. Alternatively, the rise of environmental interest groups in the 1970s caused business groups to organize or reorganize to counter them. Some corporations like the Dow Chemical Company or Exxon are so large and have so many resources that they are like interest groups all by themselves.

Most political scientists consider interest groups to be a bulwark of democracy. They believe that groups are inevitable because people always want certain things for themselves, and in opposition to other people. Therefore, they join together to promote their interests. These may be selfish like more money or privileges, or altruistic such as protection of a remote tropical park. A group begins with a disturbance, such as a proposal to build a toxic waste dump. Local citizens organize in opposition. Their response is "perhaps we need a dump, but Not in My Back Yard" (NIMBY). Leadership is important, with policy entrepreneurs mobilizing citizens, reciting their grievances, and demanding a return to the status quo. The groups often take on a life of their own. They become permanent, they gather resources, and they try to influence government and other groups. Resources are money, leadership, expertise, and a large membership. Their leaders gain permanent positions, a salary, and prestige, and in turn reward their followers with policy victories like saving a forest from destruction, or more mundanely by publishing a magazine. Interest groups are permanent, not temporary, and do not disappear once the initial disturbance is resolved. They seek new battles to fight, and form new alliances with other groups. They insert themselves into the public debate. A citizen's membership in a group is a form of participation. Although interest groups are ubiquitous in democracies, they are rudimentary in much of the Third World. Traditionally, they did not exist in Communist countries because the Communist Party claimed a monopoly on representing all interests.

Business groups typically find it easier to generate resources like money, expertise, and contacts. The conflict between environmental and business interest groups is nearly universal. In the United States, the American Chemistry Council represents more than two hundred corporations that want to minimize the expense of cleaning up. The industry employs more than a million people, and spends $400 billion a year. The Confederation of British Industry represents thousands of corporations, and the Australian Chamber of Commerce and Industry represents 350,000 businesses.

Environmental and business interest groups are not mirror images of each other. The former are more ideological, seeing environmental problems as part of the general lack of response by government and political parties. The latter has narrower goals, such as not having expenses increased due to scrubbers on smokestacks. The goals of environmental groups may be broad, such as interjecting their opinions on international treaties like the North American Free Trade Agreement, to take a US example. In this case the objective was to avoid having Mexico increase total air and water pollution in the world. Pollution was being exported to Mexico. The consequence has been more conflict in making policy.

Political Parties: In most democracies environmental interests are represented by comprehensive political parties such as the Democrats in the United States or Labour in Britain. In a few countries green parties have emerged and become quite influential. For example, the German Green Party is strong, with 55 seats in parliament and partnership with the ruling coalition from 1998 to 2005. As part of a deal with the Socialists, the Greens controlled three cabinet ministries: foreign affairs, the environment, and food and consumer affairs. The party moved the government toward more environmental protection and mandated an end to civilian nuclear power. It vigorously supported the Kyoto Protocol. In Belgium and Denmark, green parties have also been effective. In France the two different green parties have won many seats in parliament but more recently hold only four seats. In the United Kingdom, the green party has never won a seat in the national Parliament, although it has won local offices. In the European Parliament, the Green Group (i.e., party) won 59 seats, making it one of the middle-sized groups. The United States found its own tiny Green Party important in the 2000 presidential election, when Ralph Nader got the nomination and polled 3% nationwide. In two states, Florida and New Hampshire, his vote was greater than the margin of victory, causing many observers to say the Green Party vote gave the election to George W. Bush rather than to Al Gore.

A political party differs from an interest group in that its goal is to elect its people to office, whereas interest groups want to promote their interests. A party will adopt policies in its platform in order to attract votes, whereas an interest group does not seek votes. It wants to influence the government. Political scientists consider parties (along with interest groups) to be a bulwark of democracy. Parties are the means for organizing legislatures and are the means for electing prime ministers and presidents. Citizens participate in parties as members, campaign volunteers, financial donors, and candidates. This is considered conventional. In those countries without a viable green party, those goals are represented via other parties. In the United States, the Democratic Party is favorable and the Republican Party is not. Denmark has been divided among many parties, but from 1982 to 1993, several of them found they could cooperate on the subject of environmental protection, teamwork that was labeled the "Green Majority," even though it was not official. Around the world, business interests often ally more with one party than the other. In the United States, they ally with the Republicans, in Britain with the Conservatives, and in Germany with the Christian Democrats.

Outside the democracies, one-party rule is standard. From 1917 to 1990, in the Soviet Union the Communist Party was the only one permitted. In Eastern Europe, the Communists were the sole party from about 1946 to 1989. In China, it still is virtually the only party. A central tenet of Communism is the control of the means of production, that is, the factories and mines. Controlling pollution went against the goal of maximizing production. On the other hand, these governments during the 1970s and 1980s granted a small degree of toleration for those opposed to pollution. For example, during the 1980s a few party members in Siberia voiced objections to the pollution of Lake Baikal by a cellulose cord factory, and were not punished. More dramatically, the 1986 explosion of the nuclear plant at Chernobyl was so big that it could not be hidden. The new head of the Communist Party, Mikhail Gorbachev, used the accident to force reforms on the old timers in the party. Beside the Communist block, one-party governments have been found, at least in the past, in many Third World countries like Kenya and Egypt.

Structure: Political scientists comparing countries routinely analyze the importance of structures like federalism, or parliament, or the chief executive, yet these concepts do little to explain environmental policy. How governments are constituted makes little difference. One of the favorite aspects is whether the country has a federal or unitary structure. Federalism means a system such as the United States, Germany, Canada, India and many others whereby the national government is separate from the state or provincial government. The contrast is with unitary systems like France and Britain where the national government can directly control regions. Federalism has two levels of government over a single geographical area. A federal system inherently has conflicts between the two levels. Moreover, the relationship between the two levels evolves over the years, and may be different in the environmental arena than in others such as education or welfare. For example, in the United States, a major debate leading up to the Clean Air Act of 1970 and the Clean Water Act of 1972 was the proper division between Washington and the 50 states. The resolution was a hybrid, whereby the national level set detailed standards and program, which were implemented by the states, which received money for doing so. In contrast in the federal systems of Canada and Australia, more authority resides at the provincial–state level.

The alternative to a federal government is a unitary one. France is the best example. Its national government in Paris legislates and administers laws and programs directly. For example, the national government directly appoints the prefects (heads) of the departments (provinces); they are not elected governors as in the United States or premiers as in Canada or Australia. Around the world almost half of the people live in federations as opposed to unitary states. The biggest is India with more than a billion people. Russia, Brazil, and Mexico are also federations. Examples of unitary governments are Japan, Denmark, and Italy. Many are small, but China is in this category.

A federal versus a unitary structure is not the same as decentralization versus centralization. Even a unitary government like France needs to have geographic divisions. Indeed, any government larger than, say, a few hundred square miles, needs to have branch offices. The difference lies in the legal authority of the national government. While the general rule is that a country is either unitary or a federation, this dichotomy is not 100% exact. Some like Sweden do not describe themselves as federal but give a lot of autonomy to their counties. While many countries like Germany and Brazil have the word "federal" in their official names, none have the word "unitary." Moreover, there is a slight trend toward becoming more federal. Belgium used to be unitary but now is federal. In the late 1990s, the United Kingdom decided to become a bit less united by giving limited rights to Scotland and Wales. A federal structure is an inherent source of conflict. Of course, this does not mean a unitary government will have no conflict between the center and the periphery. The extent of cultural and social diversity has the potential for conflict, but in practice, environmentalists tend to be quite skilled in bridging these gaps. Although this is a major variable in many comparative studies, its impact on the environment is slight.

Political scientists like to analyze the roles of the chief executive and legislature. A presidential system such as in the United States, France, Brazil, Mexico, and Russia authorizes more power to that branch. In contrast, parliamentary systems like Britain, Canada, and Australia have the prime minister selected from the party holding the majority of seats in the parliament. For Britain and its former colonies, this is referred to as the Westminster system. Most other European countries have the parliamentary system, such as Germany, the Netherlands, Denmark, and Sweden. It is the system in Australia and India as well. In terms of environmental issues, the presidential versus the parliamentary system does not make much difference. Both chief executives and prime ministers tend to have other issues that preoccupy them such as war and peace or the economy. Their attention to the environment is sporadic and general.

The bureaucracy that implements environmental laws is crucial. Examples are the US Environmental Protection Agency; the British Department for Environment, Food and Rural Affairs; and the German Environmental Ministry. Looking around the world, these agencies tend to have similar names and histories. Most were established in the Environmental Decade of the 1970s, often directly copying agencies in other countries. Besides their function of implementing new legislation, they fulfilled a symbolic function. Their creation demonstrated to voters that the politicians were doing something. Once in existence, they attacked the problems with the techniques of science and administration. They analyzed the problems, devised solutions, started programs, and promulgated regulations. They were specialized, technical, and autonomous. While these offer important skills, bureaucrats sometimes overconform, block new approaches, and move slowly.

In all countries, different agencies will have responsibility for different areas, and they may conflict. For example, in the United States, the Office of Surface Mining has jurisdiction over reclamation of coal mines, but EPA is to set the standards for the water discharged from the mines. In Australia, the Department of Agriculture, Fisheries and Forestry shares responsibility for water quality with the Department of the Environment.

The final government structure to consider is the court system. In the United States, courts have been very influential. They have often intervened directly in the inner workings of agencies and carved out new and unexpected rights. For example, in 1960, the US Supreme Court ruled that an obscure provision of an 1899 law required all polluters of waterways needed a permit to discharge their effluent. This interpretation came as a great surprise to industry and the government. To take another example, in 1972, a district court ruled that a few words listed as a vague goal in the Clean Air Act required that EPA rewrite its regulations to prevent significant deterioration. In Canada, a court overturned the permit from the national government on the export of water from Lake Superior. In Australia, the high court overturned settled law on Aborigine ownership of the land in the *Mabo* case. Countries that do not trace their legal system back to England find the courts much less likely to intervene.

The *diplomatic agenda* is a special case of policy diffusion, and an important one for the environment. The nations of the world more and more relied on cooperation, especially through the United Nations. The pattern of a large international conference to address a problem has become standard. Specialized UN agencies like the World Health Organization, the World Meteorological Organization, and UNESCO disseminated scientific information. In 1972, the United Nations established its environmental program.

International conferences have played an important role in spreading alarms about environmental dangers and in demonstrating solutions. In June 1972, diplomats, scientists, and experts from 113 nations convened in Stockholm for the world's first environmental summit, a meeting that marked the emergence of the movement internationally. This paralleled the movements within the United States, Europe, and other industrial countries. Since the Environmental Decade of the 1970s, concerns in one country have influenced other countries, and the global aspects have been apparent. The world has now held three additional Earth Summits in 1992, 2002, and 2012, and international conferences meet every year on problems like climate change, oceans, biodiversity, and so forth. These conferences do not always result in success, however. For example, the 1997 conference on climate change in Kyoto seemed to agree on a solution, but by the 2009 annual conference of the parties in Copenhagen, it is was obvious that the Kyoto Protocol was dead.

Big conferences are a common method of transferring policies. Some countries lag behind others in their environmental concerns, thus they may first become aware of an issue because they are invited to attend a conference to sign a treaty. For example, the Japanese people and politicians were not particularly aware of the problem of global warming until they were asked to host the 1997 conference in Kyoto. Suddenly, the government leaders had to determine their negotiating position, which in its first iteration was quite proindustry. Yet as hosts, they recognized their obligation not to oppose the draft protocol with reductions in greenhouse gas emissions. In the week preceding the opening, the Japanese delegates met with the Americans and some Europeans in Tokyo to hammer out their differences. Because of their obligations to their guests who were already arriving, the Japanese were forced to take a bargaining position less favorable to industry than would have been the case if the conference were convened elsewhere. Five years later a similar situation occurred for India. Because the meeting was scheduled for New Delhi, the government had to prepare its diplomats and enhance its scientific expertise. The average Indian citizen had no opinion on the topic.

This book starts with the United States under the rationale that it has a strong environmental program and that more readers are familiar with it than any other country. Next come the leaders in Europe, starting with Germany, with briefer discussions of the Netherlands, Denmark, and Sweden. Chapter 4 covers Britain, France, and the European Union. Canada and Australia share many features with Britain as well as with the United States. All are industrial democracies. India and Brazil are both big developing countries, with vibrant democracies. They were described as the Third World by classification with the industrial First World comprising Western Europe and North America; the Second World, Communist Russia, Eastern Europe, and China; and the rest as the Third World. Kenya and Costa Rica are also developing countries but are small compared to India and Brazil. Many consider them to be environmental paradises, in which the governments have protected the land, plants, and animals in parks. In Russia, the Communist Party took power in 1917, and its ideology was that of materialism, which emphasized heavy industry and deemphasized environmental protection. Unlike Western Europe, it was not democratic. Finally, China is a developing country where the Communist Party won control in 1949 and imposed a regime even harsher than that of the Soviet Union. Environmental damage was great. However, in recent years, its government has introduced some environmental protections.

Analysis addresses the five themes of participation, interest groups, parties, structure, and diplomatic agenda but in a flexible fashion so not every theme is addressed for every country. Major historic commonalities like the Environmental Decade of the 1970s are covered for all countries, but less important threads are woven less systematically. For example, a precursor to environmentalism by 220 years was the fad for the Chinese garden. Early European travelers to China in 1685 and again in 1738 were impressed with its naturalistic style, and soon sent drawings and diagrams to England. English gardeners planted in this fashion, and the idea spread to Germany, France, and the Thirteen Colonies. A more important precursor was the Romantic Movement starting about 1790, whereby Europeans fell in love with nature, celebrating it in song and in poem.

2

The United States

Christopher Columbus's discovery of the New World revolutionized the Old World's understanding of nature, science, and civilization. Within 6 years of the first Spanish landing in the Caribbean, the English had dispatched Captain John Cabot to explore the land that is now the United States. Soon Ponce de León, Hernando de Soto, and Francisco Coronado were exploring on behalf of Spain, and Giovanni da Verrazano was sailing from North Carolina to Maine on behalf of France. They found a land rich with forests, savannas, rivers, and mountains. They also found native peoples (mistakenly labeled Indians) who lived with nature in a way the Europeans had not done for more than a thousand years. Some believed they had found paradise. Columbus believed that he had located the Garden of Eden.

As exploration gave way to settlement over the next century, the next wave of explorers extolled the beauty and resources of the country. Captain John Smith rhapsodized over the Chesapeake Bay with its rivers teeming with fish and oysters, and shores lined with fertile land suitable for farming. Farther north, the early settlers in New England extolled the riches of the land. Furthermore, they believed that its isolation from the corruption of old England would make it ideal for establishing a pure Christian community. The Pilgrim John Winthrop wrote that "God has provided this place as a refuge . . . ," and recalled the Book of Genesis, saying "the whole earth is the Lord's garden."[1]

Yet while the early explorers and settlers valued American nature, most had practical aims, too. Many sought gold and silver. They planted colonies with the aim of growing crops like tobacco for export to Europe and engaging in trade with the Indians. Even the New England Puritans praised their land for the abundance of its timber, the wealth of its furs, and the bounty of its fisheries. Yet while early American settlers exalted their natural setting, they also found it oppressive and dangerous. William Bradford wrote that when the Pilgrims looked about, "what could they see but a hideous and desolate wilderness, full of wild beasts and wild men?"[2]

As settlement moved inland from the Atlantic, filling the Tidewater and the Piedmont Plateau, the settlers found land almost perfectly suited to agriculture. Rainfall was ideal. Within a few years a newly arrived farmer could chop down the forest for fields for crops and pasture. The fertility of the soil led to prosperity. The early farmers were not only productive, they were reproductive. Their birthrate far exceeded that of England and Europe. Many families had 10 and 12 children, most of whom survived to adulthood, unlike the situation back across the Atlantic. In turn the children could move to the frontier and start their own prosperous farms. Many regions doubled their populations within 20 years. The virgin forest gave way to corn and cattle. Yet, in fact, some of the forests were not quite virgin. The Indians had systematically burned them to improve hunting and increase fertility for their own occasional crops.

In 1763 the British government had tried to stop the westward expansion at the crest of the Allegheny Mountains in order to prevent clashes with the Indians. The restriction incensed the Americans and was one of the causes of the Revolution. After the Revolution, settlers flowed across the mountains to Kentucky, Tennessee, and Ohio. This land proved even better for agriculture, and soon the forests were destroyed.

In 1790 the infant United States conducted the first national census in the world. It was required by the new Constitution in order to apportion seats in the House of Representatives. The total was nearly four million, about half the size of England, and an eighth the size of France. The growth came from natural increase due to large families and a high survival rate. The number of immigrants into the country in the colonial period was actually quite small. At home the War of 1812 discouraged immigration, and in Europe the destruction and need to conscript soldiers during the Napoleonic Wars limited emigrants, but by 1850, the population was 20 million, and the frontier reached to the Great Plains.

Although 18th-century Americans were not much concerned about nature, they were interested in science. Benjamin Franklin experimented with electricity, wrote on population statistics, and founded the Philosophical Society. While living in London and Paris as a diplomat, he met the leading scientists of the day. After the 1783 volcanic explosion at Laki in Iceland, he correctly concluded that its emissions were the cause of atmospheric haze and colorful sunsets, and even suggested that the introduction of large quantities of volcanic particles into the Earth's upper atmosphere could cause a reduction in surface temperature, because the particles would lessen the amount of solar energy reaching the Earth's surface.

Thomas Jefferson was an avid scientific experimenter. Monticello, his home near Charlottesville, Virginia, featured a museum displaying many minerals, fossils, bones, and antlers. He wrote to refute a theory proposed by the French scientist Georges-Louis de Buffon who argued that the New World's life-forms—plant, animal, and human—were smaller and inferior to those of the Old, because the New World itself was inferior. America was, according to Buffon, "a land best suited for insects, reptiles, and feeble men." Jefferson rebutted this point by point with charts of the sizes and weights of American animals. His chief evidence was the buffalo. As president, Jefferson sent Lewis and Clark to explore the west as far at the Pacific Ocean. They traveled up the Missouri River, across the Great Plains and the Rocky Mountains to the Columbia River in Oregon Country, as it was known.

19th-Century Expansion: By 1850, pioneers were going all the way to Oregon. Like the East and Midwest, it had fertile land with enough rain for farming. That was not the situation on the Great Plains, however, for this region lacked the rainfall. West of the 100th meridian, the land was too dry to farm. The southwest of New Mexico, Arizona, and southern California was even drier. Settlers who tried might be lucky for a few years when precipitation was above normal, but sooner or later, arid conditions would return.

Besides conquering the West, 19th-century Americans were eagerly building factories. In New England, textile mills sprang up along the rivers and streams that supplied water power. In Pennsylvania, abundant coal mines supplied power. The iron and steel industry grew. Mill towns and mining towns were filthy with smoke and dirty water. Coal and ore were dug with no regard to the damage to the land. When a coal mine was depleted and closed, water filled the shafts, absorbed acid, and eventually seeped out to poison streams and rivers. Life in these towns and in the cities was hard, with many deaths due to pollution. Sanitation was poor. Cholera spread from contaminated wells, and smallpox and typhus spread from garbage. The more progressive cities laid wooden pipes for drinking water, and later built sewers, which emptied into the nearest river. They began to collect garbage. As the century progressed, medical knowledge increased. Lemuel Shattuck's 1850 *Report of the Massachusetts Sanitary Commission* laid out the appalling statistics on the high death rates of workers. Public health physicians and nurses improved sanitation, quarantined the sick, and developed vaccinations. Epidemiology became a science, and after about 1870, physicians learned of the germ theory.

Even though the majority of Americans were intent on chopping down virgin forests, building factories and digging mines that polluted the air and water, there were a few bright spots. Jean Jacques Audubon came to America to escape conscription into Napoleon's army. He began painting birds, traveling as far as Florida, Missouri, and Newfoundland. His paintings were drawn from life and were full sized in his *Birds of America,* first published in 1827. The complete set had 435 hand-colored engravings. Another artist, George Catlin, went west in 1832 to paint the Indians and the scenery. Back east, artists collectively referred to as the Hudson River School, painted that river as well as Niagara Fall, the Catskills, and the White Mountains. It was a shift from earlier American preference for portraiture. Its leader was Thomas Cole.[3] Albert Bierstadt, who had studied art in Dusseldorf, painted the West, as typified in his landscape of the Valley of Yosemite. The artistic school was influenced by ideas of the European Romantic Movement and depicted nature as beautiful rather than threatening.

In literature James Fenimore Cooper was the first to write novels, like the *Last of the Mohicans* and the *Deerslayer,* based on American themes of nature, the frontier, and Indians. Near Concord, Massachusetts, Henry David Thoreau rejected urban life for a cabin he built with his own hands on Walden Pond. He lived detached from civilization for two years. He championed nature and the human spirit over social conformity and materialism. Thoreau published accounts of his travels in the remote mountains of Maine and on the Concord and Merrimack rivers. Besides his love of nature, he wrote on civil disobedience, with influence all over the world. His mentor was Ralph Waldo Emerson, who won fame in 1836 for his essay "Nature," which outlined his ideas of transcendentalism, the mystical unity of nature. Emerson visited England where he met William Wordsworth, Samuel Taylor Coleridge, and Thomas Carlyle, leaders in the Romantic Movement. As an old man Emerson was one of the first passengers of the new transcontinental railroad, visiting California, including Yosemite Valley.

By the end of the 19th century, a romantic and sentimental view of nature was widespread. Inspired by a trip to Pikes Peak in Colorado, Katharine Lee Bates composed what became a classic song, "America the Beautiful."[4]

O beautiful for spacious skies, For amber waves of grain,
For purple mountain majesties, Above the fruited plain!

In 1870 in the new town of Bozeman, Montana Territory, a group of 19 ranchers and town men had heard tales of an area just to the south of them at the headwaters of the Yellowstone River. Only a few mountain men who trapped beaver had even been there. They told fanciful stories of a mountain made of glass, mud that boiled, and steam that shot hundreds of feet into the air once an hour. This was the Age of the Tall Tale when humorists competed to relate the most outlandish lies. The group organized a pack trip to investigate. They discovered a mountain of obsidian, a volcanic glass, boiling pools of minerals, and geysers like Old Faithful that spouted 150 feet into the air every hour.

These wonders were set among beautiful mountains and valleys filled with buffalo and elk. Park lore relates how, sitting around the campfire on their last night before going home, they decided that the area was too spectacular to leave to the vagaries of the US government Land Office, and should become a national park. Of course, at the time no national park existed anywhere in the world. They prevailed on their friends in Washington, and only two years later Congress passed the Yellowstone Park Act. Encompassing two million acres, it was the first national park anywhere and remained the biggest for over a century.

Establishing another park—Yosemite—was not so smooth. Its narrow valley, hidden in the Sierra Nevada Mountains, was not discovered until 1851. Because most of it lacked legal protection as a park, it was exploited by ranchers, miners, homesteaders, and early tourists. The US Land Office transferred ownership of the valley and its giant sequoia trees to the state of California, but the state was unable to prevent abuse. Finally, in 1890 the US government established Yosemite National Park surrounding the California park. The US Army ran it, as it did Yellowstone. In 1906, California ceded back the valley and sequoia grove to the US government. The army continued to run the park for another 10 years until civilian park rangers took over the management. In 1916 Congress created the National Park Service to administer Yosemite, Yellowstone, and other parks.

Yosemite's most influential resident was John Muir, who arrived in 1868. Muir had worked at a millwright in Indiana before rejecting factory life for nature. His first big adventure was to walk to Florida. In Yosemite he worked as a carpenter and sheepherder. Wandering over the mountains, he recognized that ancient glaciers had carved the valleys, a phenomenon only recently discovered in Switzerland. Muir was a talented writer with a flair for publicity and a gift for friendship with influential people. Emerson sought him as his guide when he visited. Later he took President

Theodore Roosevelt camping. Muir successfully backed the effort to create the national park and its merger with the California properties. In 1892, Muir and others formed the Sierra Club "to make the mountains glad." He was the club's first president, continuing until his death 22 years later. In its early days, the club was active politically, promoting Yosemite and the idea of parks in general, but after Muir's death, it reduced its political role to concentrate on horseback trips, mountain climbing, and education. Muir himself did not confine himself to California, traveling to Alaska, Siberia, Switzerland, China, Egypt, India, and the Amazon.

In 1882 the United States cooperated with 10 other nations in the first Polar Year. The inspiration had come from Lieutenant Carl Weyprecht of the Austro-Hungarian navy, who had led an expedition that had wintered over in its ship in the Arctic Ocean 8 years before. Eleven nations established 12 stations in the Arctic and two in the Antarctic. The United States had one at Point Barrow in Alaska, and another at Lady Franklin Bay on Ellesmere Island across the strait from Greenland. The stations took simultaneous readings of temperatures, weather, magnetic force, sunspots, and so forth.

The Conservation Movement: Theodore Roosevelt developed his love of nature as a boy, when he collected and stuffed birds and small animals, and traveled with his family to the Adirondacks, to Germany, and even to Egypt. As a young man, he often visited the West, buying a ranch in the Bad Lands of the Dakota Territory. He helped found the Boone and Crockett Club for outdoor adventure and protection of wildlife and parks. Other organizations founded at the time include the Audubon Society, the Izaak Walton League, and the National Parks and Conservation Association. The popularizing of an appreciation of nature was labeled the Conservation Movement.

A parallel urban manifestation was the City Beautiful Movement. Architects designed imposing government and civic buildings with broad tree-lined avenues and grand parks. The model was the White City constructed for the 1893 Columbian Exhibition in Chicago. In turn, this had been inspired by the École des Beaux Arts in Paris. All around the country, magnificent courthouses and city halls were constructed. The purpose of the movement was to uplift the people. Washington, DC, already a planned city, was enhanced with designed beautification. Central Park in New York, Belle Isle Park in Detroit, and the Emerald Necklace of parks in Boston were created by landscape architects like Frederick Law Olmsted. Olmsted himself also devoted his efforts to the western national parks like Yosemite.

During his presidency, Roosevelt persuaded Congress to pass the Antiquities Act of 1906. The impetus was the plundering of petrified wood and Pueblo Indian antiques in Arizona and New Mexico. With the extension of railroads, pillagers would simply go to the Petrified Forest or historic pueblos and load up their wagons, then ship them east for sale. No law prevented this. The Antiquities Act gave the president authority to declare an area to be a National Monument. To protect another aspect of nature—forests—Roosevelt appointed his friend, Gifford Pinchot, to head the new Forest Service in the Department of Agriculture. Its purpose was to manage and protect forests owned by the national government. Most were under the control of the Department of the Interior, which had a reputation for not caring much therefore; it needed to be policed by another department. Later ownership was transferred to the Forest Service. Pinchot's goal for the forests was less to preserve, and more to provide lumber for houses. With a growing population, Americans needed housing.

Pinchot was the first American in the new profession of scientific forestry. As a young man, he became interested in the subject but realized that no US school taught it, so he went to France where he enrolled in a forestry school. The French and German schools, however, concentrated on managing the cultivated, private forests of rich landowners, not the virgin forests found in the United States. Taking the European approach often put Pinchot into bitter conflict with John Muir. Pinchot's legacy was that the US Forest Service saw its mission as providing timber, with protection being only one of several further purposes, along with grazing, mining, and recreation.

During this period, a conflict developed between the United States and Canada over an attempt to divert water in the St. Mary's and Milk rivers that flowed across the border between Montana and Alberta. The solution was the Boundary Waters Treaty of 1909, which embodied a compromise, and went on to establish a framework to mediate future conflicts. It established the permanent International Joint Commission with three members from each country. Two years later the Americans, Canadians, Russians, and Japanese signed the Fur Seal Treaty to protect seals and otters in the Pacific.

Protection of migratory birds was another US–Canadian issue. Fashionable ladies of the era wanted elaborate hats with big plumes from wild egrets and herons, threatening them with extinction. To protect at least some, President Roosevelt proclaimed a bird refuge on Pelican Island in Florida. A further problem was that hunters shot millions of birds like ducks and geese. Congress tried to protect them by passing the Migratory Bird Act in 1913, but the Supreme Court declared it was unconstitutional because the national government did not have specific authority to regulate hunting. The Constitution left that to the states. The creative solution was to negotiate a treaty with Canada, under the rationale that the birds migrated across the border. The Constitution clearly gave the national government the authority to agree to treaties, and to pass laws to implement them. Because the birds migrated into Mexico as well, that country was added, and because in Alaska some migrated to Russia and Japan, those countries were added.

The Conservation Movement eventually declined. With the beginning of World War I in Europe and the United States entry 2 years later, protecting nature seemed less urgent. When the Republican Warren G. Harding won election as president in 1920, the situation got worse. The Secretary of the Interior, Albert Fall, transferred oil lands in Wyoming and California to a petroleum company owner in exchange for a bribe. The scandal discredited the Harding Administration, and Fall went to prison. The next president, Calvin Coolidge, had little interest in protecting nature, and is famous for saying "the business of America is business." The third in the line of Republican presidents, Herbert Hoover, took a strong interest in water resources. In 1922 while serving in Harding's cabinet, he had encouraged the western states along the Colorado River to sign an interstate compact regulating its flow. An early result was to start construction of a giant dam at Boulder Canyon, later named Hoover Dam. Unfortunately, the Great Depression, beginning with the Wall Street Crash of 1929, meant that people were mostly concerned with survival rather than protecting nature. Ironically, one benefit was that with factories closed, there was less air pollution. Hoover believed that there was little the government could do to help.

The Democratic candidate Franklin D. Roosevelt won the 1932 election by promising to try to get the country out of the Great Depression. His willingness to experiment boldly was the opposite of the three previous Republican presidents. Giant hydroelectric dams were one of his chief means. He immediately persuaded Congress to build several dams on the Tennessee River. The region had been about the most impoverished in the entire nation. The dams were to generate electricity and improve navigation. The Tennessee Valley Authority also manufactured fertilizer with the electricity, instructed farmers how to prevent soil erosion, and provided schools for their children. The New Deal, as the Roosevelt program was known, also built dams on the Columbia River at Bonneville and Grand Coulee, on the Missouri at Fort Peck, and on the Mississippi in Minnesota. Construction employed thousands of workers at high wages. At the worst of the Depression, unemployment was 25 percent. By today's standards, these dams did a lot of damage by flooding valleys, destroying habitat, and displacing people, but in the 1930s, they were applauded. Observers sometimes refer to the dams as an example of "gigantism."

Roosevelt personally inherited many of the tenets of the Conservation Movement, although the term had fallen out of favor. His New Deal established the Civilian Conservation Corps, which recruited thousands of unemployed young men from the cities, and sent them to rural areas to plant trees, build trails, and restore the land. In the Great Plains drought had created the Dust Bowl. Centered in Colorado, Kansas, and Oklahoma, lack of rain for many years dried up the soil. Farmers could not grow wheat, grazing was impossible, and the dry land literally blew away in terrible storms lasting days, depositing the dust hundreds of miles away. The New Deal bought the abandoned farms so the farmers would at least have a grub stake to move on. The land was given to the Department of Agriculture as National Grasslands. Elsewhere the government fought against soil erosion by encouraging contour plowing and by paying farmers to take vulnerable land out of production. In Pennsylvania and West Virginia, New Deal workers sealed up abandoned coal mines that were leaking acid. Roosevelt created a number of new national parks and recreation areas like the Shenandoah and Olympic parks and Jackson Hole Monument, later to become Grand Teton Park. His administration expanded the Bird Treaty to cover mammals and signed the Convention on Nature Protection in the Western Hemisphere.

Aldo Leopold captured the desolation of eroded land during the Great Depression in *A Sand County Almanac*. Written in the 1930s but not published for another decade, his book recounted his efforts to rehabilitate an abandoned farm in Wisconsin. His description moves through the seasons from the snow-covered fields in January to the flowers of June and back to the snow of December. Leopold also told of his young manhood in New Mexico as a forest ranger, where he realized the futility of interfering with the natural cycles of prey and predator. He led in establishing the first wilderness area in the Gila National Forest, and later was a founder of the Wilderness Society. The book sets out his philosophy of the "land ethic," in which humans see themselves as part of a natural community.

With the outbreak of World War II in Europe, Britain and France urgently ordered military supplies. The economy in the United States picked up, factories reopened, and unemployment dropped. Once the United States entered the war, there was little time for planting trees and fighting erosion. Coal companies unsealed the mines. Factories belched smoke. Young men went into the army and navy.

After the war, industrial production continued to soar. People wanted the new houses and automobiles not available during the war. European companies wanted machinery for reconstruction. Millions of automobiles were manufactured every year. With the outbreak of the Korean War and the Cold War, military spending fueled the economy. This meant more air and water pollution, and little attention to cleaning up. World War II had sparked the "Chemical Revolution." The number of artificial chemical compounds grew sharply. These had never existed in a natural state, and were not tested for safety. DDT had first been a military secret because it was so closely related to poisonous nerve gas. Military spraying to kill insects had made it popular all over the world, and it was soon used indiscriminately. At first no one recognized its insidious dangers.

On the other hand, the economic boom of the 1950s and 1960s contained the seeds of salvation. One was that the increased prosperity gave the average worker money and leisure time to travel to the "crown jewels" of natural tourism like Yellowstone and Yosemite parks, where they could witness their beauty firsthand. Education improved as millions of veterans went to college paid for by the GI Bill. Photo magazines, such as *Life* and *Look*, found their audience eager to read about nature, parks, and travel. Later television found the genre of nature and science programs were popular. Big coffee-table books of photographs sold well. Besides a general rise in educational levels, thousands of young men studied science, hence could understand the details of chemistry and biology. Greater prosperity meant corporations had more profits that eventually could pay for pollution control, and government had more tax receipts to pay for regulation.

At the local level, citizens in Pittsburgh became concerned about their city's horrific air pollution. Its factories and homes burned huge amounts of soft coal, and its mountainous terrain trapped the pollution. Early citizen efforts had an elite cast. In 1941 the Chamber of Commerce, the Civic Club, and the League of Women Voters took the lead. Part of their concern was for the city's public relations image. The mayor appointed a Commission for the Elimination of Smoke, leading to a Smoke Control Ordinance. The next concern was enforcement. Citizens organized the

United Smoke Council, consisting of 80 groups in the metropolitan area. This soon merged with the Allegheny Conference on Community Development, a business sponsored group concerned with economic development of the downtown. A strong supporter was Richard King Mellon, head of the Mellon Bank, and the richest man in town. In 1945 the voters elected David Lawrence mayor on a platform of controlling smoke. Pittsburgh was successful in cleaning its air, partly because of the Ordinance, and partly because of changing fuels. Natural gas became available for heating houses. Railroads switched to diesel engines. Old steel plants within the city limits closed, and in general heavy industry declined.

In California in 1952, the new director of the Sierra Club, David Brower, learned about a proposal by the US Bureau of Reclamation to dam the Green River in Colorado. The reservoir would flood Echo Park Canyon in Dinosaur National Monument, established 40 years earlier under the Antiquities Act. Building a big dam fit the New Deal tradition of gigantism and public employment. Area farmers and ranchers wanted the electricity and irrigation water. The new Republican administration of Dwight Eisenhower agreed with the proposal. Brower and leaders of the Sierra Club disagreed. The club had decreased its political activity after John Muir's death, and when Brower took over, its membership was only 2000. The new director began a campaign of visits to Washington to see members of Congress and officials in the Department of the Interior. He mobilized the public with press releases and direct mail. The Sierra Club purchased full-page advertisements in the *New York Times* and the *Washington Post*, and published photographs showing the ravages of environmental exploitation on animals and the environment, a previously unused tactic. Brower and the Sierra Club were successful in preventing the Bureau of Reclamation from building the dam at Echo Park Canyon.

This inspired the club to block other dams, most notably one in the Grand Canyon. Sierra Club membership went up to 80,000. The club's victories against dams inspired a citizen group in the Hudson Valley to sue to prevent the Consolidated Edison Company of New York from building a massive pumped storage unit on Storm King Mountain (a favorite landscape to paint a century earlier). The Court of Appeals ruled for the first time that the Federal Power Commission was required to consider non-economic factors and that a citizen group had the right to sue. Other groups came into being. The Defenders of Wildlife organized in 1947, and the Nature Conservancy organized in 1951.

The Sierra Club's success was modest, however, in view of the total threats to parks and wilderness areas. Moreover, air and water pollution was increasing. At this juncture, in 1962 Rachel Carson published *Silent Spring*, a book describing how DDT was poisoning birds. The title refers to the danger that so many songbirds would die that none would remain to sing in mornings in the spring. Carson was an employee of the Department of the Interior, working in the Biological Survey, and writing in her spare time. She described the manner in which rampant use had spread the insecticide everywhere. When the birds ate insects, the DDT accumulated in their little bodies, causing death. Eagles were particularly vulnerable because the fish they ate accumulated the poison, and when the hen laid her eggs, the shells were too thin, so that when she incubated them, she crushed them. The insecticide also caused a birth defect of the beak becoming crossed so that the chick could not eat. Carson's book was an instant best seller, spreading the alarm widely.

During the 1960s, the national government took small steps to address environmental problems. President John F. Kennedy convened a White House Conservation Conference (still using the old terminology). In 1963 he signed a treaty with the Soviet Union and Great Britain to outlaw testing nuclear weapons in the atmosphere, ending the damage from fallout. The following year Congress created the National Wilderness Preservation System, fulfilling the dream of Aldo Leopold. Initially, the system contained nine million acres, and eventually expanded to 90 million acres. In 1968 Congress passed the Wild and Scenic Rivers Act protecting free-flowing rivers for their "scenic, recreational, geologic, fish and wildlife, historic, cultural or other similar values." Dams no longer automatically had top priority.

Congress began to tackle the much tougher issue of air pollution at this time. Leadership fell to Democratic Senator Edmund Muskie, who chaired the new Subcommittee on Air and Water Pollution upon its establishment in 1963. Muskie had no background in science or technology, being an attorney, and took the chair as a favor to Senate leaders. At that time attention focused on Los Angeles, where the many automobiles combined with the bright sun and stagnant circulation generated smog. Although southern California had the most dramatic crisis, other cities like Houston, Denver and New York suffered too. At this time it was viewed as a health problem. The terms environment and ecology had not come into popular use. Taking a medical approach, the early legislation directed the US Public Health Service to develop air quality criteria for the states and cities to use in regulating themselves. The next step was to establish standards for emissions from automobiles.

Muskie and his colleagues needed to determine the guiding principles for controlling both air and water pollution. Muskie himself believed the key was science. Senator Howard Baker, a leading Republican, believed it was technology, and the chairman of the full committee, Jennings Randolph, believed it was economics. In the end Muskie and Baker prevailed. It was not to be economics. Environmental laws would be based on science and technology, not how much it would cost.

Government in America is a presidential system, meaning that the president is very powerful and is elected by the people rather than being chosen from parliament as in most European countries. The Constitution was adopted in 1787 in order to strengthen the executive function, and the president is often referred to as the Chief Executive. Presidents are elected every 4 years for a fixed term. According to Article II of the Constitution he is to implement the laws. He is also commander in chief of the army, navy, and air force. According to the Constitution he can veto a bill passed by Congress. His powers are greater than this, however. Congress and the people routinely turn to the president for leadership. He routinely proposes bills to Congress, which are known as "the President's Bill" or "the Administration Bill." In fact they are actually written in detail by the administrative department such as the Environmental Protection Agency. Particular laws give added authority. For example, the Antiquities Act of 1906 gives the president the authority to declare government-owned land to be a National Monument, in effect a park. The president is the focus of television and newspapers. Every word he speaks is publicized, so he can concentrate the national attention.

Congress consists of two houses, the House of Representatives and the Senate. It passes all laws, and can override a veto by the president with a two-thirds vote. The former has 435 members elected directly by the people in districts based on population. The latter has 100 members, two for each state, elected directly by the people. All the work of Congress is done by committees and subcommittees, of which there are dozens. Many share responsibility for environmental issues, for example, the Senate Committee on Energy and Natural Resource or the House Committee on Resources. The two houses duplicate their committee structure, although not with exactly the same jurisdiction. To become a law, a bill must be passed in precisely the same form by both houses. When they disagree (which is frequent), the two houses appoint a conference committee with members from both sides, who negotiate a compromise. Members of Congress tend to specialize, hence become knowledgeable and powerful in that particular area. Although the president is powerful, his attention is spread widely so members of Congress can usually get most of what they want in the narrow area.

Courts are much more important in the United States than in any other country. They have the authority to decide the meaning of a law and even whether it is valid according to the Constitution. Over the years the Supreme Court has declared many laws to be unconstitutional. Courts can examine all laws and regulations, including procedures. They must have an actual case to decide; in other words, a court cannot answer, "What if?" nor can it probe into an agency without a real lawsuit. The national courts have three levels: district, appeals, and supreme. Many important victories for the environmental movement have come through court decisions.

Many departments and bureaus are responsible for controlling pollution and managing natural resources. The Environmental Protection Agency has wide jurisdiction, covering air pollution, water pollution, solid waste, and hazardous waste. The Nuclear Regulatory Agency is responsible for safety for civilian nuclear plants. The Department of the Interior includes the National Park Service, the Bureau of Land Management, the Fish and Wildlife Service, and the Office of Surface Mining. The Forest Service is in the Department of Agriculture. Almost every department has some environmental tasks. The Department of Energy is concerned with nuclear waste disposal. The Department of Commerce has the National Oceanic and Atmospheric Administration, and the Department of State has the Bureau of Oceans, Environment, and Science.

The United States is a federation of 50 states. Each has its own government with an elected governor, legislature, and courts. Each has its own bureaucracy. Each is a miniature version of the national government. In some cases, it is not actually miniature, since California has a population of 38 million and Texas has a population of 24 million. The states are independent of the national level, and often prickly about infringement of their authority. When there is a direct conflict of authority, the Constitution says that the national government is the supreme law of the land, but most jurisdictional issues are carefully worked out over many years. Pollution control for air and water are delegated programs with the national government setting the standards and the states enforcing them. In return the national government pays the state agencies millions of dollars each to participate.

Two political parties have dominated the United States since 1856: the Democrats and the Republicans. Besides the national level, they are active in all 50 states. Since 1980 the Republicans have been less favorable to the environment and the Democrats have been more favorable. Occasionally, small third parties emerge, but they usually do not last more than a few years.

Interest groups are very important. The Clean Air Coalition and the American Lung Association favor clean air. While no groups actually admit they favor dirty air, the Edison Electric Institute and the Alliance of Automobile Manufacturers want minimal limits on air pollution.

The Environmental Decade: Congress passed the National Environmental Policy Act (NEPA). President Richard Nixon signed it on New Year's Day of 1970 on television, making a speech about how it was a new decade in which the environment would be important. He said it would be the Environmental Decade, and in this he was absolutely right. At the time NEPA appeared to be the definitive law on the topic. It addressed how the national government would handle its own actions that resulted in pollution. Direct examples are pollution from military bases or nuclear waste from facilities owned by the Atomic Energy Commission (AEC). Indirect examples are licenses from the Federal Power Commission or the AEC for a nuclear plant to begin operation. The law has two key provisions. First is that any time the government undertakes a significant action, it must write an Environmental Impact Statement. The EIS would lay out the issues but was not required to offer any solution, nor was the agency required to adhere to any recommendations. The rationale was that once an agency and the public knew the situation, they would do the right thing (presumably protect the environment). Hardly anyone anticipated the importance of the EIS requirement. The second provision of NEPA established a Council on Environmental Quality. This small agency was to receive the Statements, advise the president, and coordinate policy throughout the national government.

Within months it became apparent that CEQ was too small to coordinate government-wide. Air was the responsibility of the National Air Pollution Control Administration. Originally this agency had been part of the Public Health Service, and then became a separate bureau in the Department of Health, Education and Welfare. Water was the responsibility of the Water Quality Administration under the Department of the Interior. Originally it too had been part of the Public Health Service, and then spun off to become a bureau in the Department of Health, Education and Welfare before moving to Interior. Other environmental responsibilities belonged to the AEC, the Food and Drug Administration, and the Department of Agriculture. To bring order out of the confusion, President Nixon created the new Environmental Protection Agency, using presidential authority to reorganize without going to Congress for permission. Its unglamorous legal foundation is Reorganization Plan 3 of 1970. Nixon wanted to avoid Congress because at that time both the Senate and the House of Representatives were controlled by the Democratic Party. Even though the issue enjoyed strong bipartisan support, he did not want to expose himself to unnecessary complications and pressure.

Public participation was high. On April 22, 1970, 20 million Americans rallied in cities from New York to San Francisco to proclaim the first Earth Day. The idea was the brainchild of Democratic Senator Gaylord Nelson of Wisconsin. Popular support for the environment had been growing for several years. In January of the previous year, the Union Oil company was drilling in the Pacific Ocean five miles off the coast of Santa Barbara, California, when the casing blew out, and crude oil gushed out. Enough escaped to cover 800 square miles of ocean, and coat the shore for 35 miles with crude oil up to 8 inches thick. The public was outraged. Senator Nelson decided this was the time to organize, copying the anti–Vietnam War movement. He issued a call to action, and immediately thousands of people volunteered to help. The Common Cause organization gave office space, and Nelson recruited a Harvard student, Dennis Hayes, to head the effort nationwide. In Coral Gables, Florida, citizens marched in front of an electric utility carrying dead fish to call attention to the fish its plant had killed. In New York City 100,000 people attended an ecology fair in Union Square, and in Omaha, students paraded wearing gas masks. The holiday was an instant success and has been repeated ever since. Twenty years later, 200 million people participated in 140 countries.

During the 1950s the environmental movement began to use public rallies, marches, and picket lines. This was both spontaneous and copied from the Civil Rights and the anti-war movements. In 1954 citizens from Maryland and Washington, DC, had walked 184 miles on the towpath of the old Chesapeake and Ohio Canal when they learned of plans to pave it as a highway. The abandoned canal ran from Cumberland to Georgetown. They found a prominent leader in Supreme Court Justice William O. Douglas, who personally led "the blister brigade." Four years later Douglas organized a similar hike along a primitive section of beach in Olympic National Park in the Pacific Northwest to protest a roadway planned for the area.

At the time, one of the first converts to the movement was Richard Nixon. Although he had no personal devotion to the environment, Nixon realized that the rallies offered a partisan political advantage to the Republicans. Demonstrations like Earth Day were better than demonstrations against the war in Vietnam, which was going badly. Moreover, protection of nature fit logically with the values of middle-class members of the Republican Party.

The president had favored NEPA, and now lent his support to a bill in Congress that became the Clean Air Act. Earlier laws directing the Public Health Service (and later the Air Pollution Control Administration) to conduct research and set standards for the states and cities now seemed inadequate. But what was to be the next step? Muskie had advocated leaving most of the authority at the state level, but Nixon suggested the national level do more. Rather than appear to be weak on the subject, Muskie then proposed the national government do more. Nixon in turn talked about even more authority for the national level. Both politicians were looking forward to the 1972 presidential election. Nixon, of course, intended to run for reelection on the Republican side. In the Democratic Party, Muskie had his own ambitions. He was nationally prominent, having served in the Senate for 12 years, and having been his party's nominee for vice president in 1968. The two men dueled over the provisions of the bill, each seeking credit as the one most in favor of clean air.

Besides the question of national versus state authority, another issue was technical—the catalytic converter for automobiles. The engineering was under development. The Big Three automobile manufacturers argued that they could not be expected to install a device that was barely invented. Some companies, however, wanted converters to be mandatory. The Corning Glass company, which manufactured the components, saw this as a source of future profits and established a lobbying office in Washington. Muskie's opinion (which eventually prevailed) was that the law would require them at a future date, and this would give the auto industry the time to perfect them. He called the process "technology forcing." Ironically, the Japanese auto manufacturers were able to meet the deadlines and the Big Three were not. Congress extended the deadlines to mollify the American manufacturers. Muskie was not surprised that the time had to be extended but wanted to be sure the law gave that responsibility to Congress rather than delegating it to an administrative agency. He called it a hammer with which to hit the auto companies.

After the passage of the Clean Air Act, Congress took the obvious next step and passed the Clear Water Act in 1972. Every few years starting in 1948 Congress had enacted water legislation for research and for planning, but now it seemed time for a comprehensive law. This one gave the national government, with its functions now centralized in EPA, the authority to set water quality standards nationally. Implementation was assigned to the state agencies. This had been done to a limited extent in the Clean Air Act, but now it was more explicit, not so piecemeal. Unlike the Air Act, this one required all polluters to have a permit. The system evolved from the authority of the Army Corps of Engineers to issue permits under an 1899 law. Although the original intent was to protect river channels dredged for navigation, courts had seized on the old law to require permits for polluters. Enforcement was to concentrate on effluent—what came out of the pipe—rather than on the quality of the receiving water.

Again like the Air Act, this bill set deadlines. It grandly declared that the goal was for all waters to be fishable and swimmable by 1983. The law's standards were to be technical, but defined rather legalistically as "best practicable technology." EPA would determine the engineering details. Uniform national standards eliminated the competition in leniency among states and cities trying to capture industrial development by allowing dirty water. Municipal sewage treatment plants were key to success. Many cities still did not purify their sewage before piping it into the river. Now treatment was required. EPA was to give out billions of dollars to the cities to pay for upgrades, which made the program quite popular. Congress recognized the importance of regional cooperation. It would not be enough for one city to clean up its plant if another city discharged raw sewage into the same river. Therefore, the Clean Water Act Section 208 required that all units in the region join a Council of Governments to cooperate in order to get the grants of money. Over the years, these "208 COGs" proved to have many benefits in coordinating environmental and other issues, such as transportation.

During the mid-1970s Congress enacted a series of laws, most being delegated to the states for implementation. The Coastal Zone Management Act regulated development near oceans and the Great Lakes. The Resource Conservation and Recovery Act regulated solid waste from the cradle to the grave, that is, from manufacturing to final burial. The Surface Mining Act of 1977 regulated coal mining. This law was the purest form of a delegated program. A new agency in the Department of the Interior, the Office of Surface Mining, established the standards, but the states implemented them. Every state had to pass its own law on coal mining, establish its own agency, train its own personnel, and provide its own budget. The national government paid half the costs. Unlike most previous programs, the one for surface mining collected a fee. It was collected on every ton mined to pay for restoring abandoned mined land.

These delegated programs typified legislation during the 1970s. A few years before, President Lyndon Johnson had used the method for aid to states and cities to fight poverty. One of his goals was to avoid having the national government try to do everything, as had been the case during Franklin Roosevelt's New Deal in the 1930s. Although a few delegated programs dated back to at least 1862, for the most part the national government did its own work. For instance, it managed the national parks through the Department of the Interior and the national forests through the Department of Agriculture. One exception during the New Deal was the welfare program for children, yet in the same law Congress set up the US Social Security Administration to handle old age pensions directly.

While most programs of the Environmental Decade were delegated, this was not 100% the case. Congress passed laws to control ocean dumping, protect marine mammals like porpoises and seals, strengthen protection of endangered species, and regulate toxic chemicals. The 1980 Superfund law was also kept at the national level. The Federal Insecticide, Fungicide, and Rodenticide Act (FIFRA) had been passed originally in 1947, well before the period when delegation became popular, so when it was extensively amended, it still remained centralized under the aegis of the US Department of Agriculture.

In 1973 Congress strengthened protection of endangered species. As early as 1940, it had safeguarded the bald eagle, the county's official bird. In 1966 it had responded to outcries over the decline of the whooping crane, then down to its last few birds. The plight of a few other big and colorful species, like whales and Key deer, aroused concern that more help was need, so with the support of the Nixon Administration, Congress enacted, by a nearly unanimous vote, a revised law. The new version gave the species in danger the highest priority. Cost was not supposed to be a factor. The law also protected endangered species outside the United States, such as tigers, and prohibited importation of animal products, such as ivory.

The Superfund law was another case of the national government taking the responsibility rather than working cooperatively with the states.

In retrospect, many considered the approach to have been an error. The inspiration came from citizen action in the suburban town of Niagara Falls, near Buffalo, New York. One summer the mother of a six-year-old boy about to enter first grade discovered that his school was built over an abandoned toxic waste dump. For 10 years the Hooker Chemical Company had dumped its waste into an abandoned canal (named for the man who dug it years before, Mr. Love). When the Hooker company finished, it filled in Love Canal. Some years later, the school board asked to buy the property to build a new school. At first Hooker refused to sell, pointing out that it was toxic. The school board persisted, so finally the company sold it for $1. Contamination extended beyond the school grounds into the neighborhood, where people complained that smelly ooze seeped into their basements and that their hands blistered when they dug in their gardens.

The mother, Lois Gibbs, had few resources. She was only 26 years old, lacked an education in science, and had no experience speaking in public. She began by talking to other parents, and then circulated a petition among her neighbors. The school board, the Hooker Company, and city officials all tried to discourage her. She went to Albany, the state capital, to talk to health commission officials, but was not welcomed. Yet as she persisted, people began to pay attention. She organized the Love Canal Homeowners Association. They held rallies, wrote letters, appeared on television, went to Washington to testify before Senator Al Gore's committee, and picketed the Democratic National Convention in 1980. President Jimmy Carter went to inspect the site, and received a 20-minute lecture from Mrs. Gibbs.

The Love Canal plight persuaded Congress to pass the law, formally known as the Comprehensive Environmental Response, Compensation, and Liability Act (CERCLA). It provided for a fund of $1.2 billion paid by fees on chemicals and some general tax revenues. Once a contaminated site was discovered, EPA was supposed to swoop to clean it up. Then companies who had dumped there over the years were supposed to be assessed the liability costs. The motto was "shovels first, lawyers later." In practice, the clean ups were delayed, and wrangling in court over who was liable was lengthy and expensive. Furthermore, the number of sites discovered was huge. Congress originally anticipated a few dozen, or a few hundred at most. In fact, more than a thousand sites were soon listed. At that point EPA gave up, and stopped listing additional Superfund sites. The costs would be too high. Although the Superfund program is not set up as a delegated one, in practice EPA has made arrangements with state agencies to implement it on a case-by-case basis. Thus, the centralized program took on characteristics of a delegated one. As the bill was speeding through Congress, the chemical industry lobbyists tried to block it, because it would cost them money, but enthusiasm was too great, and they capitulated.

Along with domestic legislation, the United States entered into a number of international treaties to protect the environment. It often took the lead, such as for the 1972 World Heritage Convention. The first sites to be listed were overseas like the Galápagos Islands and Simien Park in Ethiopia, but eventually American sites were listed like Yellowstone, Grand Canyon, and Independence Hall. Sites can be both natural and man-made. Although the United Nations Education, Scientific, and Cultural Organization (UNESCO), which administers the program, has little power, many Americans do not like the idea of it being able to have any influence on domestic policy. The following year the United States signed the Convention on International Trade in Endangered Species (CITES). To implement it, Congress amended the Endangered Species Act to include nondomestic animals. For example, Americans are not permitted to buy and sell skins, horns, tusks, and so forth of protected animals. Later it passed several laws such as Rhinoceros and Tiger Conservation Act. In 1975 the United States signed the Convention on Wetlands of International Importance, known as the Ramsar Convention after the city in Iran where it was negotiated.

With the passage of the Superfund law, the Environmental Decade was over. Under three presidents, both Republican and Democratic, Congress had passed over a dozen major laws. Most of these passed with large bipartisan majorities. Nixon had established EPA, and the Department of the Interior had shifted its mission toward a more environmental orientation. When Gerald Ford became president after Nixon's resignation due to the Watergate scandal, he continued Nixon's pro-environmental policies. Carter solidified the policies, added the surface mining program, and established five big parks as part of the Alaskan Lands Act. This bipartisan support changed abruptly with the election of Ronald Reagan in 1980.

The Reagan Revolution: Reagan won the Republican Party nomination as the champion of its conservative side. Since at least 1940 it had always nominated moderates, but that changed. Reagan described himself as conservative, and was surrounded by advisors and friends who opposed environmental protection and favored business. Reagan was like an empty vessel, into which those around him poured information and policies. Advice from outside came from the Chamber of Commerce and the Heritage Foundation. This think tank was sponsored by businessmen, and advocated less regulation, less protection, and more adherence to the market. The new president got personal advice from friends like Joseph Coors, the brewery owner, who opposed almost any government program.

A key appointment went to James Watt to be Secretary of the Interior. Originally from Wyoming, Watt was a skilled attorney who headed the Mountain States Legal Foundation, a group dedicated to promoting the rights of business and the free market. He promptly proposed selling or giving government land to the states and to private owners. He wanted to decrease the power of his department when it conflicted with business and to remove the burden of regulation. This meant not just the red tape, but the substance. Surface mining regulations were rewritten to help the coal industry. Career civil servants identified as too pro-environmental were forced out. Reagan created a new Cabinet Council on Natural Resources whose duties included supervising EPA. Yet Watt, who took pride in his cowboy image and blunt talk, was forced to resign in less than two years because of blunt talk.

Reagan's second key appointment was Anne Gorsuch to be administrator of EPA. Gorsuch had served in the Colorado state legislature, where she affiliated with a group of extreme conservatives known as the Crazies. They advocated states' rights and opposed environmental protection. Her goal at the EPA was to minimize its protection of the environment. Reducing costs for industry was important. Gorsuch was not a skillful manager, and she had trouble recruiting and retaining good employees. She had a "hit list" of career employees to remove given to her by the Chamber of Commerce. She also had a poor relationship with important members of Congress. When Representative John Dingell, chairman of the environmental committee, asked for her cooperation in considering revisions to the Clean Air Act, which were expected in the spring of 1981, she rebuffed him. Her quarrel with another representative led the House of Representatives to vote that she was in contempt of Congress, and subject to arrest. One of her top aides, Rita Lavelle, was found guilty of corruption and sent to prison for her mismanagement of the Superfund. These problems led to Gorsuch's resignation after 2 years in office.

The resignations of Watt and Gorsuch marked a diminution of Reagan Administration hostility toward the environment. Incompetent and abrasive appointees, including many at lesser levels, were replaced by those who were better managers, and less likely to offend members of Congress. At Interior, Reagan appointed Donald Hodel, a man with extensive experience in government, and the good judgment not to quarrel with Congress.

He was, nevertheless, quite conservative. At EPA, Reagan persuaded William Ruckelshaus, the first administrator under Nixon, to return, and later appointed Lee Thomas.

After Reagan: In the 1988 presidential election George H. W. Bush made environmental protection a campaign issue, promising to be "an environmental president." He accused his opponent, Michael Dukakis, governor of Massachusetts, of ignoring the pollution right in front of him. Specifically, he challenged the governor to explain why he had not even bothered to apply for EPA grants to clean up the Boston Harbor. Bush made a television advertisement showing him in a boat sailing around the dirty harbor. Once in office, however, Bush did not do much. While he did not return to the hostility of the early Reagan administration, he did not push forward. Business concerns usually trumped environmental ones. To head EPA, Bush appointed his friend and head of the World Wildlife Fund, William Reilly. Reilly proved a good manager and advocate for nature. On the other hand, opposition came from elsewhere in government. The Interior Department, under Secretary Manny Luhan, continued policies of helping industry, mining, and ranching. Business interests found access by way of a newly created Council on Competitiveness. This was a cabinet-level group chaired by Vice President Dan Quayle that was supposed to monitor any government action that would harm exports. EPA regulations were often the target because they make production and transportation more expensive.

The brightest spot for the Bush administration was its support of the Clean Air Act Amendments of 1990. In this area, the president made good on his campaign pledge. The law had not been changed for 13 years. The amendments dealt with acid rain. The problem occurs when coal-burning plants, many in the Ohio Valley, emit sulfur high into the atmosphere, where it forms sulfuric acid that blows east and north, finally falling as rain or snow on upstate New York, New England, and eastern Canada. Soils in those regions lack natural buffering, so the rain contaminates lakes with the acid, killing fish. The amendments adopted a technique from the marketplace to establish a cash value on each ton of sulfur emitted. All electric plants and factories received a fixed number or tons for each year. If they emitted fewer, they could sell their excess for a profit, and if they were short, they could buy sulfur emissions from others. Additionally, EPA got a number of tons it could sell. Each year, the total tonnage for the country decreases, so the air will get cleaner. For the first time, all sources emitting air pollution were required to get individual permits, something the Clean Water Act had required in 1972. The electric industry was not too happy to have the permits and limitations imposed. Its chief lobbying organization was the Edison Electric Institute. Once the industry recognized the inevitability of the amendments, however, it shifted to lobbying for a maximum number of permits and the highest tonnage. It was quite successful, and for the first years until the screws tightened a bit, it had more allowances than it needed.

President Bush needed to determine the American stance at the Earth Summit to be held in Rio de Janeiro in June 1992. This was to be the successor to the Stockholm conference 20 years before. Presidents and prime ministers were coming from 140 nations. At Rio the delegates were to sign two treaties. One was on biodiversity and the other was on global warming. For the previous 7 years, the scientific evidence was piling up such that greenhouse gases, primarily carbon dioxide, were causing the earth to heat up like a greenhouse. Experts from all over the world had been meeting at the United Nations headquarters in New York, preparing a draft of the Framework Convention on Climate Change. It began a process of limiting the amount of carbon dioxide each country could emit into the atmosphere. Support was strong from nearly all the other industrial democracies. Within the Bush administration, however, opinion was divided. EPA and the scientific agencies believed the danger was serious, but business-oriented ones like the Department of Commerce, the Office of Management and Budget, and the Council of Economic Advisors opposed signing. This reflected the pressure on these agencies from environmental or business groups. Bush himself was torn between the two camps, but in the end decided to fly to Rio. Although he gave an enthusiastic speech to all the delegates, many thought US support was insincere, and the treaty was already weakened by US pressure on the negotiators in New York.

By this time—June 1992—the presidential campaign was already under way. Governor Bill Clinton, soon to receive the Democratic Party nomination, attacked Bush for not doing enough for the environment. For a Democrat to favor the environment, while the Republican favored business, fit the pattern since the Reagan Administration.

With Clinton's election in November, a pro-environmental administration was back in power in the tradition of Nixon and Carter. For his running mate, Clinton chose Al Gore, the senator from Tennessee. As vice president, Gore advocated for the environment, and personally directed certain efforts such as global warming policy. EPA returned to enforcing the laws vigorously. It put a moratorium on toxic waste incineration. The president signed an order to restrict logging in old growth forests.

Difficulties followed, however, after the 1994 congressional elections, when Republicans won control of both the House and the Senate for the first time in 42 years. The Republicans, especially in the House, did not pass any pro-environmental bills, of course, but were frustrated because EPA continued to implement existing laws from a green perspective. The next fall presented a target when the annual appropriations bill came up. The Republicans simply refused to vote funds for the agency to do its routine work. Without money, the agency was forced to shut down, and send its employees home without pay. After a few weeks, the Republicans relented, to give temporary funding to reopen, but after a few more weeks again shut the agency down. This happened a third time, but now the Republicans had read public opinion polls showing that the American people supported EPA and wanted it to continue its work. Rather quickly the House passed the appropriations bill. The remaining years of the Clinton administration were a stalemate for the environment. The Republicans were hostile but feared direct attacks. No important bills about environmental protection were passed.

Clinton and his administration proceeded in areas that did not need new legislation by the Republican Congress. A dramatic one was to give a huge area in southern Utah protection under the authority of the Antiquities Act. The Grand Staircase Escalante region is a spectacular desert with high cliffs, deep canyons, bright sun, and dozens of endangered plants and animals. Paleontologists can find rare fossils. The proclamation that it was a Monument greatly irritated many local people who would have preferred economic development. The Kaiparowits Plateau has rich deposits of coal. The proclamation was motivated by the politics of the 1996 presidential race. Clinton hesitated for a long time, but in September decided he was never going to win the votes of Utah but could pick up votes among pro-environmental voters in California, Arizona, and elsewhere. Clinton did not even go to Utah for the ceremony, but signed it at the Grand Canyon in Arizona. On Election Day, he got only 34% of the vote in Utah. Clinton used the technique of proclaiming national monuments to protect other areas as well, for a total of 58 million acres during his two terms. Furthermore, he ordered protection for eight million acres of forests.

After the Rio Earth Summit, not much happened regarding global warming policy as far as the public was aware. Now it was time for the experts to work quietly to draft specific provisions. Five years later they were ready with a protocol to present to a meeting in Kyoto, Japan. (A protocol is a treaty limited to a specific problem within the Framework Convention.) The protocol had three major provisions. First, all industrial countries were to agree to specific limits to greenhouse gas emissions to be imposed over a 13-year period. Second, underdeveloped countries would not have any limits. This was because it seemed unfair to deny the Third World an opportunity to develop their industries, when the First World had had a 150-year head start. This included China, which was the second largest emitter, even though its people were poor. Third, the protocol provided that the industrial countries would give money to the underdeveloped ones to help them. After 10 days of bitter debate in Kyoto, including an all-night session, the delegates signed. The US delegation was not happy, but Clinton wanted the United States to sign, and Vice President Gore made a special trip to Japan to strengthen their resolve and gain the agreement of allies.

Having signed the Kyoto Protocol, however, Clinton was in a quandary. Business opposition was intense. Under the provisions of the Constitution, the Senate has to pass all treaties with a two-thirds vote, and a few months earlier the Senate had passed a resolution 95 to zero announcing it would not approve the protocol. Hence, Clinton did nothing, except to make a speech saying that he hoped that within a year or two China and the other under-developed countries would sign—an impossible dream. Clinton ignored the situation for the rest of his term. When Gore sought and received the Democratic presidential nomination in 2000, he was afraid the controversy would cost him votes, so he did not want Clinton to do anything.

The Energy Crisis: Presidents from Nixon to Reagan had to deal with the energy crisis that burst upon the world in October 1973, when the Arab oil exporters suddenly raised the price of oil from $1.50 a barrel to $3, followed over the next year with increases to $6. It impetus was the Arab inability to win back much territory after the Yom Kipper War. Besides raising the price of crude oil, they embargoed countries that had supported Israel. The Arabs were backed up by the Organization of Petroleum Exporting Countries (OPEC). The United States was in turmoil. Motorists waited in line for hours to purchase a few gallons of gasoline, and heating oil was scarce. President Nixon invoked wartime authority to allocate gasoline from one state to another. Also Congress quickly passed a law to limit the price domestic oil producers in Texas and Louisiana could charge. The crisis was a transportation and economic disaster. Supplies were short, and businesses were subject to strict regulation. As a result getting more oil often meant sacrificing the environment.

OPEC was only able to hike prices so dramatically, however, because the world supplies were growing short. American production had been declining for many years, while demand was growing. Furthermore, electricity and natural gas were short, also. Since the end of the Great Depression, consumer demand for electricity had been growing 7% percent a year, and utilities were not building enough generating plants. The early hope that atomic energy would be cheap and safe had not proven true. Natural gas was strictly regulated for interstate sales under laws dating to the New Deal, and these laws prevented sales where demand was greatest. The immediate action of Nixon and Congress was regulation of the prices. This turned out to be a great failure, because it discouraged production. Nixon proposed that the government embark on a multibillion-dollar effort to manufacture synthetic fuels—gasoline from coal and shale. These facilities would destroy mountains, forests, and prairies.

One immediate solution appeared to be building a pipeline in Alaska from the newly discovered oil fields on the North Slope to the warm water port of Valdez 800 miles to the south. Environmentalists foresaw the destruction of the delicate land and permafrost with danger to caribou and other wildlife. For the first time their lobbyists in Washington organized jointly to persuade Congress. It was the beginning of permanent cooperation. The final version of the Trans-Alaska Pipeline Act required added precautions such as raising the pipeline off the ground and safety equipment to prevent spills. So the environmental coordination met with partial success.

Jimmy Carter campaigned in 1976 on the platform of developing a national energy plan. When finally in place 2 years later, it continued much of the Nixon program of detailed regulation and government-sponsored synthetic fuels facilities. Carter insisted on protecting the environment, however. Energy conservation was an important method for the president. The automobile speed limit was set at 55 miles per hour, and houses and offices were required to turn down their thermostats. Yet Carter was inconsistent. Less than two years after Congress passed the National Energy Act he had devoted so much effort to enacting, he began a gradual decontrol of the price of crude oil in order to encourage conservation through higher prices. Each month the companies could charge a little bit more for a barrel.

Reagan rejected Carter's policy of detailed regulation, originally put in place by another Republican, Nixon. His answer was the free market. This had a big element of ideology. Reagan and his advisors were under the sway of economists like Milton Friedman, who advocated market solutions for everything. He was also inspired by the success of British Prime Minister Margaret Thatcher, who was deregulating and selling off government industries. She divested the coal industry, the steel industry, and the oil industry. Reagan, within days of his inauguration, totally decontrolled the price of crude oil. His appointees to the Federal Energy Regulatory Commission, which had regulated the price of natural gas, ended the controls that had been in place for 48 years. The president saw the leniency in surface mining control as a way to lower the price of coal. He terminated the synthetic fuels program. Although done to save money, it prevented the destructive mining of millions of acres of oil shale in Colorado and Wyoming.

Radioactivity: Pollution from atomic energy followed a different course than other environmental issues. The danger began during World War II with the Army Manhattan Project to invent and build the first atomic bomb. The secret plants refining the fuel in Oak Ridge, Tennessee, and Hanford, Washington, discarded the lower-quality ore. Indeed, until the bomb was dropped on Hiroshima, scientists did not realize how deadly the radiation was. After the war, nuclear waste piled up at Atomic Energy Commission facilities. The first commercial electric plant began generating in 1958 near Pittsburgh, adding a further big source of contamination.

Nuclear safety was regulated by the AEC, which neglected this aspect in favor of building more plants. Citizens had little way to influence decisions. That began to change with opposition to the proposed plant in Shoreham on Long Island begun in 1966. The AEC promoted its construction, local officials saw it as a clean way to provide electricity and increase taxes, and the Long Island Lighting Company (LILCO) wanted profits, but a group of local residents did not agree. The nearby village of Lloyd Harbor was a wealthy community, and home to scientists from the Cold Spring Harbor Laboratory, a center for biomedical research. They asked to intervene at hearing before the AEC staff to voice their objections. These scientists made persuasive witnesses, even though their specialties were not in nuclear engineering. One of them was James Watson, the co-discoverer of DNA, who couched his criticism in nearly philosophical terms. About the same time in Maryland, citizens opposed building a nuclear power plant at Calvert Cliffs on the Chesapeake Bay. By this time Congress had passed NEPA, which required an Environmental Impact Statement for a significant action. The AEC maintained merely issuing a license was not significant, but the US Court of Appeals disagreed. Now citizens had the right to intervene at many steps in the process. It became a powerful tool.

Widespread complaints that the AEC should not be responsible for regulating the industry, at the same time as it was promoting it, led to reorganization in 1974, whereby the Commission was split in two. The smaller part, the Nuclear Regulatory Commission, concentrated solely on safety, while the bigger part promoted the industry, conducted research, and built weapons (a function the agency had had since World War II). This was named the Energy Research and Development Administration, and got additional responsibilities for nonnuclear energy projects. Three years later under President Carter, it became the Department of Energy. About 1989 the new department discovered its own facilities were contaminating the ground and water with radioactive waste. Its plant in Barnwell, South Carolina, was leaking radiation into the Savannah River.

Storage of radioactive waste from civilian electric generating plants was a continuing issue. Never since the Manhattan Project has a permanent site been found. Plutonium is the most dangerous material known, with a half-life of 24,000 years, meaning that after that time, it will still be half as dangerous as now. Utilities store their old uranium in temporarily in pools of water and in vaults next to their plants. In 1982 Congress passed the Nuclear Waste Policy Act requiring the Department of Energy to identify several sites, but all of them had drawbacks. Eventually, the Department decided to use Yucca Mountain in Nevada. Citizen Alert is a local group opposed to storing the waste in the state. It organized in 1975 when this idea first arose. In the presidential elections of 2004 and 2008, Nevada voters found themselves in a key position. Although the state has only four votes in the Electoral College out of a total of 538, candidates were afraid of losing them, so they promised that the waste site would not be built.

George W. Bush began his term by denouncing the Kyoto Protocol, the international treaty to protect against global warming. At home he directed Vice President Richard Cheney to develop a national energy policy, a concept not seen since the Carter administration. The Reagan administration had staunchly opposed central planning in favor of the free market. Cheney promptly alienated many environmentalists by consulting only industry people. He had just resigned as president of the Halliburton Corporation, a petroleum company. Cheney talked of opening the Arctic National Wildlife Reserve to oil exploration. Bush himself had begun his career in the oil business in the Arbusto, Spectum 7, and Harken companies. Some of the president's early acts seemed almost deliberate slaps at protection. For example, he withdrew regulations limiting the amount of arsenic in drinking water. The Interior Department allowed snowmobiles into Yellowstone, Grand Teton, and Voyageurs parks. The Forest Service permitted more logging.

To head the Department of the Interior, Bush appointed Gale Norton, an attorney who had been on the staff of the Mountain States Legal Foundation (James Watt's organization). She believed strongly in the rights of business and in the free market. The department staff included former Reagan administration officials. Her chief deputy was Steven Griles, whose career had been devoted to advancing the interests of the coal industry, and who was a bitter enemy of the surface mining program.

On the other hand, to direct EPA, Bush appointed an environmentalist, Christine Todd Whitman, the Republican governor of New Jersey. As a girl she had been raised on a farm in New Jersey, and spent summers on a ranch in Wyoming. As governor of the Garden State, she had worked to clean up smog and prevent beach closings due to contamination. In spite of her good intentions, Whitman made little progress at EPA. Her attempts were blocked by the White House. Right at the beginning of the Bush administration, she was disheartened to find that other Republicans were blaming environmental protection for the economic recession. Vice President Cheney's energy policy rode roughshod over the Clean Air Act. Whitman wanted to resolve problems caused by New Source Review, whereby old power plants faced restrictions on installing new equipment. She believed the solution was to have a comprehensive program for both old and new plants. Labeled the Clear Skies Initiative, it used the market concept of trading modeled on the sulfur trading program in the 1990 Clean Air Act Amendments. President Bush lent his prestige to the plan by announcing it personally. It met predictable criticism from environmental groups, who objected that it was voluntary and would replace the existing program ready to go into effect. With its 10-year timetable, the pace would be slower. To Whitman's surprise, it also met criticism from business groups who thought it still had too much regulation. After his initial speech, Bush barely mentioned it again. Regarding global warming, Whitman tried to be a good soldier by making the case against the Kyoto Treaty at international meetings but received little thanks from Republicans at home and much hostility from the Europeans. After three years, she resigned in frustration.

The president also took time to personally announce his Healthy Forests Initiative, supposedly a way to reduce the danger of fires. The rationale of the plan was that because fires need fuel, the Forest Service and the Bureau of Land Management would encourage loggers to harvest the fuel, in other words, cut down trees. As an incentive to do this, the Forest Service would reward loggers with the right to harvest more trees. The Tongass in southeast Alaska is the country's largest forest, encompassing 17 million acres, virtually all of it old growth and much of it steep mountainsides. Under previous rules, logging was not permitted in areas without roads. Besides giving access to equipment, the roads themselves damage the land due to erosion. Logging is not profitable there without subsidies. The Bush administration removed those restrictions and encouraged harvesting.

To succeed Whitman at EPA, Bush named the governor of Utah, Michael Leavitt, praising him for his ability to work cooperatively between the national and state levels. One instance was negotiating an agreement to build the Legacy Highway across a wetland near Salt Lake City. The other was a deal with the Department of the Interior to reduce the amount of land that was eligible for reclassification as wilderness. The method was to argue that Utah and its counties were entitled to rights of way across these lands, including national parks, monuments, and wildlife refuges. The legal basis was the 1866 mining law that was designed to promote mining and settlement in the Old West. The Federal Land Policy and Management Act of 1976 repealed this provision but grandfathered in existing highways. Governor Leavitt and Secretary of the Interior Norton claimed that these existing highways were very extensive, including on their list many hiking trails, cow paths, off-road vehicle tracks, and dry stream beds. Thus, these regions could not qualify as wilderness areas. Once in office, Leavitt was likeable and moderate, but little seemed to happen. He announced a plan to reduce mercury emissions from coal-fired plants by capping the level and allowing trading and sales of allowances like the sulfur allowances in the 1990 Clean Air Act Amendments. This was aligned with the Bush administration's desire to use economic principles rather than command and control. Leavitt called it "markets before mandates."[5] Critics pointed out that the reduction in mercury would actually be from 50 tons a year only to 34 tons rather than the 5 tons under the latter. They also argued that EPA policies were fitting another Bush desire, which was to give industry major influence. Earlier EPA announced it would drop investigations into 50 electric-generating plants for violating the Clean Air Act. This had been a recommendation of the Energy Task Force headed by Vice President Cheney. Little more than a year after being appointed, Leavitt resigned to become Secretary of Health and Human Services. Bush next appointed a career civil servant to head the agency, the first ever. Stephen Johnson had served 24 years, chiefly in the pesticides division. In spite of his background as a scientist and bureaucrat, he stressed the importance of cooperating with industry.

Two crises shaped the Bush environmental policy: September 11 and Hurricane Katrina. The Al Qaeda attacks on the World Trade Center in New York and the Pentagon in Washington permanently changed the Bush agenda. Public attention was riveted on the terrorists. In November the United States invaded Afghanistan to oust Al Qaeda and the Taliban regime that allowed it to operate. In March 2003, the United States invaded Iraq, under the claim that that country harbored Al Qaeda and possessed weapons of mass destruction. Environmental issues were pushed to the background. When Hurricane Katrina caused the levees protecting New Orleans to break, flooding most of the city, a few environmental issues jumped back into focus. The water was highly polluted from sewage, the bodies of human victims and animals, and toxic wastes stirred up from refineries and dumps. Congress asked EPA to relax the regulations for 120 days to accelerate cleaning up, but environmentalists took a hard line against making an exception.

Beginning about 2004 the dangers of fracking jumped into attention. This was the technique of producing natural gas by hydraulic fracturing of rocks deep underground. Wildcatters would drill very deep, 5,000 to 10,000 feet, then turn the bore horizontal. Next they would pump down water and chemicals to fracture the rock and release the gas. It was a bonanza, estimated to be 500 trillion cubic feet—enough to heat US homes and power electric plants for two decades. Even better, the gas was located in the northeast from New York State to West Virginia to Ohio, the heart of industry and houses that needed the fuel. Amazingly, geologists had not recognized the presence of this energy resource in an economically recoverable form.

The environmental danger came from contamination of underground and surface water and damage to the land from the drilling activity. The wastewater and chemicals had to be disposed of, and when injected into extremely deep wells, occasionally caused earthquakes. Regulation was fragmented among county and state governments. National regulation under the Safe Drinking Water Act would have been logical but is not allowed. US EPA's jurisdiction was curtailed by an amendment to the act, known as the "Halliburton loophole." The provision excluded from the law "the underground injection of fluids or propping agents . . . pursuant to hydraulic fracturing operations."[6] This was put in the law at the request of Vice President Richard Cheney, who was previously president of the

Halliburton Corporation, a company that is a major supplier of equipment for shale drilling. Dispersion of authority to the state or local level was advantageous to the drillers.

Exotic species were recognized as a new threat. These were plants or animals introduced into North America accidentally (or even intentionally) from Europe, Asia, or Africa that flourished in their new home, often because they had no natural enemies. These invasive species could quickly overrun native species. In their home countries, they were kept in check by natural predators. Actually, the phenomenon had been occurring since colonial times, but increased international commerce accelerated the threat. One avenue was the ballast water of ships. Zebra mussels arrived this way from Russia and quickly spread through the Great Lakes, displacing native mussels and clogging intake pipes for drinking supplies and cooling water. Their damage has been estimated at $500 million a year. The round goby invaded as well, also from Russia. It ate the eggs of native fish like bass, walleye, and salmon. At first the shipping companies denied the problem and resisted regulation. Congress passed the Invasive Species Act in 1996, but this expired 6 years later.

The Asian carp was a threat everyone could recognize. During the 1970s fish farmers in southern states like Arkansas and Louisiana imported the fish to reduce the amount of plants and algae in their ponds. They consume up to 20% of their body weight per day in plankton and can grow to over 100 pounds. Soon many escaped and began reproducing vigorously. The carp spread up the Mississippi River. Fishermen found they were eating the food that supported native game fish. Recreational boaters encountered them literally in the air. When frightened by the sound of an outboard motor, the silver carp jumps several feet out of the water and may strike a boater. One fear has been that they might enter the Great Lakes via the Chicago River, then spread widely. An answer was to totally close the river, but Illinois businesses and politicians resisted. In an unusual step, the state of Michigan sued the state of Illinois in the US court.

Burmese pythons drew a lot of attention in the Florida Everglades. Hobbyists bought these tropical snakes as pets, and when they grew too big, had to get rid of them. An adult can grow up to 17 feet long and weigh up to 165 pounds. They eat muskrats, storks, and small deer. One snake was filmed eating an alligator. While pythons cannot survive the winter climate in most of the United States, the Everglades are warm enough that abandoned pets thrived and reproduced. The state Fish and Wildlife Commission sponsored a python hunt for amateurs to shoot them. Prizes of $1000 were offered, and

1567 hunters enrolled. After 30 days, they had killed or captured 50 out of an estimated 150,000 feral snakes. It was hopeless.

As a candidate in the Democratic Party primaries in 2008, Barack Obama strongly supported biofuels, in particular ethanol, to be added to gasoline. The program had begun in the Clean Air Act Amendments of 1990 to reduce air pollution and to reduce American dependence on imported petroleum. The Energy Independence and Security Act of 2007 was the latest version, in which Congress mandated adding 36 billion gallons by 2022, up from 5 billion gallons at the time. Most of this came from corn that the Department of Agriculture subsidized. The program distorted farming in the Midwest, with acreage shifted from food to fuel. Farmers, of course, loved it since the price went up even as production went up. Indeed, the prices went so high that the prices of hogs and cattle went up, raising meat prices for consumers. In Mexico, ordinary people had to pay more for their cornmeal. The state of Iowa, in the middle of the Corn Belt, holds the first event of the presidential primary season—a caucus. Candidates from both parties flocked there, promising support for ethanol. On the Democratic side, the most persuasive was Barack Obama, who won, thus launching his eventual victory of the party's nomination. As president he continued to support ethanol in the face of environmental criticism that it was distorting the market and harming the land.

When Obama became president in 2009, he returned to policies more in keeping with the usual Democratic lines of Carter and Clinton. Carol Browner, Clinton's EPA head, was appointed to the White House staff with a portfolio for energy and climate change. The new head of EPA was Lisa Jackson, a 16-year veteran of the national agency, and more recently head of the New Jersey state agency. The overriding question was how much Obama would emphasize the environment when balanced against the national financial crisis. His rhetoric was positive. He claimed the bail-out of $850 billion would have green projects like eliminating toxic waste dumps and saving energy by investing in photovoltaics and high mileage automobiles. Yet a $30 billion infusion of cash into the auto Big Three was not a logical match for reducing air pollution. SUVs are the most profitable vehicle for the manufacturers. During the campaign Obama promised to reduce greenhouse gas emissions but did not endorse the Kyoto Protocol. Regarding methods, Obama urged entrepreneurial approaches to pollution control, as the Bush administration had advocated. EPA seemed unlikely to return to the Golden Age of regulation as in the Nixon and Carter administrations. Furthermore, to the dismay of environmentalists,

Obama canceled two major sets of air regulations at the last minute. In September 2011 he told the EPA Administrator to withdraw regulations limiting ozone within hours after they were promulgated. In December regulations on emissions of mercury and toxics were blocked by the White House. The president seemed to want to avoid criticism from Republicans that he was harming the economy in the coming election year.

The 2012 election between Obama and the Republican Mitt Romney largely ignored the environment. The particular issue that did not appear was global warming. Romney spent much of the primary season trying to make the topic disappear, and he was largely successful. Although in previous years he had stated that he believed in warming as a threat, he soon learned that that was going to cost him votes. Most Republicans who voted in primaries and caucuses denied that it existed; therefore, Romney denied it. Democrats considered this was just one more example of changing his beliefs to pander to voters. Obama, for his part, also avoided mentioning warming in spite of many environmentalists who demanded that he take a stand. Obama wanted to avoid agitating voters. Suddenly on election night in his victory speech in Chicago he said "We want our children to live in an America that isn't threatened . . . by the destructive power of a warming planet."[7] The line drew sustained applause from the crowd and praise from environmentalists in general. Nevertheless, the steps to take were uncertain in view of the hostility of the Republicans who again held a majority in the House of Representatives. One option was to use executive action that did not require new legislation. The Clean Air Act authorized EPA to promulgate regulations, and presumably these could limit greenhouse gas emissions. The previous year EPA had issued CAA regulations to double fuel efficiency for cars and trucks by 2025.

The environment intruded into the campaign peripherally. In October Hurricane Sandy struck New Jersey and New York, raising the specter that global warming was a cause. Costs were estimated at $75 billion with 285 deaths. Often the campaign questions were framed in terms of energy. The Republicans solicited the votes of coal miners in the swing state of Ohio, in which the outcome was narrowly divided. In the televised debates, Romney accused Obama of discouraging drilling for oil. Both candidates advocated "energy independence," meaning more specifically oil import independence for North America. The supposed benefits were reduced vulnerability from the unstable Middle East and Venezuela and reduced costs. During the fall, Republicans blamed Obama for blocking construction of the Keystone XL pipeline from the tar sands of Canada to refiners in Texas. The route crossed the Ogalala Aquifer in the Great Plains, the underground source of irrigation. And although Obama had often touted the benefits of solar energy, Republicans criticized him when the Solyndra company that manufactured thin film solar cells went bankrupt in spite of generous grants from the Department of Energy.

CONCLUSION

Citizen participation has always been important in American environmental policy. After all, the country prides itself on being a democracy where the people rule. Yellowstone became the first national park because of the agitation of the ranchers and townspeople who explored it in 1870. In California Yosemite largely owes its status as a national park to the agitation of John Muir. To mobilize other citizens, he established the Sierra Club. Two generations later, the Sierra Club director, David Brower, mobilized its members and others to oppose construction of a dam at Echo Park Canyon. In Pittsburgh citizens fought the steel industry and railways to enact the Smoke Ordinance. When the Long Island Lighting Co. wanted to build a nuclear generating plant at Shoreham, citizens in the nearby village of Lloyd Harbor united to block it. When Lois Gibbs discovered the school her son was scheduled to enter was on a toxic waste dump in Love Canal, she carried a petition door to door to rally opposition, an act that climaxed when Congress established the Superfund. Earth Day 1970 mobilized 20 million people to demonstrate and has continued to bring out crowds every year since.

Citizen movements, when successful, often end up as interest groups. Muir organized the Sierra Club, which while he still lived, had a political function as well as a recreational one. Later it returned to its political roots with Brower. The citizens of Pittsburgh did not act individually, but in the form of United Smoke Council and the Allegheny Conference on Community Development. At the earliest stages they worked through the Chamber of Commerce, the Civic Club, and the League of Women Voters. Lois Gibbs organized the Love Canal Homeowners Association.

Political parties have played key roles. Under President Theodore Roosevelt, the Republican Party supported the Conservation Movement. Later the Democratic Franklin D. Roosevelt, who was personally quite devoted to nature and country life, established many new parks, rebuilt existing one, planted millions of trees, and worked to rehabilitate the Dust Bowl. The most crucial presidential administration was that of Republican Richard Nixon. He believed that the Republican Party fit naturally with the environmental movement. He established the EPA and asked Congress to pass the National Environmental Policy Act, the Clean Air Act, and several other important laws. His Democratic successor, Jimmy Carter, continued to protect the environment. Republican support for the environment ended abruptly with Ronald Reagan, who stifled pollution control and gave away protected land in the West and Alaska. George H. W. Bush was not so hostile, but except for advocating the Clean Air Act Amendments, neither did he do much to help. Since Reagan the lines have been sharp with Democrat Bill Clinton returning to protection and George W. Bush relaxing protection and opposing the Kyoto Protocol. The Republican Party advocates helping business and industry, and has denied that global warming is a threat. Obama returned EPA to an active role in the Democratic Party tradition.

Governmental structure makes a difference. Congress is different from most legislatures in European democracies in that it is separated from the president, that is, the executive function. Moreover, congressional committees and even individual senators and representatives can be very powerful, and don't shy away from interfering in the agencies. The US government implements many environmental policies through its federal system of two levels. Control of air and water comes from national laws and regulations implemented by state agencies. EPA sets the standards, and then delegates enforcement to the states. For mining, the national agency is the Office of Surface Mining, which in turn delegates enforcement to the states. On the other hand, many other programs do not operate in a delegated fashion. Radiation, parks, land management, fish and wildlife, and hydroelectricity are managed directly by the national government.

The influence of the diplomatic agenda as an avenue for environmental events is limited because the United States is such a dominant country on the world scene. Very seldom is it a follower. It is often a leader, such as the Migratory Bird Treaty, CITES, and the Framework Convention on Climate Change. An early example of the United States becoming acquainted with an issue by following the diplomatic agenda was the first Polar Year. More recently although the United States is seldom surprised by items on the diplomatic agenda, it is not necessarily the greenest country in the world. The 1963 Test Ban Treaty with the Soviet Union elevated concern with radioactive fallout. In preparation for the 1992 Rio Earth

Summit, preliminary negotiations in New York at UN headquarters found the United States participating but seeking a less stringent draft of the Framework Convention on Climate Change.

The United States has followed news of events around the world (although having a preference for those that speak English). The 1952 Great Smog in London garnered more publicity than domestic tragedies. The Clean Air Act copied language from the British law. The Environmental Decade of the 1970s unfolded parallel to that in Europe. Jacques Cousteau's films and books of underwater exploration were popular. The United States made numerous contributions to other countries. The idea of national parks started with Yellowstone and was soon copied in Australia and Canada. The creation of EPA in 1970 inspired similar agencies in other countries.

NOTES

1. John Winthrop, "Conclusions for the Plantation in New England," in *Major Problems in American Environmental Policy*, ed. Carolyn Merchant (Lexington, Mass.: D. C. Heath, 1993), p. 72.
2. William Bradford, "Of Plimouth Plantations," in *Merchant*, p. 68.
3. Gregory Clark, Michael Halloran, and Allison Woodford, "Thomas Cole's Vision of 'Nature' and the Conquest Theme in American Culture," in *Green Culture: Environmental Rhetoric in Contemporary America*, ed. Carl G. Herndl and Stuart C. Brown (Madison: Univ. of Wisconsin Press, 1996), pp. 261–280.
4. Katherine Lee Bates, "America the Beautiful," *The Congregationalist*, July 4, 1895.
5. PBS News Hour, "Newsmaker: Mike Leavitt," Interview by Margaret Warner, December 11, 2003.
6. Energy Policy Act of 2005, Section 323, Oil and Gas Exploration and Production Defined.
7. President Obama's acceptance speech, *Washington Post*, November 7, 2012.

3

Germany, the Netherlands, Denmark, and Sweden

A few European countries have been leaders in the environmental movement. Their citizens have agitated for laws and programs, their parliaments have enacted legislation, and their diplomats have promoted treaties and cooperation. Germany, because of its big population and economic power, has been the most influential. The Netherlands, Denmark, and Sweden have often set an example. Sweden, for instance, proposed and sponsored the 1972 Earth Summit at Stockholm.

Germany: The forest has long been a symbol of this nation, dating back to prehistoric times. The Roman historian Tacitus wrote of the German tribes' attachment to their forest. It offered refuge from the Roman invader, and was a source of food and clothing. In pagan days, it was the home of spirits and gods. Rivers also held mythic significance. Along Father Rhine, the Lorelei maidens sang to tempt sailors to their deaths. In 1824 Heinrich Heine wrote the folk story in a poem, later set to music.

> The air is cool under nightfall.
> The calm Rhine courses its way.
> The peak of the mountain is sparkling
> With evening's final ray.[1]

Compared to France, England, and the Low Countries, 18th-century Germany was less developed in terms of its government and economy. The empire was not established until 1871. Industrialization, and therefore pollution, lagged behind. Germany was not at the heart of scientific

53

knowledge of the Age of Enlightenment, which centered in France and England. Politically, it remained fragmented into dozens of kingdoms, duchies, and free cities. As the years went on, a few centers appeared. The region had universities such as Jena, Heidelberg, Gottingen, and Leipzig. In 1700 King Frederick I founded the Prussian Academy of Sciences. His grandson, Frederick the Great, surrounded himself with a group of educated men, mostly French, who advanced the ideas of the Enlightenment.

In 1792 Alexander von Humboldt started his scientific career with an appointment as an assessor of mines in Brandenburg. In 1799 he began his explorations in South America, where he discovered the current off Peru later named for him. He also analyzed the relationship between altitude and temperature and between geography and plant distribution. To study terrestrial magnetism, Humboldt organized one of the first projects involving international scientific cooperation by coordinating meteorological stations throughout Russia and the British Empire. Later in the 19th century, Germans participated in the Polar Year. They hosted a preliminary meeting in 1872 at Leipzig and sent expeditions to Kingua Fjord in the Canadian Arctic and South Georgia Island in the South Atlantic.

Germany was also the location of one of the earliest examples of international cooperation for a river, the Rhine. The Congress of Vienna, which convened in 1814 to restore Europe after the Napoleonic Wars, addressed the problem of navigation on this river. Multiple governments restricted boats and charged them tolls. Indeed, it had been the home of the notorious "robber barons." Furthermore, the channel was difficult to navigate in places due to rapids, rocks, and low water. The congress established a commission that first met in 1816 and had a permanent secretariat, making it the oldest international organization still in existence. Eventually, the commission assumed responsibilities for cleaning up pollution. The commission inspired those for other rivers: the Elbe in 1821, the Weser in 1823, the Ems in 1853, and the Danube in 1856.

Although the Industrial Revolution came late to Germany, by the middle of the 19th century, factories were belching out smoke and fouling the rivers. Lumbermen chopped down forests, and miners dug coal and ore. To improve navigation, governments dredged, narrowed, and canalized rivers. A few Germans spoke out against this damage and pollution. In 1815 Ernst Moritz Arndt wrote to criticize shortsighted exploitation of woodlands and soil and to condemned deforestation. Arndt's stance was based less on the scientific evidence of the risk, and more on a Romantic love of esthetics.

Germany was a leader in the Romantic Movement, a glorification of nature and emotion that emerged in reaction to the perceived over-emphasis on rationality during the Enlightenment of the 18th century. The new movement stressed the individual, as manifested both in popular government and folk culture. The Romantic Movement was strong in the arts. Paintings depicted dramatic landscapes and storms at sea. In literature, Johann Wolfgang von Goethe and Friedrich von Schiller wrote prose, drama, and poetry. Goethe wrote of the unity between humans and nature. His ideas had elements of a pantheist religion. Other authors wrote of how the landscape shaped the national soul. In 1789 construction began in Munich on the Chinese Tower, a pagoda, in a naturalistic garden in the Chinese style, but styled the "English Garden" because the fashion had been transmitted via England. Romanticism also had a strong element of patriotism in reaction against Napoleon's conquest that had imposed elements of the Enlightenment at the point of a bayonet. While Germany was a leader in Romanticism, the movement extended beyond its borders to affect all of Europe and America.

The Romantic study of nature tied to emerging science. Ernst Haeckel was a skilled marine biologist, who saw a religious side to nature, growing out of his deep aesthetic response to the beauty of the world. He is famous for coining the word "ecology," which he defined as the relation of the animal both to its organic as well as to its inorganic environment. Haeckel had earned a degree in medicine but switched to biology when a professor took him on a field trip to the North Sea. He also considered a career as a landscape painter. Upon reading *On the Origin of Species*, he became an enthusiastic Darwinian. He spent his career as a professor of comparative anatomy at the University of Jena, specializing in radiolarians, sponges, and segmented worms. Haeckel is famous for originating the biogenic law that ontogeny recapitulates phylogeny, meaning that the embryonic development of an animal repeats its evolution. In spiritual terms, he was a pantheist who believed that all animals, not just humans, contained a divine spark. In his personal politics, he was a conservative and a German patriot, shaped at least in part by his experience growing up during the turmoil of the 1848 revolutions. In one of his most controversial statements, he wrote that politics is applied biology.

In 1852 Wilhelm Heinrich Riehl appealed for "a right to wilderness," in opposition to the monotony of capitalist expansion. He praised the traditional countryside of peasants, woodcutters, and fishermen who engaged themselves with nature on a daily basis. Riehl's ideal was a politically conservative peasantry in a land dominated by rural estates. Others wrote against the decadence and degeneration due to industrialization. They despaired that life in the dirty, overcrowded cities without fresh air and contact with nature was leading to a long-term decline of the human species. Data from the army showed that recruits from the big cities were unhealthy compared to those from the countryside. Besides concern with nature, these reformers also wanted to preserve old buildings. City planning developed as a profession, with the first journal published in Berlin. Critics of urban decay and of capitalism closely followed the writings of Englishmen such as John Ruskin and William Morris.[2]

By the turn of the 20th century, more and more Germans were participating in outdoor recreation. They spent their Sundays and their summer vacations in the mountains and countryside hiking, climbing, and boating. Young people joined *wandervogel* clubs. Hundreds of thousands of people engaged in "life reform" activities such as vegetarianism, nudism, temperance, and unconventional living arrangements. Others worked to bring nature back to the city by forming garden clubs. Ernst Rudorff sought laws to preserve hedgerows and to prevent streams from being straightened.[3] In the 1890s, Prussia and other states (Lander) within the empire enacted laws to protect natural monuments such as old trees, waterfalls, and geological formations.

Ordinary citizens had protested against air and water pollution. Three times in the 18th century—1714, 1721, and 1778—people in Stuttgart petitioned to stop the silting and pollution of the Nesenbach River. In the 19th century, citizens of Hamburg objected to pollution of the Elbe River. In 1895 residents of a suburb of Hamburg blocked construction of a foundry because it violated the residential and agricultural character of the area. The national government in 1869 adopted an industrial ordinance providing for permits for effluents and licenses prior to construction of new facilities.[4] In 1895 the government passed the Technical Guidelines for Air Purity.

As early as 1817 hydraulic engineers began straightening and diking the Rhine River to control floods and improve navigation. The negative consequences were to erode alluvial soil, lower the water table, increase sediments, and destroy floodplains and marshes. Nevertheless, floods continued. Cities and industries dumped their wastes. Factories on the banks of the Rhine emitted sulfur dioxide, resulting in acid rain that killed the forests. The Ruhr River suffered more. In this coal mining region, engineers dumped untreated waste into its tributary, the Emscher, described as "the river of hell."[5]

Many people had established local groups, known as Heimatschutz: protectors of the homeland. In 1903 they organized a national federation, with a scope extending beyond nature to architecture, art, handicrafts, folk clothing, and more. Almost immediately, the federation tried to prevent a dam from being constructed on the Rhine in south Baden. Although unsuccessful, its intervention brought favorable publicity and more members. Members agitated for a law to protect townscapes and landscapes. When promulgated in 1907, the regulations required the city government to consult with local experts, in other words, the Heimatschutz. This semi-official role was an impetus for expansion and attracted new members. The federation also forged links with similar groups in France, the Netherlands and Austria.[6]

Bird lovers organized nationally as early as 1875. In cooperation with societies for botany, gardening, and animal protection, they lobbied successfully for the first law to protect birds. In 1899 Lina Hahnle led in establishing the League for Bird Protection. Its membership climbed from 6,000 to 41,000 in 12 years. The league sold birdhouses, purchased refuges, educated children, and lobbied for laws and international treaties. Inspired by the American examples of Yellowstone and Yosemite, the Nature Park Society agitated to preserve the Luneburg Heath, a unique region of heather and scrub vegetation in Lower Saxony. In Bavaria, the Isar Valley Society agitated to protect the river from industry and urban sprawl. One technique was to purchase land along the banks. A second was to lobby government to promulgate regulations and to discourage industrialization. The society managed to block a proposed hydroelectric dam.[7]

The outbreak of World War I crippled the nature movement for years. During the war, fighting took priority, and after the Armistice, Germany was impoverished. Millions of men had been killed. The Weimar Republic, established to replace the Empire, had more pressing needs. Then the hyper-inflation began that sapped the economy, and plunged it into depression. Group membership was down greatly. The government did not respond to calls for legislation. On the positive side, the Weimar constitution actually had a provision to protect nature. Section 150 said "Artistic, historical and natural monuments and the landscape enjoy state protection and care."[8] Yet this remained an empty promise, as the government did not implement it.

As the Nazi Party emerged during the 1920s, it found commonalities with the nature movement. They shared an esthetic sensibility, a dislike of materialism and modernity, an idealization of peasants, and a call for national regeneration. Both adhered to the motto of "Blood and Soil," meaning the connection between the German race and the environment that nurtured it. Many of the young *wandervogel* hikers joined the Hitler Youth. The League for Bird Protection said, "Joyously we stand behind the Fuhrer," and the Bavarian League for Nature Conservation praised "converting the love of Nature into the great love of nation and Fatherland."[9] The minister of agriculture and Fuhrer of the Peasants, Walther Darré, advocated organic farming and worked to prevent erosion.[10]

In constructing the autobahns, engineers were obliged to blend them with the terrain and preserve the landscape. The Reich adopted a hunting law qualifying as one of the most progressive in the world in terms of protecting animals. In 1935 it enacted the progressive Conservation Law, codifying regulations and centralizing administration under the Reich Forest Master, Hermann Goering. Goering was also the head of the Gestapo (secret police), the air force, and the economics ministry. The new law overrode the authority of the states. The government banned all billboards in the countryside and established an unprecedented number of nature preserves.[11] The Nazis cooperated with local nature clubs, protecting sites and giving them patronage. Prior to ascending to power, the Nazis had added to their electoral totals in 1930 by attracting peasant votes.

Adolf Hitler spoke numerous times of the importance of the land for shaping the German people. For instance, he declared that "the German countryside must be preserved under all circumstances, for it is and has forever been the source of strength and greatness for our people."[12] Hitler himself was an animal lover, and a strict vegetarian, who hated the sight of blood. In his book *Mein Kampf*, he argued that the German national decline was due to its divergence from biological laws. He believed that in the 19th century, the Germans had neglected these laws in their pursuit of industrialization and materialism. To Hitler, existence was a Darwinian struggle where the fittest survived. Yet Hitler's conception of the homeland differed from the nature groups. It equated the German people with a species in competition with other races. Racial mixing was a cause of degeneration, and the influence of the Jewish race was the worst. Moreover to Hitler, land was not just for inspiration and molding people; it was to give living space to the German race. The land he sought extended outside the borders of the country to encompass parts of Czechoslovakia,

Belgium, Switzerland, Poland, and the Ukraine where ethnic Germans lived. It even included lands to the east, which were the prehistoric homes of the ancestral tribes.[13]

Once war broke out in 1939, protection of nature evaporated. Factories, railroads, and fortifications were built on sensitive land. Mines stripped coal without regard to damage. Youth groups became recruiting channels for the army. Top leaders like Darré, who favored nature and peasant farming, were dismissed from their positions of power. During the war, American and Royal Air Force bombing destroyed the cities, railways, and autobahns. Ground combat destroyed the rest.

After the defeat of the Nazis in 1945, the country was in ruins. People were near starvation and needed to find housing in the bombed-out cities. Protecting nature and controlling pollution were impossible luxuries. The victorious Allies divided the country into three western zones controlled by the Americans, British, and French, and an eastern zone controlled by the Soviets. By 1949 the western zones became the Federal Republic of Germany. Its Basic Law—that is, constitution—ended control of nature at the national level, giving authority back to the states. The new republic was federal, with 10 states, a form similar to the United States. As a substitute for the end of authority at the national level, the German Conservation Ring was organized as a private umbrella group. Eventually, it grew to a hundred groups representing two million individuals. The League for Bird Protection found its membership cut in half at the end of the war. In the following years it recovered gradually, under the leadership of Herman Hahnle, son of the founder. By 1965 it had 57,000 members, more than its prewar high. In 1962 it decided one of its projects should be to promote Rachel Carson's book, *Silent Spring*.[14]

Government: Germany is a parliamentary democracy. The head of the government is the chancellor, equivalent to the prime minister in other countries. He or she is elected by the Bundistag, the lower house. There is also a president with little power other than ceremonial. The chancellor heads a cabinet with 14 ministers whom he or she appoints. This includes a minister for the environment, nature conservation, and nuclear safety. The cabinet ministers come from all parts of the ruling party and sometimes another party when it is necessary to build a coalition. A chancellor selects cabinet members to give support from all sectors, and without support he or she may be removed from office in a vote of no confidence. The ministers are politicians who are elected members of the Bundistag. They administer the bureaucracies composed of permanent civil servants.

The Bundistag is equivalent to the lower house in other parliaments such as the US House of Representatives or the British House of Commons. It has 600 members, with the number varying a little depending on election results. Half are elected directly and half are elected by proportional representation, a system of allotting seats according to the votes for a party. A party must receive a minimum of 5% to qualify for proportional representation.

The Bundesrat, or upper house, is in some ways equivalent to those in other parliaments such as the US Senate or the French Senate, but its authority does not cover the full range. For instance, foreign affairs and defense policy are not under its sway. Its participants—councilors—are appointed by the governments of the various states (Lander). Different ones attend depending on the topic. For instance when debating an environmental bill, they may be the land environmental ministers. It has similarities to the United Nations General Assembly. Their jurisdiction is confined to issues that involve federal relations with the states, but in fact these are extensive so they are involved in over half the legislation.

The Federal Ministry for the Environment, Nature Conservation and Nuclear Safety, sets national policy and is responsible for air quality, water quality, waste management, noise abatement, nuclear safety, and chemical safety. It has special duties for remediation in eastern Germany. Its minister, appointed by the chancellor, sits in the cabinet. It is headquartered in Bonn with a branch office in Berlin. It was established in 1986 after the Chernobyl disaster in the Soviet Union. The Federal Environment Agency (Umweltbundesamt), established in 1974, implements the national laws on emissions trading, chemicals, pharmaceuticals, and herbicides provides scientific support to other branches of the federal government.

The federal republic has 16 states (Lander) much like the American states. In some areas they may have more power than the national government. For example, during the 1950s and 1960s, they had authority over environmental issues, and the national government did not. Even when authority is at the national level, the states may be responsible for implementation and enforcement. Again this parallels the American system of delegated programs. The largest state is North Rhine–Westphalia with a population of 18 million. Second is Bavaria with 12 million. The states are smaller versions of the national government, with environmental ministries of their own.

Post-War Events: During the 1950s people organized to oppose threats to nature. In Bavaria the League for Conservation fought proposals by the government's electric utility for dams, with mixed success. It formed alliances with the Isar Valley Society, the national Conservation Ring, and the Alpine Society. As the post-war Economic Miracle began, the now prosperous workers flooded out of cities in their new automobiles to remote beaches, lakes, and mountains. A ski resort company proposed to construct a lift to the peak of Jenner Mountain, famed for its jagged beauty. Preservationists objected. Eventually, they compromised with the tourist industry in return for its promise never to build any other ski lifts nearby. When forests were endangered by clear cutting and demands for fuel, people organized the Protective Association for the German Forest. High demand for coal prompted a proposal to strip mine near the Hohe Meissner, a unique geological formation. This triggered formation of a group to protect the site. Ultimately, the government permitted strip mining, but with safeguards.[15]

Water pollution loomed as a problem. The Rhine was labeled "Germany's Biggest Sewer." One study recorded more than a hundred major fish kills in the country every year. Detergent suds caused foaming in streams and canals. Run off from oil and gasoline fouled them. The Alliance for Protection of Germany's Waters, founded in 1951, called for a national water pollution control law. The group was a federation of nature groups plus individual members. It cooperated with groups like the Federal Union of German Industry.[16]

During the 1950s concern emerged that the industrial recovery of West Germany was damaging the workers' mental and physical health. Diseases like high blood pressure, chronic fatigue, and cancer were increasing. The solution advocated was to get back into closer contact with nature. Therefore, the country needed more parks and peaceful oases. These did not necessarily have to be wilderness areas, of which virtually none existed but could be recreated with rehabilitated forests, streams and lakes. By 1962 21 parks had been established with an extent of 2½ million acres, and more were added later.[17]

Air pollution became an issue in the 1961 federal election, with Willy Brandt, the Socialist candidate for chancellor, calling for "Blue Skies over the Ruhr." Not enough voters were persuaded (since his party lost), and industry was opposed. Although the effort was not effective at the national level, in 1962 the North Rhine–Westphalia state (Land) legislature enacted a comprehensive air pollution control law.[18] The Socialist Party was strong in this state. Soon four other states passed similar laws. The national government had passed the Clean Air Maintenance Law in 1959 in order to modernize and expand the program, but not until five years later did it issue the Technical Guidelines, which in turn required implementation by the state governments.

Brandt finally led his Socialist Party to victory in 1969, forming a coalition with the small Free Democratic Party to gain a majority in parliament. Brandt personally did not do much for the environment immediately, but he did appoint Hans-Dietrich Genscher from his partner party to become the minister of the Interior, in which capacity Genscher promoted environmental programs.

East Germany: After 1945 the Soviet occupation zone became a country separate from West Germany. Only the Communist Party was allowed. Devastation from the war had been severe, and the Soviets demanded reparations in the form of money and machinery. Food was scarce. The Communists seized most private property and established government ownership of the means of production following the Soviet model. The government built heavy industries like steel, and planned the total economy. An uprising in Berlin in June 1953 spread throughout the country, causing the Soviet Red Army to suppress it. Afterward, the Soviets tried to improve economic conditions, especially food and consumer products. Nevertheless, four million people from the East fled to the West, which was easy to do in Berlin where people routinely traveled between the eastern and western sectors. In 1961 the Soviets erected a wall through the middle of the city to cut off the emigration. Besides forcibly retaining its best workers in the East, the Communist regime tried to improve economic conditions by easing up on the central planning, which was stifling efficiency. Productivity improved during the 1960s.

The relations between the two halves of Germany were close to war. The border was fortified with barbed wire, concrete tank barriers, and explosive mines. NATO troops patrolled on one side and Soviet and East German troops patrolled the other side. Both had nuclear weapons aimed at the other. After the Wall was built, Berlin became totally divided. Both sides spied on each other.

Environmental conditions were horrendous. Government heavy industries emitted tons of smoke and fumes into the air and chemicals into the water, and the main fuel was coal. Communist economic theory gave no place to protection. Worse still, the factories were not very efficient, and their products were not attractive to consumers. The Trabant automobile typified the backwardness of the country. Using obsolete engineering, these cars drove badly, were uncomfortable, and spewed out pollution. When in

1981 a small group of pacifists demonstrated against the presence of Soviet nuclear missiles on East German soil as well as civilian nuclear reactors and industrial pollution, the government quickly suppressed them. Their motto was "Swords into Plowshares." Other mass demonstrations had little to do with the environment. In the summer of 1987 crowds of East Berlin youths gathered on their side of the Wall to hear two rock concerts being held in West Berlin near the Reichstag building. When the crowd broke into spontaneous cries for freedom and unification, police charged in.

Suddenly in 1989 the gates of the Berlin Wall were opened. In the popular parlance, the Wall fell. Political changes in the Soviet Union had undermined support for the Communist government in East Germany. In 1985 the Soviet Politburo had recognized that its tired, elderly leadership needed to be replaced and appointed Mikhail Gorbachev to head the Communist Party and the government. Gorbachev realized that oppressing the satellites in Eastern Europe was dragging down the Soviet Union. The unwillingness of the Soviets to prop up the Communist regimes in East Germany, Czechoslovakia, Poland, and elsewhere, encouraged people to be bolder in demanding more freedom, and soon the entire system collapsed. By August 1989 East Germans were permitted to travel to Czechoslovakia or Hungary and then to West Germany, where they were granted political asylum. Thousands did so. When the East German top officials asked Gorbachev for Soviet troops to prevent this, he declined. Without the troops, the situation rapidly disintegrated. During the autumn, people in Leipzig held mass demonstrations every Monday night. In Berlin in November, 500,000 Easties went to the Wall, and hundreds of thousands of Westies massed on their side. Once the gates were opened on November 9, people began spontaneously to tear down the Wall. The phenomenon surprised the West German leaders as much as their counterparts on the East.

East Germany held free elections in March 1990, but the idea that the two Germanys would remain separate was soon dismissed. On October 3 the two states were unified, and in December the united country held its first nationwide election since before Hitler came to power. The eastern portion, having about a fifth of the land and population, faced difficult problems in becoming integrated. Its industry was so backward that most was simply shut down. This dramatically improved the air and water quality. But it meant high unemployment.

Nuclear Power was controversial. As the loser of World War II, Germany had had enough of war. Yet it did not have much choice. After the surrender, the Soviet Union continued its military occupation of East Germany (as the American, British, and French did of the West). The Soviets also kept the Red Army in place in a de facto military occupation of Poland, Czechoslovakia, and other eastern countries, establishing Communist governments by force and trickery. The Americans, British, and French feared that the Soviets would invade with tanks across the plains of central Germany, so they deployed troops on their side. In 1949 they joined Italy, the Low Countries, and others to form the North Atlantic Treaty Organization (NATO), and in 1955 West Germany joined. The Americans backed up their troops with atomic bombs, soon deploying the weapons on German soil. The West German government accepted this reluctantly, but many citizens objected. They did not want to become the target of a nuclear holocaust that would fry the entire region, especially when the Americans would have some safety on the other side of the Atlantic Ocean, at least before the Soviets developed intercontinental missiles.

Germans became alarmed about the dangers of nuclear fallout from American atomic tests. They read news stories of how radioactive dust from the 1953 bombs tested in Nevada fell in measurable quantities thousands of miles away. Then the hydrogen bomb explosion at Bikini Atoll in the Pacific accidentally contaminated the crew of a Japanese trawler. Soon the Soviet Union, as well as the United States, had a stockpile of thousands of weapons. A magazine article described how an all-out attack would kill or maim 70 million people and contaminate hundreds of square miles for a generation. Next, an American general announced his estimate that an atomic war would kill several hundred million. The Germans knew they were at Ground Zero.

In 1957 the German public discovered that its NATO allies, the United States and Britain, were about to station tactical nuclear weapons on their own soil, including some to be in the hands of the Germany Army. This was literally too close to home for many. The protesters called themselves the Fight Against Atomic Death (Kampf dem Atomtod). The Social Democrats declared their party was opposed, as did groups of scientists, some labor unions, and the Evangelical Lutheran Church. Opinion polls showed two-thirds of the public were opposed. Several big demonstrations protested the atomic weapons. But the opposition disappeared within a year or so.

A different danger came from civilian nuclear power plants to generate electricity. These plants would emit radioactivity and would be likely targets in case of war. Because of the promise of cheap electricity, the city of Karlsruhe was eager for a plant but decided to locate it away from town near the Black Forest village of Friedrichstal, with only 2000 inhabitants. Its citizens feared the direct radiation, damage to their farm crops, and depletion of groundwater to supply cooling. They tried to fight the plant in the law courts but lost, so the plant was constructed in 1958.[19]

The first time citizens were successful in blocking a nuclear plant was in February 1975 when several hundred residents of Wyhl, in southwestern Germany near the French border, occupied a construction site. People believed the state government of Baden-Wuerttemberg had ignored their petition and their complaints during public hearings. Police responded with water cannons and arrests, but by the following week, 28,000 people had joined the occupation. The protest was inspired by an occupation of a proposed sulfur plant only a dozen miles away just across the border in France. Many Germans had crossed the border to participate in the French demonstration, and many French participated in the German one. Even earlier, citizens had demonstrated against a nuclear plant under construction in Kaiseraugst, Switzerland, not too far away.

The next protest occurred at the opposite end of the country in the northern town of Brokdorf in Schleswig-Holstein. In October and November 1976, thousands of demonstrators clashed with the police. The courts temporarily suspended the construction permits. The next year the most violent conflict to date occurred in Lower Saxony when 4000 police clashed with protesters who attempted to storm barriers around a reactor site. And in September 35,000 people demonstrated against a fast-breeder reactor under construction at Kalkar. The fast-breeder reactor seemed particularly dangerous because it produced plutonium, suitable for weapons.

These victorious protests occurred in spite of the Energy Crisis of 1973. West Germany had little in the way of coal or oil. Its once bountiful mines in the Ruhr were nearly depleted. National production declined rapidly from a peak in 1957 in spite of government efforts to subsidize it to help workers and owners. Strip mining brown coal (lignite) destroyed the countryside and villages, although the reclamation methods were exemplary. The country had only a few oil wells onshore. In the North Sea, reserves of oil and gas were better, but the German sector of the sea was small compared to Norway and Great Britain. Oil imports grew steadily. The federal government decided that the answer was to increase nuclear power, proposing to build 50 plants in the following 10 years.

In 1977 environmentalists asked for a moratorium on nuclear construction. The company manufacturing nuclear reactors, Kraftwerk Union, objected that it would destroy the industry, cost 260,000 jobs, and cause a shortfall in energy. This in turn would lead to an economic recession that would cost 1.6 million additional jobs. At first, the Federation of German Trade Unions came out against the moratorium, too. But later it revised its position to ask that safety be assured and that coal plants be constructed to prevent a shortage of electricity and unemployment.[20] In effect, it now endorsed the moratorium.

Until this point the political parties had said little about nuclear energy. In April 1977, the Social Democratic Party held a conference solely on energy policy. The moderate wing, including Chancellor Helmut Schmidt, did not want the moratorium because it seemed likely to hurt the economy and raise unemployment. Those on the ideological left favored the moratorium. They wanted to protect the environment and believed energy conservation measures could make up any shortfalls. The small Free Democratic Party, which was in coalition with the Socialists, split along the same lines. A few months later parties voted, both by narrow margins, to back the moratorium, but after a few more months, they edged away from it. The Socialists feared alienating its core labor union support. The opposition party, the Christian Democrats, criticized the equivocation of the Socialist and Free Democrat parties, but not being in office, they did not have to do anything. All politicians began to focus on the 1980 election.

Nuclear politics was about to become the catalyst for the Green Party. By the late 1970s many opponents of nuclear power and nuclear weapons believed they had reached the limits of their effectiveness. In spite of dramatic mass demonstrations, construction of reactors was continuing. Moreover, weapons were being deployed by both NATO and the Soviet Union. An alternative was to enter electoral politics. This is easier in Germany than in many countries because it uses proportional representation, whereby citizens vote for party lists, and after the election, the parties are entitled to a number of seats in proportion to their vote. For example, if the Socialists win 40% of the votes, they get 40% of the seats in parliament. This contrasts with Britain and the United States where every candidate for Parliament or Congress runs in a district with a single member, and the winner is the one with a plurality, that is, more than his or her opponent. In other words, the candidate who gets the most votes wins. In fact, the German system is a hybrid, with half the members of the Bundestag (lower house) elected proportionately and half elected by single member districts. Additionally, it requires a minimum of 5%, as a means of preventing very small parties. The advantage of proportional representation for the Greens was that they could get the 5% by combining small numbers of votes from many different places.

The Green Party had its first success at the local and state (Land) levels. In 1977 Greens ran in local elections in Schleswig-Holstein and Lower Saxony, both regions affected by nuclear construction. The next year they ran at the state level in Lower Saxony, Hamburg, and Hesse. At first, they won only a few local elections. In 1979, they exceeded the all-important 5% level in Bremen, which entitled them to seats in the state (Land) parliament. The Greens first put forth a list at the federal election in 1980. Disappointingly, they won only 1.5%.

The federal election of January 1983 was a breakthrough for the Greens, who won 5.6% of the votes, thus entitling them to 27 seats in the national parliament. The nuclear power issue had been crucial in attracting support to add to their other environmental planks in their platform. They also opposed deployment of US intermediate range nuclear missiles. When the Greens arrived in Parliament, they did not fit the conventional model of politicians. They said they did not want to be just a "stinking normal party," and claimed they were a movement, not a party. On the floor of Parliament they wore jeans and sweaters, carried flowers and banners, and flouted standard speech. In their early years, the Greens refused to form alliances with other parties.

The most celebrated member elected that year was Petra Kelly. She was born in Guenzburg, but moved to the United States at 12 years of age when her divorced mother married an American army officer, and Petra took his name. Kelly attended university in Washington, DC, where she participated in the civil rights and anti–Vietnam War movements. She was a lifelong admirer of Martin Luther King, Jr., and Mahatma Gandhi. In 1970 Kelly returned to Europe to begin her studies for a master's degree at the Europa-Institut of the University of Amsterdam. She took a job at the European Community headquarters in Brussels. At this time she became active in the environmental, anti-nuclear, and peace movements. Kelly was elected leader of the Greens in parliament. She explained the reason for seeking political office:

> At the moment, the party system is still the main mechanism for selecting and deciding which issues figure on the political agenda. Consequently, it is imperative, I believe, for many people in the ecology and peace movements to push themselves to the forefront of the party political stage.[21]

Upon entering parliament in 1983, the Green Party was in opposition, that is, not a member of a ruling coalition. A few months earlier in a dramatic about-face, the Free Democrats had deserted their coalition partners, the Socialists, and formed a new coalition with the Christian Democrats. This continued. The only logical partner for the Greens would have been the Socialists, and together they did not have enough votes to make a majority coalition. At the state level, however, the Greens held the balance of power in Hamburg and Hesse. Negotiations broke down in Hamburg, but in Hesse the Greens cooperated with the Socialists to make a deal. The combination voted for the budget and confirmed the Socialist candidate for premier, in return for halting construction of nuclear plants, among other concessions.

These decisions on whether to cooperate with other parties in parliament sparked dissension within the party between the "realos" and the "fundis," in other words, the realists and the fundamentalists. The fundis opposed cooperation. They wanted to control their parliamentarians by votes and directives from the grassroots. They wanted members of parliament to serve only one term, and then retire so other Green candidates could be elected. The two sides differed on policy as well as procedures. The fundis demanded that nuclear power plants be closed, that the US missiles be removed, and that Germany withdraw from NATO. The realos ignored these demands, solidified their positions of authority, and compromised on policy. An accommodation within the party was to have co-presidents and co-chairmen at many levels, one from each faction. In the 1987 election, the Greens increased their share of the vote to 8.3% giving them 44 seats.

The Greens were overtaken by the events of 1989 when the Berlin Wall came down and the East German government collapsed. In anticipation of the all-Germany elections, the Greens made contact with a parallel movement in the East, the Alliance 90 (Bündnis 90) but decided not to cooperate formally. The eastern group focused more on civil rights and had been leaders in the fall of the Communist regime. The Greens did not favor unification of the country, preferring two Germanys, both militarily neutral. Furthermore, the Socialist Party added some pro-environmental planks to its platform, sucking votes away. The result was a disaster for the Greens, who won only 4.8%, thus failing to break the 5% threshold, and resulting in no seats in parliament. Alliance 90 won 6% of the eastern vote, thus winning eight seats. Had the two cooperated, they would have won 40 seats.

The Greens learned their lesson and formed a coalition with Alliance 90 for the 1994 national election. The combination won 7.3%, thus getting

49 seats, making it the third largest party in parliament. In the 1998 election, Alliance 90/Greens (as they styled themselves) won 47 seats with 6.7% of the vote. The Socialist Party out-polled the Christian Democrats to become the largest, but still needed a few votes to make a majority, so they formed a coalition with the Greens. As a reward, its leader, Joschka Fischer, became vice chancellor and foreign minister in the new government. The Greens were further rewarded with two additional ministries—environment and health. Wags spoke of the Red–Green coalition. Like a watermelon, it was green on the outside and red on the inside. Being a member of the ruling majority was a new experience and produced strains. It became apparent that the civilian nuclear industry could not be shut down because the electricity was needed. Two foreign issues split the Greens. Germany was cooperating with NATO by sending troops on a peacekeeping mission to Kosovo in the Balkans and later assisted the United States in its invasion of Afghanistan after the September 11 attack on the World Trade Center and the Pentagon.

In the 2002 election, the Greens did even better, winning 8.6% to get 55 seats. This saved the Red–Green coalition, since the Socialists had slipped to 39%. The combination got a bare majority of 306 out of 603 seats in parliament. Again they got the foreign ministry and two other ministries. Public opinion polls showed that Joschka Fischer, the Green leader, was the most popular politician in the country. Campaigning in a flashy bus with "Joschka" painted in big letters, he drew large crowds. On the other hand, many fundis believed he had sold out. A further factor in increasing the vote for the Greens was their embrace of nonenvironmental issues such as opposition to troops in Kosovo or Afghanistan. Moreover, they favored feminism and rights for gays and lesbians, such as the bill they had initiated for a Registered Partnerships Law. From their own perspectives, the Greens believed they were the brains behind the governing coalition with the Socialists, contributing most of the ideas that appealed to the voters.

The 2005 election ended the Greens' place in a governing coalition. The Socialists (their partners for many years) received only 36% of the seats, yet their opponents, the Christian Democrats did only slightly better with 37%. Neither of the two major parties could find enough additional votes to form a majority coalition. After weeks of negotiation, the two big parties formed a Grand Coalition with the Cabinet divided evenly. The Socialists got the Environment Ministry. The 2009 election gave the Christian Democrats a majority in coalition with the Free Democrats leaving the Greens out again. They had 68 seats for 11% of the lower house of parliament.

The Netherlands has been a leader in environmental protection, comparable to Germany in its zeal, but smaller in terms of its population or economy, being only one-fifth as large. Dutch history has been the story of the people's battle with the sea. Since prehistoric times they have been pushing it back to create land by building dikes and filling in marshes. The old saying is that "God made the world, but the Dutch made Holland." By the Middle Ages its cities were some of the largest and richest in Europe. One consequence of the early urbanization was that cities had to enact regulations to control garbage and sewage. In the 19th century, rapid industrialization and more urbanization caused air and water pollution and diseases like cholera and tuberculosis. Early 19th century laws addressed these problems, culminating in the Nuisance Act of 1875, based on public health goals. That century also saw the influence of the Romantic Movement on literature and painting. The turn of the 20th century marked the establishment of early conservation and nature groups like the Foundation for the Protection of Birds and the Foundation for the Preservation of Natural Monuments.

Being located at the heart of Europe, the Netherlands was constantly at the center of wars between the Great Powers. The Congress of Vienna in 1815 declared the country to be permanently neutral, and it was able to maintain that status in World War I. But in World War II the Nazis ignored its neutrality with its blitzkrieg, conquering the country in a few days. That trauma left the Dutch even more convinced of the need to cooperate with their neighbors to guarantee their safety. In 1949 the country opted for collective security by joining NATO. The second reason to cooperate was its desire for free trade. The Netherlands has been a center of commerce for centuries. Rotterdam is the biggest port on the Continent. Even before the end of World War II, the Netherlands, Belgium, and Luxembourg formed the Benelux customs union to promote free movement of workers, capital, goods, and services. The country cooperated with the United States on the Marshall Plan and was a founding member of the Coal and Steel Community. It was a founding member of the Common Market, signing the Treaty of Rome in 1957. Since then it has become more integrated by evolving into the European Community, and then the European Union.

The government is a constitutional monarchy, nominally headed by King Willem Alexander. Its constitution was originally set forth in 1815 and has been amended many times. The First Chamber of parliament, which has limited power, is elected by the councils of the twelve provinces. The Second Chamber, which is the core of the government, is elected directly by the people. More than eight parties are represented, including a Green Party with four seats out of 150 (a recent decrease from ten). No one party can command a majority, so they must organize a coalition after each election. In recent years, politics has been unstable. One coalition collapsed in less than three months. Immigration policy has been the chief controversy because some do not welcome newcomers from the Middle East and Africa, especially Muslims. Support for the environment has remained strong, with backing in most parties.

The Green Left Party began in 1989 with a small coalition of four leftist parties, which won six seats in parliament. The following year the four merged to become a single party. Besides favoring the environment, it advocated drastic income redistribution and more benefits for immigrants. The Green Left Party won victories at the municipal and provincial level. It opposed economic growth based on the market, calling for government intervention and decentralization. In 1998 the Green Left won 7% of the vote in the national election to get 11 seats in parliament, and the next year won 12% of the vote in the European Parliament election. More recently, it has had four members in the national parliament. Democrats 66, although without the word "green" in its name, is a liberal party that firmly supports environmental protection. It has had as many as 14 seats out of 150 in the Second Chamber of Parliament, and held portfolios in the cabinet.

In 1972 the government established a Ministry of Public Health and Environmental Hygiene, and in 1982 the functions were moved to the Ministry of Housing, Spatial Planning, and the Environment. The ministry issues comprehensive plans every 4 years. To implement the plans, the government favors negotiating individual agreements with industries instead of mandating universal controls. The Netherlands passed the Water Supply Act in 1957, the Pesticides Act in 1962, the Surface Water Pollution Act in 1969, and the Air Pollution Act in 1970. As in other Western democracies, the Environmental Ministry often finds itself in conflict with three other ministries: Economic Affairs, Agriculture, and Traffic and Waterworks. The provinces have limited power, with their heads appointed by the central government. It is a unitary rather than a federal system. Mayors of municipalities are also appointed by the central government.

Decision making in the Netherlands is highly cooperative. The county's divisions between Protestants and Catholics, its rural-urban split, and its vulnerability to foreign invasion have put a premium on solving problems smoothly. A frequent metaphor is called "the polder model." A polder is a section of land reclaimed from the sea with dikes and pumps. Dutch citizens are quite aware that this can only happen through cooperative effort extending over many years and needs constant vigilance to ensure the polder does not flood. The metaphor illustrates the importance of consensus, consultation, and solidarity.[22] It contrasts with the majority rule utilized in Anglo-Saxon countries.

The emphasis on cooperation has gone too far, according to some critics. They point to the shift from enforcement to conciliation. Inspectors would rather be advisors than policemen. In 1995 facts finally came out that the TCR company, a waste disposal firm in Rotterdam, had pumped huge amounts of poisonous chemicals directly into the Maas River without any questions being asked by the government. In the meantime the company had received an International Standards Organization (ISO) certificate and $11 million in subsidy. (These are environmental criteria set out by the ISO, a federation of standards agencies from more than 150 countries.) Four years later news came about two companies that were mixing fat wastes from the sewers into animal food, while earning certificates for Good Manufacturing Processes.[23] A less serious criticism is that the process is too slow, leading to endless discussion.

Traditionally, the country was organized into four pillars (verzuiling) of Protestant, Catholic, Liberal, and Socialist. Each community had its own schools, clubs, newspapers, social work agencies, farm cooperatives, radio stations, and so forth. The witticism was that on Sunday morning the Protestants went to church, the Catholics went to mass, the Liberals tended their gardens, and the Socialists washed their motorcycles. National decisions were carefully and slowly negotiated in private among the pillars at the elite level. In recent years the pillars have not been as strong due to declines in religious and ideological devotion. The environmental movement has been a force toward more openness. Protests against nuclear energy at Almelo, Kalkar, and Dodewaard between 1978 and 1981 marked the emergence of direct citizen participation.[24]

The government has engaged in comprehensive planning for many years. In the past these plans used to be drawn up by government experts and coordinated with leaders of the affected groups, but now they involve direct consultation with citizens and businesses. Because business has more resources to gather data and present its arguments, this sector has tended to be more influential. The Third Plan sought to address problems broader than merely cleaning up pollution such as overconsumption and the destructiveness of economic growth. The Fourth Plan in 2003 was even more global, looking ahead 30 years, and addressing issues like climate change, loss of biodiversity, and resource scarcity. The Fifth Plan emphasized compact cities.

The number one Dutch environmental threat is the sea. More than a third of the land is below sea level, and the polders are subject to flooding. The worst disaster occurred in 1953, when a severe storm, coupled with a high tide, breached the dikes in Zeeland, drowning 1835 people. Even with reclamation, the land has a natural tendency to sink. Higher sea level caused by global warming is a particular threat because then North Sea storms could destroy the dikes. The government already has increased the required height of the dikes. Increased rainfall due to warming could cause the Rhine and Meuse rivers to flood frequently. A 1995 flood forced 200,000 people to evacuate. The government has decided to give the rivers more room, allowing them to flood naturally, rather than trying futilely to contain them. Over the next 50 years 222,000 acres of land will be returned to floodplain as natural forests and marshes as in ancient time. Another 62,000 acres of pasture will be available for temporary flooding, and 185,000 more acres of farmland will be modified so they can tolerate soggy conditions in the winter and spring.

In addition to the dangers from the sea, the Netherlands suffers from more mundane forms of pollution found in all industrial countries. Factories and power plants discharge water contaminated by nitrates, phosphates, heavy metals, and organic compounds. The Rhine and Meuse Rivers bring pollution from Germany, France, and Switzerland. Air pollution comes from vehicles and refineries. In turn, its own dirty air wafts into Germany and Belgium, and dirty water flows into the North Sea.

Acid rain first became an issue at the 1972 Earth Summit in Stockholm. The Scandinavians complained that sulfur and nitrogen oxides emitted by industries burning coal and oil from the Netherlands (as well as a swath from England to Poland) were drifting north and falling as rain that acidified their lakes. Little was done at first. Later Germany began to feel the effects as its own forests died back. Research showed that about 80% of the sulfur and nitrogen oxides from the Netherlands were exported via the atmosphere to neighboring countries. In 1979 most European countries signed the Convention on Long Range Trans-boundary Air Pollution. Although this treaty did not contain any concrete commitments, it was a start. In 1984, 10 countries agreed to reduce sulfur dioxide emissions by 30% over the following nine years. At the same time the Netherlands implemented specific plans to reduce emissions for this as well as for nitrogen oxides and ammonia. In the following years, emissions limits were further refined and tightened.[25] In its policy making, the Netherlands tended to follow Germany, both as a model and as a source of pressure to reduce trans-boundary pollution.

Jan Pronk typifies Dutch leadership both at home and internationally. He was elected to the Second Chamber multiple times between 1971 and 1989 as a member of the Labor Party, serving as a minister for development cooperation. In 1998 he was appointed Minister of Housing, Spatial Planning, and the Environment. Internationally, he served in high positions in the United Nations and its agencies. He chaired the conference of the parties for the Kyoto Protocol in 2001 in the Hague and its follow up at Bonn. Unfortunately, the Hague negotiations ended in collapse, partly blamed on Pronk's trying to force through an agreement. On the other hand, the conflict between the Europeans and the United States (now that Bush had become president) was probably too great to allow an agreement.

The Oostvaardersplassen is a unique experiment in rewilding, that is, recreating a natural wilderness like what existed thousands of years ago before humans lived there. This is a park of 15,000 acres of grassland populated by red deer, horses, foxes, geese, and egrets. In prehistoric times one would have found aurochs, gigantic ancestors of modern cattle. But because aurochs have been extinct for a century, their substitutes are Heck cattle. The biologists in charge set the scene but do not manage the park. Tourists can take a Pleistocene safari for a daily charge of $45. Other experiments in rewilding are beginning in Siberia, Spain, and the Balkans.

The Dutch pride themselves on taking a leading role in the environment. One method is to set a good example as with pollution control and returning parts of rivers to wetlands. Regarding global warming, the Netherlands in 1993 offered to reduce its output by 3%, then prior to the Kyoto conference raised that to a 10% reduction. In the mid-1990s, it entered into a half-dozen international projects to reduce carbon emissions, mostly with Costa Rica. In order to advance international cooperation, the Dutch use several techniques. One is to sponsor conferences. Another is very thorough preparation. They do their homework carefully by researching and marshaling information. Their delegations are large, considering the small size of their population.

Today, many interest groups exist. Domestically, leading groups include Codename Future, the National Youth Coalition on Environment and Development, and Young Environmental Activists. The Dutch affiliate of Friends of the Earth, Milieu Defensie Holland, has 85,000 members in a hundred local chapters. It advocates more mass transportation and opposed expansion of the giant Schiphol airport. The Environmental Ministry pays several million dollars annually to subsidize the operations of about 30 groups, mostly for specific projects. Some groups have taken the duty of monitoring the implementation of covenants between businesses and the government.[26] Internationally, the world headquarters for Greenpeace is in Amsterdam.

Denmark is also a leader in protecting the environment, along with Germany and the Netherlands. With a population of only five million, it is a low, sandy country composed of the Jutland peninsula and many islands. The Atlantic Drift, an extension of the Gulf Stream, keeps it warm despite its northern latitude. With its Viking heritage, it was late to become integrated with European institutions, and with its peripheral location, it was slow to develop industrially. The Romantic Movement in nearby Germany influenced its art and literature. Landscapes were a popular subject to paint. In 1819 Adam Oehlenschläger wrote a poem that became the national anthem.

> There is a lovely land with spreading, shady beeches
> Near the Baltic's salty strand, its hills and valleys gently fall.
> Its ancient name is Denmark, and it is Freya's hall.

By the turn of the 20th century, Danes were becoming interested in protecting nature. The Danish Conservation Society (Naturfredningsforening), founded in 1911, promoted outdoor recreation, but was not particularly interested in wilderness or controlling pollution. Its members tended to be professionals who wanted opportunities for hiking, fishing, sailing, and summer cottages, often opposing local landowners. Society members were well connected with government, and many were civil servants. Rural planning was often an issue. This fit the extensive government role in welfare and progressive education.

During the Great Depression of the 1930s, cooperation had developed between the government, industry, and labor, making it a leading example of a communitarian nation. In World War I Denmark maintained its neutrality, but in World War II, the Nazis ignored its declaration of neutrality, invading in 1940 and occupying it for 5 years. In the 1950s the government expanded its welfare state with old-age pensions, health insurance, disability insurance, and more generous unemployment benefits. These were universal, not just for the poor. Schools, vocational training, and higher education were expanded too. The economy prospered from the late 1950s on, increasing wealth, but also pollution. Industry spread from the old cities into the countryside, displacing established agriculture.

Environmentalism came to Denmark via the antinuclear movement. It was inspired by the British demonstrations against atomic weapons manufacturing in England and US submarines based in Scotland. This gave it a more radical and purist cast than in other countries. In 1962 30,000 people marched in Copenhagen to protest nuclear weapons and power plants. A number of the leaders came from the old Left with ties to the Danish Communist Party dating back to the 1930s. As the demonstrations evolved, younger leaders took over with more of a New Left perspective. Protests were also connected to opposition to the US War in Vietnam and to solidarity with the Third World.

In the 1960s two new groups appeared: NOAH and the Organization for Information about Nuclear Power. The first was a radical offshoot of an old natural history organization that decided to play with its acronym to tie to the Biblical rescue of the animals from the flood. It held to Marxist ideology, and believed little could be done to protect the environment as long as capitalism existed. It did not believe in "half solutions" or technological fixes. It said "no" to growth and maintained that excessive consumption is the problem. In addition NOAH expressed solidarity with the Third World. Later it affiliated with Friends of the Earth. The other group was more practical and aimed solely at condemning nuclear power, both weapons and electric generation. In 1975 a third group began, the Organization for Renewable Energy. In the 1980s a younger, more active members took over control of the Conservation Society.

Like other Western countries, Denmark fashioned its policy during the Environmental Decade. It passed a Conservation Act in 1969, a Zoning Act in 1970, and planning acts in 1973 and 1975. On the non-planning side, parliament passed the General Protection Act in 1973 and the Chemical Act in 1979. In 1971 it established the Ministry of the Environment, now consisting of the Environmental Protection Agency, the Forest Agency, the Cadastral Survey, and the Geological Survey. It also has a Research Institute and a small Environmental Assessment Institute.

Denmark is a constitutional monarchy, nominally headed by Queen Margrethe II. Its parliament is unicameral, with eight parties. Election is by proportional representation, whereby a citizen votes for a party rather than an individual member. Of the 175 seats, after the 2011 election the Red Green Alliance held 12, but other parties supported the environment. In the 2001 a Liberal-conservative coalition had come to power, replacing the Social Democrats who were originally a labor party, but had moved to a more general middle-class position. In spite of the name Liberal, the party is quite conservative by European standards, advocating a tax freeze and tight immigration control. Yet it favors strong environmental protection. The coalition won again in 2005 and 2007. This Liberal-led majority is less favorable to the environment than its predecessor, led by the Social Democrats. With many parties, no permanent coalition can be put together, so majorities have to be put together for each vote.

From 1982 to 1993 environmental proposals had found support in parliament from the so-called Green Majority, which was not a permanent majority. Fragmentation meant that the cabinet had to cobble together majorities on particular votes. Members from the governing coalition would entice members from the opposition parties to pass a single bill. In 1993 the Social Democrats won the election which enabled them to forge a majority with the Social Liberals, the Center Democrats and the People's Party. Thus, most of the green-leaning parliamentarians were in the same coalition. The minister for the environment declared that "green issues would be the red thread of the government's policy."[27]

The country is divided into 14 counties and two cities: Copenhagen and Frederiksberg. Its form is unitary rather than federal. Additionally, Greenland and the Faeroe Islands are self-governing dependencies.

The Liberal-led coalition elected in 2001 and reelected four years later had a mixed record. On the positive side, it pledged in its platform to protect the environment, demonstrating this commitment when Denmark held the presidency of the European Union in 2004. This is the rotating headship, during which it pushed the EU for stronger control of chemicals; adopted new regulations on water, mining, and transporting waste; and asked the commission staff in Brussels to set more ambitious goals. After a long gestation, the new EU Environmental Agency began operating out of its headquarters in Copenhagen. The agency concerns itself with the technical and statistical aspects, not policy. In terms of saving energy, Denmark is acclaimed for using wind energy, with windmills spotting the landscape. One small island, Samso, has gained world attention by generating all of its electricity by windmills. It even exports a surplus to the rest of the country.

On the negative side, the government appointed Bjorn Lomborg, author of *The Skeptical Environmentalist*, to direct the Environmental Assessment Institute. Lomborg was a statistician who won fame as a vigorous opponent of the Kyoto Protocol. He attacked it as based on weak science and not being efficient from the economic perspective. Under his direction the institute advocated getting the most for the money, finding cheap solutions, and trading emissions allowances. Within a few years, Denmark became the first country to buy carbon allowances from Russia. Earlier it had purchased half of the carbon emissions quota of Moldova, the maximum that former Soviet republic was allowed to sell. Critics argued that Denmark should reduce its emissions at home.

Even prior to assuming his position directing the institute, Lomborg had come in for bitter criticism. The Committee on Scientific Dishonesty, a branch of the National Research Agency that draws together some of the country's most senior scientists, officially condemned his work. The committee's 6640-word verdict concluded that his book "is deemed to fall within the concept of scientific dishonesty" and that it "is deemed clearly contrary to the standards of good scientific practice." The committee said that "The defendant . . . based on customary scientific standards and in light of his systematic one-sidedness in the choice of data and line of argument, has clearly acted at variance with good scientific practice."[28] Later the Science Ministry, reflecting the views of the conservative political leaders, overturned the committee's dishonesty verdict.

Denmark has another aspect to its environmental policy: Greenland. This largest island in the world had been under Danish sovereignty since 1605, based on claims of ancient Viking settlement. The most important threat comes from global warming. Virtually any scenario of the future puts Greenland at the center. If the ice cap melts, the water will raise the sea level. Furthermore, the freshwater will be enough to disrupt the Gulf Stream–Atlantic Drift due to lessened salt content of the North Atlantic. Over the years, many scientific expeditions have drilled cores in the ice of Greenland to measure temperatures in the geologic past. The giant island has some potential for oil, for which the government hopes to drill. At present the number of tourists is small, but the government has aspirations here as well. To entice them, the Greenland provincial government plans to permit tourists to hunt polar bears. Native hunters earn $1000 or more per skin, and expect that visitors would pay in the range of $10,000.

Today, many believe that the center of Danish environmental activity is no longer in Denmark, but in Brussels at the EU headquarters. For instance, the Society for Nature Conservation lobbies there, and in turn tries to keep the Danish public aware of what is happening in Brussels. It cooperates with organizations from around Europe. Its main partner is the European Environmental Bureau, a federation of 140 citizens groups. The Danish Ecological Council, a research and educational group, is also a member. Besides policy within their own country, Danish groups are interested in environmental problems in the Third World. The government has donated 1% of its budget to environmental aid overseas.

Denmark was the center of attention in 2009 when the Conference of the Parties met in Copenhagen to consider how to repair the Kyoto Protocol. For the prior year or so, it was obvious to all that the industrial countries were not going to honor their agreement to reduce greenhouse gases. Moreover, China, not a country with a reduction target but growing industrially, was now the second-largest emitter after the United States. Optimists hoped China and India would join the industrial countries to make new, firm commitments. They talked buoyantly about the "Road to Copenhagen." Many countries sent their presidents and prime ministers instead of lower-ranking diplomats. But by the time the conference convened, pessimism reigned. Agreement was impossible, and the distinguished world leaders left in embarrassment.

Sweden, like Germany, the Netherlands, and Denmark, has been strongly pro-environmental. Its first major act of leadership was to sponsor the 1972 United Nations Conference on the Human Environment, the first Earth Summit. Most of Sweden's population of 11 million live in the south. The northern part of the country is cold and mountainous. Two-thirds of the total land mass is forested, and only a tenth is arable. Although humans have lived in the region since the end of the Ice Age, their numbers were small and their impact was slight. Much of the land was not settled intensively until the second half of the 19th century, when the so-called "timber frontier" moved across the pine-dominated northern forests to provide lumber for export and domestic use. Many trees harvested then were as old as 300 to 500 years.

Like its Scandinavian sister, Denmark, Sweden's peripheral location meant it was slow to integrate with Europe during the Middle Ages. In the 17th century, much of the contact took the form of wars with Denmark, Germany, and Russia. In the 18th century, the Enlightenment produced an intellectual flowering. The botanist Carolus Linnaeus developed the binomial system of nomenclature and originated the modern scientific classification of plants and animals. The Swedish Academy was founded in 1786.

By the 19th century, the country turned from Enlightenment rationality to the emotionalism of the Romantic Movement imported from Germany. Themes in painting and poetry glorified nature, the countryside, and peasants. Science blossomed as well with exploration of the polar regions. In 1895 the chemist Svante Arrhenius discovered the greenhouse effect and calculated its impact at every latitude. In 1903 the kingdom passed a modern forestry law based on sustainable yield.

Sweden has not fought a war since 1814. Its neutrality during the First and Second World Wars spared it the catastrophes of the century, and encouraged the kingdom to take a role in diplomacy and peacekeeping. Internally, it enjoys advantages in its homogeneous population. Its generous welfare programs began in 1910 with workers compensation insurance law.

Like Denmark and the Netherlands, Sweden is a constitutional monarchy, nominally headed by King Carl Gustaf. Its unicameral parliament has 349 members elected by a system of proportional representation. Eight parties hold seats. On the left, the Social Democrats and the Left Wing usually form one coalition and on the right Moderates, Liberals, and the Center Party usually form an opposing coalition. The parties of the so-called left are actually quite moderate. The Social Democrats, who were in power for a half century, have been weaker in recent years but are still the single largest party.

In 1988 the Environmental Party Greens won 20 seats, entering parliament for the first time. In this election it crossed the threshold of 4% to qualify. Ten years later it found itself in a crucial position. The Social Democrats had done poorly in the election, and its coalition with the Left Wing was a few votes short, so they invited the Greens to become part of the ruling block. Recently, it has not been officially part of the government but has cooperated in votes in parliament on a case by case basis. The 2006 election shifted power from the Social Democrats, who had long led the government, to a moderate coalition, that is, more conservative. It was slightly less favorable to the environment. In 2010 the Environmental Party Greens won 7%. The Greens also put up candidates for the European Parliament. In 2009 they won two seats out of seventeen for Sweden.

The Party advocates green taxes, protecting primeval forests, safeguarding rivers, animal-friendly agriculture, and opposes genetically modified food and crops. Furthermore, the platform includes many issues beyond the environment. It favors human rights and disarmament and opposes exporting weapons. The Greens want Sweden to leave the European Union. They maintain that too many decisions are made in Brussels behind closed doors.

The government is led by a prime minister and cabinet, who are selected from parliament. Although not officially a federal system, the government is decentralized, so that elected county and municipal governments play a major role in running the country. For example, the national EPA does not directly impose regulations but designs targets, measures, and control mechanisms, and then monitors and assesses them.

Sweden is famous for its belief in equality and solidarity. It is a leading example of communitarianism. During the 1930s, it evolved the concept of *folkhemmet*, a utopian form of social engineering for a paternalistic welfare state, characterized by a classless society, government provision of many services, and the quest for social justice. Decision making was by consensus. The elite negotiated agreements and compromises and prided itself on avoiding conflict. Neutrality in World War II spared the country a Nazi invasion, and after the war steady economic growth resulted in prosperity, which reduced social conflict. In foreign affairs, the nation set goals of being a good neighbor, criticizing exploitation and military aggression, aiding the Third World, and setting a good example. On the negative side, Swedish decision making can take a long time as all the various interests are reconciled. Moreover, the system favors existing interests, and new ones like environmental groups have had difficulty breaking in.

At the individual level, Swedes believe in *allemansratt*, all humans having the right of access to nature, meaning that anyone can hike in the countryside or swim off a beach without excessive concern with private property. Hikers can ramble about picking berries, mushrooms, or rosehips. Paths go across the fields, with gates or stiles at the fences. People can even camp on private property for one night. They do have an obligation to not get too close to the owner's house, however, and to leave the campsite clean. Swedes are also enthusiastic recyclers, dropping off their waste at ubiquitous collection points. This includes heavy items like white goods, old mattresses, and construction material.

In 1967 Sweden established the Environmental Protection Agency (Naturvardsverket), and two years later passed a law to regulate air, water, and noise pollution. It concentrated on point sources such as sewer discharges. In 1987 it established the Ministry of the Environment with EPA as part. The kingdom uses taxes and charges to protect the environment. For example, leaded fuel and sulfur are taxed to discourage their use. When introduced in 2000, this was labeled the Green Tax Shift.

In 1999 Sweden redrafted its laws by adopting a comprehensive Environmental Code. Besides consolidating existing legislation, the code introduced environmental courts, set ambient quality standards, clarified the function of impact assessments, and integrated the European Union water regulations. It uses economic instruments like taxes and charges. The code promulgates seven principles: precaution, best possible technology, appropriate location, eco-cycle, product choice, and polluter pays. City and rural planning is another method of environmental improvement. The country is famous for it city planning, dating back more than a century. The first planning law in 1874 addressed health problems caused by air and water pollution. Today, the 1987 national Planning and Building Act assigns primary responsibility to the municipalities. The biggest cities of Stockholm, Gothenburg, and Malmo have metropolitan area plans. In rural areas, protecting the landscape is a county function.

Industry is more prone to cooperate on environmental protection than in other countries. The Confederation of Swedish Enterprises published a *Vision for Sustainable Industrial Development* in 2000. Nearly three thousand companies are certified according to ISO 14001, giving Sweden the highest rate of certification in the world. The government has signed many voluntary agreements with industry in areas such as shipping, gasoline, and pesticides. Nevertheless, industry still favors its own interests. The confederation lobbies for tax cuts, opposes regulation, and advocates letting private companies take over government activities like health care and education. The organization has a staff of 200 in its headquarters plus 21 regional offices around the country and a branch in Brussels for lobbying the EU. Its *Vision* report brags that the industry is doing a good job so far in cleaning up the environment.

Acid rain was the first environmental problem Sweden faced internationally. By the mid-1960s scientists recognized that sulfur emissions from England, the Low Countries, and Germany were drifting north to fall as rain, snow, or solids on the delicate boreal soil. The post-glacial soil lacks buffers found farther south, so the acid washed into lakes, where it increased the acid balance causing fish and plants to die. For a long time, the acid-emitting countries denied their responsibility, claiming scientific evidence was not conclusive. Sweden presented incriminating data at the 1972 Stockholm Conference and at other European meetings without much success. Finally, in 1982 the polluting countries acknowledged the damage they were doing. Germany, for one, recognized its own problem of trees dying in the Black Forest. Finally, in 1985 Sweden and other affected countries signed a protocol under the Convention on Long Range Trans-boundary Air Pollution, and three years later another on nitrous oxides.

The Stockholm Conference on the Human Environment, known as the first Earth Summit, was a turning point. Credit for the idea goes to Inga Thorsson, an employee at the United Nations in New York. The head of the country's delegation, Sverker Astrom, promoted the idea. In 1968 Sweden introduced a resolution at a meeting of the UN Economic and Social Council. The promoters set a date for the summit four years in the future to give time for thorough preparation. Because the Swedes initiated the proposal, Stockholm was the logical site. As preparations began, public interest in the environment grew rapidly. Many Western countries debated and passed laws. The first Earth Day in 1970 was an international event. When the Conference opened in Stockholm, delegations came from 113 countries. The UN named Maurice Strong to be the secretary-general for the conference. He was a Canadian diplomat and businessman, who took an energetic role in making the meeting a success.

By its end the conference issued three documents. First was a brief *Blueprint for Survival* outlining objectives in 13 categories, with a timeline out to the year 2075, such as the elimination of pesticides. Second was the Declaration on the Human Environment, with 26 principles, such as Number 6: ending the discharge of toxic material. Some principles went beyond strictly environmental ones, such as ending racial discrimination and colonialism. Third was to set out an Action Plan later adopted by the UN General Assembly. This led to establishment of the UN Environment Program. The conference also advanced negotiations for treaties like the Convention on International Trade in Endangered Species (CITES).

The Stockholm Summit was strongly influenced by the Club of Rome *Report* issued only a few weeks before it convened. This was a massive computer simulation of the future of the earth, predicting scarcity of land for farming and resources like oil and timber, and a surplus of pollution.

The *Report* forecast that unless the industrial world acted immediately the entire world economy would collapse as early as the year 2020, leading to mass starvation, poisonous pollution, and warfare. It was a sobering way to start the conference.

Today global warming is one of the issues that concerns Sweden most. Although the Arrhenius was the first to discover the problem, for much of the 20th century, it did not seem to be much of a danger. A number of Swedes (including Arrhenius) thought a little more warmth might be good. The country burns a lot of fossil fuel, and in a referendum in 1980 it voted to phase out its nuclear electric plants. At that time 12 nuclear plants were in operation, supplying half of the Swedish electricity. In 1986 routine monitoring of them had detected the excessive radiation in the atmosphere that was the first sign of the Chernobyl accident in the Soviet Union. Yet when the government moved to actually shut down two reactors in 1997, public opposition was strong, especially from labor unions. An opinion poll showed 66% of the public opposed closing the plant.

Sweden did not join the European Union until 1995. One reason for its reluctance was that ties to Europe would violate its neutrality and might suck it into war. Another was that its environmental standards were higher than the rest of Europe. Therefore, it negotiated a transition agreement for its protection. Since then EU environmental standards have become stricter, now matching those of Sweden. On the other side, Sweden has a duty to implement the EU directives. Overall its record is excellent.

Margot Wallström typifies a political leader concerned about the environment. As a young woman, just out of high school, she joined the staff of the Social Democratic Party as the Youth League ombudsman. At the age of 25 she was elected to parliament. In 1988 Wallström became minister of consumer affairs, women, and youth, and later minister of culture and minister of social affairs. In 1999 she went to Brussels to become the EU commissioner for the environment. After heading the commission for 5 years, she was promoted to be a vice president of the European Commission, that is, the executive branch (bureaucracy) of the EU.

CONCLUSION

Citizen participation has been a hallmark of these leaders of northern Europe. At Wyhl in Germany, hundreds protested against a proposed nuclear plant, and in Brokdorf, the crowd numbered in the thousands. In Denmark in 1962, 30,000 people marched to protest nuclear weapons and power plants. Voters have consistently elected members of parliament who back green legislation and programs.

Interest groups are numerous and influential. In Germany in the 1950s, the Isar Valley Society, the Conservation Ring, and the Alpine Society mobilized to block dams for electric generation. In the 1960s, the League for Bird Protection had 57,000 members and, in an example of international diffusion, made one of its projects to promote Rachel Carson's book *Silent Spring*. The Netherlands has groups like Friends of the Earth with 85,000 members. Other groups are Codename Future, the National Youth Coalition on Environment and Development, and Young Environmental Activists. The world headquarters of Greenpeace is in Amsterdam.

The German Socialist Party was the first in the world to put the environment in its platform in 1961 with the call for "Blue Skies over the Ruhr." The country's Green Party has been the most effective such party in the world, with its partnership in the governing coalition from 1998 to 2005. It continues to elect a block of members to the Bundistag and is likely to go back into power in the future. In a similar fashion in Sweden, the Environment Party Greens joined the Socialists in a governing coalition in 1998. From 1982 on the Danish parliament was dominated by the unofficial Green Majority, and later by a coalition with strong environmental membership. All four of these northern countries have enacted strong laws to protect the air and water and to limit nuclear power.

The German governmental structure has differences and similarities to the United States. Unlike the United States, it does not have a strong president. The chancellor is a member of parliament and selects the cabinet ministers from its members. The proportional representation system makes it easier for a small party like the Greens to win seats. The other three parliamentary democracies of the Netherlands, Denmark, and Sweden are similar. Germany is a federation like the United States, and laws are delegated to the states for implementation. Indeed, compared to the United States, Germany has more power at the state level. The three smaller countries are not federations. The consequences for the environment are not apparent. Structure, by itself, does not seem to make the leaders more green or less green.

The ultimate example of diffusing ideas via the diplomatic agenda was the 1972 Stockholm Earth Summit, sponsored by Sweden. For some delegations like that from the People's Republic of China, it was the first time they had heard of environmental protection. For others like Britain, France, and the Low Countries, it was the occasion when Sweden confronted them about acid rain. For the European Community, it was the impetus for its first Environment Action Program that set forth a number of principles that have been adopted worldwide: prevention is better than remediation, prevention at the source, the polluter pays, integration among air, water, and groundwater, and precaution. In preliminary talks about the 1992 Rio Earth Summit, Germany led the world in pledges to reduce greenhouse gases, proclaiming it would cut 30%. Three years later Germany hosted the Conference of the Parties leading to the Berlin Mandate, and it provided a permanent home for the secretariat in Bonn.

These northern leaders learned about environmental protection from each other, and from the United States, and other Europeans. They read *Silent Spring* and watched films by Jacques Cousteau. They had untold connections to other countries. All read the *Club of Rome Report*. These four countries earned the label of leaders by setting the example and by deliberate leadership. Swedish sponsorship of the Stockholm summit put it at the forefront. Germany, in the period coming up to the Kyoto Protocol, pledged massive cuts in its greenhouse gases. The US Green Party was a direct copy of the German Greens. Dutch rewilding in Oostvaardersplassen makes it the first in Western Europe to act on a large scale.

NOTES

1. Heinrich Heine, "Lorelei." Translated by A. Z. Foreman, *Poems Found in Translation*, Web.
2. William H. Rollins, *A Greener Version of Home* (Ann Arbor: University of Michigan Press, 1997), pp. 70–71.
3. Rollins, *A Greener Version of Home,* pp. 72, 77.
4. Raymond H. Dominick, *The Environmental Movement in Germany* (Bloomington: Indiana University Press, 1992), pp. 42, 43.
5. Thomas M. Lekan, *Imagining the Nation in Nature* (Cambridge, Mass.: Harvard, 2004), pp. 32–33.
6. Rollins, *A Greener Version of Home,* pp. 87, 92, 97.
7. Dominick, *The Environmental Movement in Germany,* pp. 53–55, 47–49.
8. PSM, "Weimar Constitution," Web.
9. Dominick, *The Environmental Movement in Germany,* p. 98.
10. Anna Bramwell, *Blood and Soil: Richard Walther Darré and Hitler's Green Party* (Bourne End, Buckinghamshire, UK: Kensal, 1985), pp. 91, 171.
11. Dominick, *The Environmental Movement in Germany,* p. 106.
12. Lekan, *Imagining the Nation in Nature,* p. 153.

13. Lekan, *Imagining the Nation in Nature*, pp. 156–159.
14. Dominick, *The Environmental Movement in Germany*, pp. 120–123
15. Dominick, *The Environmental Movement in Germany*, pp. 131, 135.
16. Dominick, *The Environmental Movement in Germany*, pp. 140–141.
17. Sandra Cheney, "For Nation and Prosperity, Health and a Green Environment," in *Nature in German History,* ed. Christ of Mauch (New York: Berghahn Books, 2004), pp. 102–104.
18. Miranda A. Schreurs, *Environmental Politics in Japan, Germany and the United States* (New York: Cambridge, 2002), p. 48.
19. Dominick, pp. 162–163.
20. Michael T. Hatch, *Politics and Nuclear Power: Energy Policy in Western Europe* (Lexington: Univ. Press of Kentucky, 1986), pp. 84–87.
21. Petra Kelly, *Fighting for Hope* (Boston: South End Press, 1984), p. 17.
22. Pieter Glasbergen and Henri J. M. Goverde, "Greening Political Institutions," in *Greening Society: The Paradigm Shift in Dutch Environmental Politics*, ed. Peter P. J. Driessen and Pieter Glasbergen (Dordrecht: Kluwer, 2002), p. 192.
23. Herman Vuijsje, *The Politically Correct Netherlands* (Westport, Conn.: Greenwood, 2000), pp. 11–12.
24. Pieter Leroy and Jan P. M. Tatenhove, "Environment and Participation," in *Greening Society*, ed. Driessen and Glasbergen, p.169.
25. Duncan Liefferink, *Environment and the State: the Netherlands, the EU and Acid Rain* (Manchester: Manchester University Press, 1996), pp. 70–75.
26. Dagmar Timmer, "Strategic Cooperation: The Role of NGOs in the Netherlands National Environmental Policy Plan," Resource Renewal Institute Green Plans, Web.
27. Mikael Skou Andersen, "Denmark: The Shadow of the Green Majority," in *European Environmental Policy: the Pioneers* (Manchester: Manchester University Press, 1997), p. 267.
28. Michael McCarthy, "Best Selling Scourge of the Greens Accused of Dishonesty," *The Independent,* January 9, 2003.

4

Britain, France, and
the European Union

Although Germany and its northern neighbors enjoy a reputation as leaders, Great Britain and France have also promoted good policies to clean up their environments, especially since the 1970s. In recent years, the European Union has assumed a role of its own. Other countries on the continent like Italy and Spain have followed, albeit as a slower pace. Critics sometimes labeled Britain as a laggard, but in many ways it is a leader.

Great Britain has never had a natural environment completely untouched by humans. Mesolithic peoples moved into the area as soon as the glaciers retreated 10,000 years ago, burning forests and chopping out clearings. With the beginning of agriculture about 3500 BC, people cleared permanent fields and cut down trees for fuel and buildings. Bronze Age farmers knew the importance of rotating crops and manuring their fields. A combination of grazing and burning created moors devoid of trees. By the Middle Ages, Englishmen were mining tin, iron, and copper, burning charcoal, digging coal, and draining the wet fens. At the time of the *Doomsday Book* in 1085, only 15% percent of England remained wooded. For his personal hunting pleasure, the king preserved areas designated as Royal Forests, Chasses, and Deer Parks. The kingdom's first air pollution law dates to the 14th century when the Crown forbid coal fires in London while Parliament was sitting. In 1661 the problem of acid rain was first identified and understood.

Early in the 18th century, wealthy landowners began to surround their houses with gardens planted in a naturalistic style. Flowers and trees adorned their property with curving footpaths and vistas of distant faux temples and ruins seen over ponds and streams. The layout was informal and asymmetrical. The style soon acquired the name of "an English garden," and the fad spread across the Continent as a *jardin anglais* or an *Englischer garten*. In fact, the fashion owed its origin, at least in part, to the Chinese scholar's garden after English visitors to China sent back descriptions in 1692. It was an early example of an environmental concept being diffused internationally.

As the leader in the industrial revolution during the 19th century, Britain was notorious for foul air and water. Government was forced to take some action. In 1863 it established the Alkali Inspectorate to control emissions from the chemical industry, and in 1876 Parliament passed the Rivers Pollution Prevention Act. The alkali legislation introduced the terminology of "best practicable means," which became the basis of a series of individual voluntary agreements rather than mandatory national standards. This began a pattern that implementation was specific to the site and achieved through a process of bargaining and accommodation. The physical setting of the British Isles has minimized pollution damage. They are windswept, and have short, fast-flowing rivers. Sewage piped into the Channel or the North Sea was diluted with no apparent threat to bathers.

An 18th-century clergyman, Gilbert White, has earned the title of England's first ecologist. Spending his entire life near Selborne in Hampshire, he wrote down his daily observations year after year in journals and letters, eventually being published as *The Natural History and Antiquities of Selborne*. He believed in studying birds by observation rather than shooting them. White was one of the first to understand that swallows and martins migrated during the winter, rather than hibernating underground as the folk tradition said. He had a keen eye for the interconnections of a natural community:

> Earthworms, though in appearance a small and despicable link in the chain of nature, yet, if lost, would make a lamentable chasm . . . worms seem to be the great promoters of vegetation, which would proceed but lamely without them.[1]

The British Romantic Movement of the 19th century shared the German rejection of the Enlightenment with its universalism, rationality, and science. Likewise, its champions resented overidentification with French ideas, culture, and language. Nineteenth-century poets like Byron, Coleridge and Wordsworth found inspiration in nature and the untamed countryside. Wordsworth described the Lake District as "a sort of national property, in which every man has a right and an interest who has an eye to perceive and a heart to enjoy."[2] Putting his emotions to verse, he wrote:

I wandered lonely as a cloud, That floats on high o'er vales and hills,
When all at once I saw a crowd, A host, of golden daffodils;
Beside the lake, beneath the trees, Fluttering and dancing in the breeze.[3]

Nature lovers organized. In 1865 the Commons, Open Spaces, and Footpaths Preservation Society was founded, and in 1889 the Royal Society for the Protection of Birds was founded. The National Trust was established in 1895, due to concern about the impact of uncontrolled development and industrialization. The trust, a private charity, acted to protect threatened buildings, coastlines, and countryside. As people began to tour the mountainous regions, many proposed creating national parks like those in the United States, but this met with opposition from local landowners. In the 1930s hikers and conservationists in groups like the Ramblers' Association, the Youth Hostels Association, the Council for the Preservation of Rural England, and the Council for the Protection of Rural Wales joined together to lobby to protect and allow access to the countryside. In 1932 they organized a mass trespass to publicize their demands. On the political scene, the Labour Party was sympathetic, and when it came to power after World War II, it passed the National Parks Act. It also passed the Town and Country Planning Act, creating a comprehensive legislative framework for city and rural planning.

Like the United States and continental Europe, Great Britain developed a greater concern with the environment during the 1960s. A few interest groups like the National Trust dated back to before the turn of the 20th century. The Fauna and Flora Preservation Society began in 1903. A number of groups had an international or Empire-wide orientation like the International Council for Bird Preservation and the International Union for the Conservation of Nature. The World Wildlife Fund began in 1961 amid fears that habitat destruction and hunting would soon bring about the extinction of much of the wildlife in India and Africa. The British Friends of the Earth began in 1970, and it soon had a more important role there than its parent organization in the United States. At present 5 million Britons belong to environmental organizations. The National Trust alone has more than 2 million members, and the Royal Society for the Protection of Birds has nearly a million. Greenpeace has 300,000 members in the

United Kingdom. There are 100,000 Friends of the Earth, organized in two hundred chapters throughout the British Isles. Rachel Carson's *Silent Spring* had a British edition in 1962. Britain participated in the first Earth Summit at Stockholm in 1972, where the Scandinavians and the Germans took the opportunity to accuse the United Kingdom of causing acid rain because of the sulfur its factories and electricity-generating plants emitted, which drifted across the North Sea.

The government established a national Department of the Environment in 1970, which also included responsibility for housing and local government. This was a bit of a surprise because the Conservative Party unexpectedly won the election that year, and the issue of the environment had not figured in the campaign. Within a few months, the new department faced a crisis when municipal sewerage and sanitation workers went out on strike, provoking tension between the national and local levels. In 1997 it became the Department of the Environment, Transport and the Regions, and the next year it issued its first sustainability statement. In 2001 transport was split out, and it became the Department for the Environment, Food and Rural Affairs (DEFRA). The department's programs tend to rely on voluntary compliance. Local governments continue to have responsibility for water and air pollution control for minor problems, while the Environment Department addresses larger ones. In the past local programs had not always proven adequate. For example, four thousand people died from the Great Smog in London in 1952. This tragedy led to the 1956 Clean Air Act. In the 1960s evidence grew that sulfur oxides from burning coal were drifting across the North Sea to fall as acid rain in Scandinavia. Damage from coal pollution was already widely known in Britain. In 1957 an accident at the nuclear plant at Windscale had spread radioactivity across the north of England. During the 1970s Parliament passed the Poisonous Waste Act, the Water Act, the Control of Pollution Act, and the Endangered Species Act. Support was bipartisan, coming from the Labour Party when it returned to power in 1974.

From the end of World War II to the 1980s, the British economy grew slowly. One ironic benefit was less air and water pollution, but the economic situation was dismal. Many blamed the nationalization of industries like coal, steel, and transport by the Labour Party starting in 1945. Others blamed the loss of the Empire and its foreign trade. Even as the Empire disappeared, however, Britain stayed out of the European Common Market, which, to the chagrin of the British, was enjoying its Economic Miracle. At first the United Kingdom did not want to join Europe, reflecting its geographical insularity, its ties to the former Empire, and its special rela-tionship with the United States. Then when it changed its mind in 1961 and sought to join the Common Market, the French vetoed its membership. It did not become a member of the successor European Community until 1973. The island's natural resources were few and declining. This changed in 1969 with the discovery of oil off the east coast of Scotland. Production grew rapidly to more than 22 million barrels per day. The timing could not have been more propitious, because the price per barrel rose from $2.50 to a peak of $40 by 1985. The North Sea fields also produced vast quantities of natural gas. The cheap and close-by oil and gas brought a boom to the kingdom. In terms of air pollution and carbon emissions, natural gas was nearly the perfect fuel.

Government: Great Britain has a parliamentary form of government, and indeed is the model for parliaments around the world, hence, is called the Mother of Parliaments. The House of Commons represents the people, and the House of Lords represents the aristocracy. In fact, the power of the Lords has been whittled away, so today plays a limited role. The prime minister, who holds an elected seat in Commons, leads the government and appoints ministers from members of his own party. They serve both as elected representatives of their constituents and, for a few, as admin-istrators of departments like Environment, Health, or Foreign Affairs. This is called the Westminster System after the neighborhood in London where Parliament sits. Party discipline is strict. Once a party has finished its internal debate on a policy, all members of Parliament are required to vote in favor or risk expulsion.

Great Britain has a two-party system, with a few minor parties over the years. The Labour Party won a large majority of the House of Commons in 1997 and continued its majority in the 2001 and 2005 elections. As its name implies, it developed from the labor movement at the turn of the 20th century, and first came to power in a coalition in 1924. The party represented the working class in a society where class affiliation domi-nated. The Labour government elected in 1945 made sweeping changes by nationalizing (i.e., taking ownership of) major industries like coal and steel, by building public housing on a grand scale, by establishing cradle to the grave health care, and by taxing heavily. It considered itself to be socialist. Its strident left-wing ideology lost favor with the voters during the 1970s, and the party appeared doomed to perpetual minority status. Its *Manifesto* in the disastrous 1983 election had so little appeal to the average voter that it was called the "the longest suicide note in history."

This changed about 1995 when Tony Blair and a group of moderates won control of the party and adopted a centrist platform that appealed to the middle class, leading to a stunning victory in 1997.

In the past the Labour Party was not a logical friend of the environment because of its commitment to the Mineworkers Union and other industrial trade unions. The nationalized Coal Board wanted production, not regulation. Even as the country's coal reserves were being depleted to almost nothing, the government subsidized mining to maximize employment, and hence votes. Strip mining was destroying the land, but the Coal Board fought reclamation. The Board joined the government-owned British Steel Corporation to oppose air pollution controls. New Labour, as the party now liked to call itself, is pro-environment, bragging about cleaning up beaches, rivers, and drinking water, and purifying the air. In the 1997 election, Blair campaigned with strong environmental language in the Labour *Manifesto*.

The Conservative Party was not a logical friend of the environment either. For most of the 20th century, it was more favorable to industry than the Labour Party. After the 1952 London Smog, the Conservative government, in spite of holding a large majority in the House of Commons, declined to introduce its own Clean Air Bill, but waited until a private bill was agreed upon to back its own version, eventually passed in 1956. In the 1970s support came from both parties. The Conservative Party strengthened its protection at the same time it was privatizing the government role. Much of the reason was personal commitment and leadership. In 1979 Margaret Thatcher became prime minister after an election victory, introducing many ideas for a free market as a way to cure economic stagnation. She was a strong advocate of a smaller role for government, blaming the kingdom's economic woes on nationalized industries like coal and steel, heavy-handed state regulation, and lack of free enterprise incentives. Early on she began to sell state-owned corporations, including the North Sea oil and gas corporations, as well as municipal water works. Thatcher sold the government share of British Oil and British Gas. Her policy both resembled and inspired the free market approaches popular in the United States under the Reagan administration. A strong influence came from the Institute of Economic Affairs, a private think tank. The institute does not lobby or try to influence specific legislation but prefers to try to change elite opinion. Since the 1970s, both parties have been influenced by its arguments. Its spokesman claims "We try to make it easier for Conservatives to be brave, and make it harder for Labour to be socialist."[4]

Thatcher's remedy began to work, and the economy picked up. Unlike Reagan, however, she was concerned about the environment. In particular she worried about water pollution and the greenhouse effect. By training she was a chemist, having taken a degree in the subject at Oxford University. She was persuaded by the scientific facts about pollution. In 1988 she gave a speech to the Royal Society outlining environmental dangers, and the following year she addressed the UN General Assembly, calling for protocols on climate change, ozone depletion, and the preservation of plant species. Thatcher hosted an international conference on saving the ozone layer. Known as the "Iron Lady," she imposed her scientific and environmental ideas on the Conservative Party. Today, the Party continues to claim a strong commitment to a clean environment.

In late 1990 Thatcher lost her position of party leader, and thus the prime ministership. Her successor, John Major, also a Conservative, continued her environmental policies, especially about global warming. In 1992 he went to the Earth Summit in Rio de Janeiro, supporting the Framework Convention on Climate Change. In spite of Major's speeches, environmental policy moved to the back burner during his time in office. With respect to Europe, the party opposed further integration, particularly for a common currency. Most Conservatives were Eurosceptics. After losing control of the House of Commons and being in the minority, it focused on marginal social issues like immigration. The party retained its pro-business philosophy, but public opinion polls showed that voters considered Labour to be better at developing the economy. The Conservative Party acquired the insulting label of "the nasty party."

In the 2010 election, the Conservatives bounced back. Voters had tired of Labour after 13 years. Under the leadership of David Cameron, the Conservative Party won 306 seats in the House of Commons, not quite enough for a majority of 326. Cameron recruited the small Liberal Democrat Party with 62 seats to form a coalition. This was not a natural combination since the smaller party was more favorable to the environment and advocated closer ties to Europe. Nevertheless, the coalition government pledged to protect the environment, including biodiversity and tree planting. Indeed, the Conservatives recently changed their party logo to the oak tree. With the European fiscal crisis that threatened to destroy the euro as a currency and plunge Greece, Italy, and Portugal into bankruptcy, environmental policy seemed secondary.

Although two parties dominate British politics, the kingdom does have a small Green Party. It was organized in 1973, first calling itself the

People's Party, and later the Ecology Party. Throughout its existence, it has been stretched between its practical members who advocate moderation in order to attract votes, and its radical members who want to voice a purer environmental stance. While it has never elected a Member of Parliament, it has elected some to the European Parliament. In 1999 the European Parliament switched its election method to a proportional representation system that allowed the party to aggregate its votes from many different electoral districts. This system typically helps smaller parties win a few seats. The election led to the victory for two parliamentarians to go to the EU Parliament in Strasbourg from a vote of 6%. Proportional representation is not used for the British House of Commons, which continues to be based on single member districts, a method called "first past the post." The Green Party holds a number of seats in local governments, and often does well at this level, but in national elections, which are decided by the first past the post, it has yet to win a seat in Commons.

In the June 1989 elections for the European Parliament, the British Green Party had achieved startling success when it won 15% of the vote. Unfortunately, it was an empty victory since it failed to win any seats with the rules in effect at the time. Throughout Europe, green parties did well in that election, with the British one gaining the highest percentage. Analysis showed that the Green Party did best in southern England and among middle-class voters. It took votes away from the Conservatives, but not from Labour. In percentage terms, the party has never done as well since. The Green Party takes positions, generally on the left, on issues ranging from the economy and defense to crime and disabilities. It strongly opposes nuclear energy.

The Department of the Environment, Food and Rural Affairs (DEFRA) is the key agency. It is the successor to the Department of the Environment, Transport and the Regions, and farther back, the original Department of the Environment. The 2001 reorganization came about because of the crisis in the failure to control the foot-and-mouth epidemic among cattle. The public perceived the existing Ministry of Agriculture, Fisheries, and Food as incompetent. The original Department of the Environment in 1970 had included the transport function, but that was removed in 1976, only to be returned in 1997. When transport was combined again with the environmental aspects, many environmentalists were pleased because it offered the opportunity to coordinate the policies that caused so much air pollution with the goal of amelioration. Highways both pollute directly with their auto traffic, and create urban sprawl that produces indirect harm. The department was supposed to pay attention to city planning. However, in fact, the coordination did not take place.

Unlike the United States and Germany, Britain has a unitary government, meaning that it is not a federation of many states or provinces, but governed directly from London. DEFRA does have regional offices for administrative convenience, but the decisions and rules are the same for all parts of the kingdom. Presumably this is a more rational and efficient system than that found in federations. The unitary form has been slightly fragmented, however, by the devolution of power that was a campaign promise of Labour in the 1997 election. This is the permanent delegation of power to Scotland and Wales. In response to longtime demands by the Scots, the central government authorized the recreation of a Scottish Parliament for the first time since 1707. It has authority in designated areas such as housing, education, and the environment. Hence, there is now a Scottish Environment Protection Agency, responsible for air and water pollution, water supplies, and sewerage, land use planning, and the natural land heritage. They do not include energy, authority for which remains in London. Wales also received a devolution of power, but to a lesser extent, reflecting its nine centuries of integration with England.

Great Britain has a long tradition of excellence in science. Gilbert White and Charles Darwin were naturalists of the 18th and 19th centuries. In the 20th century, J. B. S. Haldane, James Lovelock, and Francis Crick were prominent. While many worked at universities like Oxford and Cambridge, their research was often sponsored by the government. British scientists were in the forefront of research on both the ozone hole and global warming. The hole was reported in 1985 by British scientists in Antarctica. A team led by Joseph Farman combined ground observations from Halley Bay with a satellite-borne spectrometer to discover that the layer had thinned every September until one year it disappeared. A Welshman, Sir John Houghton, was a leader in studies of global warming, chairing the technical portion of the Intergovernmental Panel on Climate Change for many years. He was a professor at Oxford and later served as head of the British Meteorological Office. The Hadley Centre for Climate Prediction and Research in Exeter is one of the best in the world.

Britain has a range of interest groups concerned with environmental policy. The oldest, the Royal Society for the Protection of Birds, began more than a century ago to counter the trade in grebe feathers. Today, the society has more than a million members, making it the largest wildlife organization in Europe. Besides lobbying, research, and education, it owns 180 reserves. It has a paid staff of 1,300 people and more than 13,000 volunteers. The Society has 175 local groups and 110 youth groups. It is affiliated with Birdlife International. It is concerned with how birds are impacted by governmental and private development of forests, highways, airports, rivers, and fisheries.

The National Trust, nearly as old, has more than 3.4 million members. Natural areas are only one of its concerns. It owns 166 houses, 19 castles, 47 industrial monuments and mills, 49 churches and chapels, and 35 pubs and inns. It manages 600,000 acres of countryside, moorland, beaches, and coastline. Although most property adjoins historic buildings, some are nature reserves like those at Wicken Fen, Cheddar Gorge, Blakeney Point, and the Farne Islands. Recent acquisitions are the Mournes, Orford Ness, and a large part of Snowdon. The trust owns about a quarter of the property in the Lake District National Park and an eighth of the property in the Peak District National Park. Unlike parks in United States and most non-European countries, the government does not actually own most of the property in its national parks. Instead, they were assembled during the 1950s and 1960s from a mosaic of private, charitable, and government sources. The trust has played a key role. More than in other countries, private organizations play a key role in administering government programs.

The Friends of the Earth is large and influential. The British affiliate was established in 1971, only 2 years after the organization's founding in the United States. That year it gained national attention by dumping non-returnable Schweppes soda bottles outside the company's London headquarters. The Friends successfully opposed plans by the Rio Tinto corporation to mine zinc in Snowdonia National Park. Later it led a boycott against do-it-yourself stores that imported hardwoods from unsustainable tropical rain forests. The British group soon became larger than its American parent. It has 200,000 members and three hundred local groups. Other UK groups are for Scotland, Wales, and Northern Ireland.

The Campaign to Protect Rural England was founded in 1926. It has 60,000 members organized in more than 200 district groups. It opposes urban sprawl, roadside advertising, and new motorways. It favors tranquil areas, greenbelts, and locally grown food.

The World Wildlife Federation was established in 1961 under British leadership, including Sir Julian Huxley, the biologist, and Sir Peter Scott, the painter, to be fully international in sponsorship. The initial purpose was to protect Indian and African wildlife. The former colonies in Africa were in the process of gaining independence, and the founders worried that the new nations might shortchange their wild treasures through hunting and economic development. WWF soon expanded its purpose to encompass wildlife on all continents. The British chapter was its first one, also established in 1961.

On the other side are interest groups like the Confederation of British Industry, the Society of Motor Manufacturers and Traders, and the Country Land and Business Association. The Confederation is huge, representing the complete range of industry. It has 13 regional offices, plus branches in Brussels, Washington, and Beijing. The division of its staff responsible for environmental issues has its primary liaison with the Department of Trade and Industry but continually monitors DEFRA. The Motor Society takes pride in the industry's ability to meet ever stricter emissions standards, beginning in 1992. These are Europe-wide. The Euro IV standards came into effect in 2005, resulting in emission reductions greater than 45%. In 1998, British vehicle manufacturers reached an agreement with European, Japanese, and Korean manufacturers to reduce carbon dioxide emissions by 25% to comply with the Kyoto Protocol. Because so many cars are exported, the society must consider European standards at many points. The Country Land and Business Association, which began in 1907, often is on the other side from the environmentalists. Its motto is "The rural economy is our business." It has lobbied for barriers against public rights of way across privately owned land, under the rationale that it prevents crime. Reduced property taxes and less onerous reclamation are other goals.

The United Kingdom has governmental agencies that operate with various degrees of autonomy. Natural England was established in 2006 from English Nature, the environment parts of the Rural Development Service and the Countryside Agency's Landscape, Access and Recreation Division. Its functions are conservation, promoting access, and research. Britain has a number of organizations between purely governmental and purely charitable. The jargon term is QUANGO, for quasi-autonomous nongovernmental organization. There are a thousand of them, a quarter of the government budget goes to them, and the government often appoints their directors, decreasing their voluntary and democratic nature.

Britain favors voluntary compliance rather than the firm standards and enforcement method of the United States and continental countries. Industry and government experts cooperate in setting the general requirements, and then a joint working group sets the specific requirements for each factory, electric generating plant, or sewer treatment plant.

Prosecution of violators is weak, and the inspectors tend to believe the polluter is trying hard, hence should not be sanctioned.

Issues: Although Britain first heard serious complaints about its sulfur emissions causing acid rain at the Stockholm Earth Summit, it largely ignored the issue. The Central Electricity Generating Board argued both that science did not prove the connection, and that installing flue gas desulfurization equipment would be too expensive. The National Coal Board seconded these rationales. Furthermore, the sharp increase in the prices of fuel after the 1973 oil crisis encouraged not acting. Nevertheless, pressure increased. Research, even by the Electricity Board, showed the scientific connection, and international pressure grew. In 1979 Britain signed the Convention on Long Range Transboundary Air Pollution, yet fought against specific limits. The United Kingdom was referred to as the Dirty Man of Europe. The English Friends of the Earth began a campaign for cleaning up the sulfur and coordinated it with the international Stop Acid Rain Campaign. Besides the Electricity and Coal Boards, the Confederation of British Industry fought sulfur limits for existing plants, although it admitted this might be a possibility for new plants.

The Conservative Party, while in power from 1979 to 1995, was not ideologically friendly to regulation, especially with its programs of deregulation and privatization. Yet Prime Minister Thatcher was personally interested in the scientific aspects and became concerned that sulfur was a problem. This combined with growing scientific evidence and more pressure from the Scandinavians and the Germans led to the Electricity Board reversing its position and moving toward flue gas desulfurization by 1988. It would cut its emission by 20% during the following 5 years, with more cuts to follow. These reductions would be binding on the new private corporations to which the Electricity Board was transferring ownership.

In comparison to the United States and Commonwealth dominions like Canada and Australia, Great Britain was late to develop national parks. The chief reason was that virtually no land remained under government ownership. Moreover, wilderness has not existed for thousands of years. In 1949 Parliament, under the Labour government, passed the National Parks and Access to the Countryside Act. It provided for establishment of 10 parks in England and Wales incorporating most of the unspoiled area remaining, and amounting to nearly 10% of the two countries.

The Lake District is the largest park, and one of the first established. Its many mountains mark a wide variety of geological origins, registering 500 million years of continental drift, deep oceanic sediment, and glacial carving. The park has 14 lakes. Human settlement dates back 10,000 years, with archaeological evidence of prehistoric, Roman, Anglo-Saxon, and medieval settlements. Wordsworth lived here, and wrote a *Guide to the Lakes*, which became popular. Today, millions of tourists visit each year. A joint national–local planning board oversees the park. Most of the land remains in private hands, with a quarter owned by the National Trust. Hikers have access to most areas. The second largest park is Snowdonia in Wales, named for Mount Snowdon, the highest peak in England and Wales. It is a land of mountains, valleys, and castles. Like the Lake District, it is largely privately owned, but with public access. Twenty-six thousand people live there, many speaking Welsh as their native tongue.

An issue in many of the parks is the extent to which the land should be restored to a prehuman natural state. North American visitors are horri-fied to find sheep are allowed to graze on the moors, clipping the hills to bareness. Native trees and shrubs cannot grow to maturity. On the other hand, most Britons believe that is the proper situation because sheep have been grazing there for thousands of years. Moreover, prehistoric inhabit-ants used to cut the timber for fuel and building, and later residents dug mines, plowed fields, and dammed rivers.

In 1968 the government, once more in the hands of the Labour Party, expanded parks, adding some national ones, but also creating many smaller ones more accessible to the cities under the Countryside Act. They were designed for recreation, and were not necessarily significant in terms of nature. The Wildlife and Countryside Act of 1981 established Areas of Special Protection. These incorporated Sanctuary Areas, originally desig-nated under the Protection of Birds Acts 1954. The 1981 law responded to pressure from farmers against unilateral action. Now they must be con-sulted. It also established Sites of Special Scientific Interest for wildlife habitats and geological features, categorized into international, national, and local importance. In 1991 Parliament reorganized the agency into agencies for England (English Nature), Wales (Countryside Council for Wales), and Scotland (Scottish Natural Heritage).

Fox hunting has been one of the most controversial issues in politics, pit-ting the upper class against the working class. A hunt begins with upper-class horsemen and women dressed in red coats gathering with their packs of hounds to chase a fox. England has more than three hundred packs. A fox is released with a head start, followed by the hunters and hounds gal-loping across the countryside until the hounds chase the fox into a hole. To some it is a thrilling ride, and to others it is cruelty to an innocent animal. Hunters argue that it helps nature by giving an incentive to maintain wooded land. Furthermore, it gives employment to several thousand people.

Parliament first debated whether to outlaw the sport in 1949. Neither the Labour nor the Conservative Parties wanted to confront the issue along party lines, so at various times they have proposed "a free vote," that is, without enforcing party discipline. After a bill passed its second reading in Commons in 1998, the pro-hunting Countryside Alliance rallied 250,000 protesters in London. Then the next year in a surprise move, the Labour prime minister, Tony Blair, announced the party would officially support a ban. In 2001 the House of Commons voted to outlaw fox hunting by a large majority, but it then needed a vote of the House of Lords, which rejected it by 317 to 68. While the upper house is generally not too important, this was an exception. Furthermore, the upper-class bias of the Lords fit the social status of the hunters. In 2002 Parliament voted again, with Commons favoring a complete ban and the Lords favoring a compromise of licensed hunting. This time even more protesters marched on London: 400,000. In 2004 Commons again voted for the ban and Lords rejected it. In an unusual procedure, the Commons forced the bill to become law over the objections of the Lords. The act forbids hunting foxes, deer, and hares with dogs, but does not cover using dogs to flush out unidentified wild mammals or drag hunting, where the hounds follow an artificial scent. This results in a lot of hunts with horses and hounds galloping across the countryside that look much like fox hunts but technically are not.

In March 2001 foot-and-mouth disease broke out in Essex, and soon spread throughout England and Wales, closing farms and parks. The viral sickness affects cattle and other livestock, first causing fever, drooling, and blisters on the feet, and then death. Wild deer could be victims, too. The government responded by culling sick animals, eventually killing seven million cattle and sheep. People who were on farms, moors, and open land sometimes spread the virus on their shoes, so the government set up disinfection stations. The government postponed local elections for fear those bringing farmers to the polls would spread the disease. Later the general election was also postponed. The Ministry for Agriculture was blamed for not recognizing and solving the problem promptly, so authority was transferred to DEFRA.

Like the United States, the British Isles face invasions by exotic species, many coming from North America. The gray squirrel is winning the competition against the native red squirrel, and the American mink eats seabirds, voles, and salmon. The zebra mussel from Russia has invaded Scotland. Japanese knotweed and pennywort displace native plants. DEFRA estimates the annual cost of exotic species is two billion pounds a year.

Genetically modified crops have stirred strong opposition in the United Kingdom, as well as Germany and elsewhere on the Continent. Food such as maize, beets, oilseed rape, and potatoes have their genes modified to tolerate herbicides or in some other fashion. Corporations promoting this include Monsanto, Bayer, and Syngenta, some of the biggest in the world. In the 1990s government scientists planted maize in an experiment that provoked bitter opposition. A leading group was GM Freeze. Protesters dressed up in bio-hazard suits trespassed on the fields and dug the plants out of the soil. Their theatrics gained popular attention and sympathy, despite the fact that scientists claimed there was no danger to human health. The DEFRA minister told Parliament that "There was no scientific case for ruling out all GM crops or products."[5] This was not persuasive, and the sponsor, Bayer, withdrew from the commercial market in the United Kingdom. The controversy flared again in 2012. Protesters calling themselves Take Back the Flour threatened to rip up an experimental field of spring wheat genetically modified to resist aphids at the Rothamsted Research Station in Hertfordshire. When the day came to attack the test plot, the police successfully defended it.

France. During the 17th century, France pioneered in creating and protecting landscapes, albeit not always natural ones. King Louis XIV built his palace at Versailles with endless formal gardens, laid out symmetrically and pruned neatly. This reflected the Enlightenment ideals of rationality and science. A century later, with the rise of Romanticism, aristocratic taste shifted to naturalistic gardens. Louis XV and Madame du Pompadour, and the Duke of Orleans, were royal leaders in this. Jean Jacques Rousseau wrote of the benefits of living close to nature. He, along with Diderot, Voltaire, and Delille, bought or rented country estates. Later the Romantic poet Theophile Gautier praised the greenery that symbolizes spring:

The chestnut trees are soon to flower At fair St. Jean, the villa dipped
In sun, before whose viny tower Stretch purple mountains silver-tipped
The little leaves that yesterday Pressed in their bodices were seen
Have put their sober garb away, And touched the tender twigs with green.[6]

On the scientific side, Georges-Louis Buffon published 36 volumes expounding on natural history. Under the leadership of Guy Crescent Fagon, the Garden of Plants in Paris became a center of botanical research.

The Revolution of 1789 enshrined many features of the Enlightenment as government law and policy. For example, it replaced the ancient system of weights and measures with metric ones of kilograms and meters. At its most extreme, the National Convention proclaimed a Cult of Reason to replace Christianity. The Goddess of Reason was worshiped at the high altar of the Cathedral of Notre Dame. Although the Cult soon disappeared, the French elevated the role of science. The Garden of Plants was enhanced with a museum and a zoo. Georges Cuvier pioneered the field of paleontology with his studies of fossils of elephants and mammoths. Analyzing sedimentary rock in the Paris basin, he outlined the principles of stratigraphy. Napoleon Bonaparte established the School of Mines, which advanced the science of geology. Louis Pasteur discovered the germ theory, and Marie and Pierre Curie discovered radium. The post-Revolutionary period advanced the importance of the technical expert: the technocrat.

In 1835 scientific societies addressed the issue of how the decrease in songbirds resulted in the increase of insects and recommended protecting birds. The League of Ornithology began in 1892. The government established the National School of Water and Forestry in 1824 and enacted a forestry code three years later. Some conservation began in colonies sooner than at home. Experimental ecological protection began on the Island of Mauritius in the Indian Ocean,[7] and in Africa the government worked to preserve the rhinoceros, giraffe, monkey, and elephant.

In 1854 Isidore Geoffroy Saint-Hilaire established the Zoological Acclimatization Society in Paris, the first organization in the world to worry about damage to animal habitats. It later became the National Society for the Protection of Nature. In 1906 this group helped found the Friends of the Elephant, and in 1912 the League for the Protection of Birds. In 1926 the Acclimatization Society laid the basis of the first nature reserve in the Camargue at the delta of the Rhone River designed to protect the animals and plants in their natural setting. Later, it sponsored reserves in the Pyrenees and the Alps, areas that eventually became national parks. The government passed the 1930 National Heritage Act to protect natural as well as cultural sites. In 1960 it passed a law providing for a national park system. In the 1950s and 1960s France became concerned with air and water pollution, passing an air pollution control act in 1961 and a water act in 1964.

In 1943 a French naval officer, Jacques-Yves Cousteau, made perhaps the greatest invention to advance knowledge and love of the oceans. After the defeat of France by the Nazis in 1940, Cousteau was ordered to sit out the war in Megreve, on the Mediterranean Sea. To amuse himself he began skin diving with underwater goggles. An additional purpose was to spear fish to eat since meat was scarce. His ingenious mind soon invented the aqualung, or scuba gear. From the beginning he wanted to share his love of the undersea world in film. His first was called *Eighteen Meters Deep*. His 1953 book, and later film, *Silent World*, gained worldwide fame. Over the following 40 years, he made 120 documentary films and published more than 50 books.

Cousteau was always a strong advocate for protecting the environment. He and his crew sailed their research vessel, the *Calypso*, to the Red Sea and the Great Barrier Reef to study coral and to the northern seas to study whales. In 1960 the French Atomic Energy Commission proposed to dump a large amount of nuclear waste into the Mediterranean Sea. Cousteau rallied opposition and citizens blocked passage of the train by sitting on the tracks. The commission gave in and canceled the dump. In 1973 he established the Cousteau Society, now with 300,000 members.

Several environmental groups were founded or expanded in the 1960s and 1970s. The largest, France Nature Environnement, was organized in 1968, combining many existing groups. The Friends of the Earth founded a French affiliate in 1971. Another group established at that time was Pollution Non. During the 1970s these were the only national-level organizations concentrating on the environment. Later Greenpeace established a French affiliate, targeting nuclear energy and weapons in particular. The League for the Protection of Birds now has 33,000 members and has affiliated with Bird Life International. An antinuclear group began in 1962, the Association for Protection against Radiation.

Government: France combines features of a parliamentary democracy like most European countries with a strong president like the United States. The president, who is elected by the people for a 5-year term, appoints a premier and cabinet, who in turn are responsible to the National Assembly of 577 members. There is also a Senate of 331 members. For more than a century, political parties have split along a left–right ideological continuum. The Socialists dominate the left with the Communists being the second biggest party. On the right the chief party is the Union for a Popular Movement, formerly called the Rally for the Republic. Several small parties exist, including Europe Écologie–Les Verts, a merger of the Greens with a few regional parties. They have 17 seats in the National Assembly and are part of the ruling coalition with the Socialists. French elections are determined by first past the post, as in the United Kingdom. Although this makes it harder for a small party to win, they do occasionally. Furthermore, the French have a runoff if no one gets a majority in the first round.

Officially, the authority of the national government is supreme and centralized, penetrating every aspect of life. The unitary government in Paris regulates everything in detail. The administrative bureaucracy has continued since the days of Napoleon, displaying remarkable continuity considering three devastating wars with Germany. Its centralization is notorious. Its authority is enhanced by many experts in the bureaucracy: the technocrats.

While France is not a federated republic like the United States, Canada, and Germany, it is subdivided geographically into 96 departments (like states or counties), dating to the Revolution. In 1972 22 administrative regions were imposed on top of the departments to coordinate. More authority was delegated to the regions in 1982. While the departments and regions have elected councils, departmental prefects are appointed by the national government. Most authority remains with Paris.

In 1971 the government, under the conservative president Georges Pompidou, established the Ministry of the Environment and Protection of Nature. This was the first such ministry on the continent. Over the years, it has had many different names and configurations. Often it has been more of a coordinating office than a ministry, and sometimes has been combined with the planning or culture agencies.

Some environmental laws date back to the Napoleonic era. An 1810 decree addressed foul smells generated from workshops. An 1829 law to protect fish was used to control water pollution. More recently, France enacted a weak air pollution control law in 1961, a stronger water law in 1964, and a waste law in 1975. Over the following years it amended and strengthened this legislation. The French parliamentary custom is to enact sweeping laws of principles to guide specific provisions on air pollution, water pollution, and so forth written by the technocrats in the bureaucracy. The 1995 Barnier Law, named for the environmental minister, set out general principles of the polluter pays, prevention at the source, the precautionary principle, and the public's right to information. These followed the European Community's 1973 Environment Action Program. France has incorporated many environmental provisions set by the EC-EU as that body has adopted them.

On the political side, politics since the beginning of the Fifth Republic under Charles de Gaulle in 1958 has been characterized by swings between two coalitions of parties on either the socialist or the conservative side. In 2007 the conservative Union for the Popular Movement won the presidency and a majority of seats in the National Assembly. It had also won the presidency and a majority in 2002. From 1997 to 2002 the Socialists governed in a coalition with the Communists. The Verts entered the coalition with seven seats in the Assembly.

One or two environmental parties have been active since 1974, when a green candidate, René Dumont, ran in the presidential election, winning more than 1% of the votes. In 1979 Les Verts (the Greens) won 4% of the parliamentary vote, but failed to win any seats. Ten years later, it won 11% of the vote, and got nine seats. In 1994 the Greens, now divided, won 5%, but no seats. In 1999 the Verts won 10%, and got nine seats. They had won seventy seats on regional councils the year before, and also won nine seats in the European Parliament. Three years later their seats in the National Assembly dropped to only three. Like the German Greens, the Verts were ambivalent about practical politics. They wanted to be a different kind of party, emphasizing local autonomy, complex written procedures, and initially a reluctance to compete for power. They have a libertarian streak. Many believe the answer is not better pollution control technology, but a total rejection of industrial production. Besides environmentalism, the Verts favor feminism, gay rights, racial minorities, and legalization of soft drugs. For a long time, they avoided entering into coalitions, but did so in 1997. This was with the Socialists, labeled the Red–Green coalition. After the coalition won a parliamentary majority, they entered into shared power, with Dominique Voynet as environment minister. In 2007 they won four seats.

Another green party began in 1990. Génération Ecologie was headed by Brice Lalonde. Lalonde, who started as a student radical during the 1968 demonstrations called the Events of May, became a leftist militant during the 1970s, later became the head of the Friends of the Earth, and eventually became the environment minister in a Socialist government in 1988–91. Many saw Lalonde's role as merely self-promotion. In any event, internal squabbles caused Génération Ecologie to self-destruct by 1997. A small successor party focuses on local politics. In 2012 the Greens bounced back, in a reorganized form. They won 17 seats in the National Assembly of 577 seats, and entered a governing coalition with the Socialists. They also won 12 seats in the Senate out of 348 seats.

In the early 2000s environmental issues were of only secondary importance. Attention focused on proposals for economic reform with a bigger role for the free market. Then in 2005 riots broke out in the slums of the industrial suburbs surrounding Paris. One issue was allowing employers more freedom in terminating young employees, a free-market reform aimed at reducing the high unemployment rate of 23%. This particularly affected Arab and African youths who were the children of immigrants. Their rate was as high as 40%. The government decreed a state of emergency lasting four months.

The conservative Nicolas Sarkozy won the presidency in 2007 after taking a strong stance against the rioters and in favor of the free market. Although he had said little about protecting the environment during the campaign, he soon convened a 3-month conference labeled a Grenelle, meaning a broad-based debate and resolution of a major problem. The sessions included environmental groups and industry as well as scientists and officials. Together they planned to reduce greenhouse gases, lower air pollution, and promote biodiversity. The government agreed to halt new highway and airport construction and expand rail transportation. Agricultural pesticides were to be reduced by 50%, land devoted to bio-farming was to be increased 20%, and genetically modified crops were to have a moratorium. The press called the president Ecolo-Sarko.

Interest groups: While France has had interest groups for a century or two, environmental ones got an infusion of energy by the nationwide student demonstrations against the government in May 1968. At the time it seemed possibly to be the beginning of a second French Revolution. Although in the end the Events of May were less sweeping, they did produce many changes. One was that people were more likely to question the wisdom of bureaucrats and scientists: the technocrats. Besides political and social issues, the protests flowed into environmental issues. The following year many citizens objected to plans for a ski resort in the Vanoise National Park and were able to stop it. In 1971 farmers objected to the army taking their land to enlarge its base on the Larzac plateau. The same year 15,000 people demonstrated against the Bugey nuclear plant. Nevertheless, citizen environmental groups were weak. The old nature groups did not want to be active politically.

France Nature Environnement, originally the Federation of Associations for the Protection of Nature and the Environment, organized in 1968, is an umbrella group. It has more than 3000-member organizations, representing 850,000 individuals. Groups may be for a particular aspect like birds, or may be regional. The federation emphasizes conferences, education, and the technical side of protection, rather than engaging in political action. When the government wants citizen members of advisory committees, it often goes through this group. In spite of its size, it is not especially aggressive.

The French affiliate of the World Wildlife Fund, now the World Wide Fund for Nature, has 170,000 members and a staff of 60. WWF projects include protecting the Loire River, one of the last free-flowing ones in Europe, protecting dolphins and whales in the Mediterranean Sea and the brown bears in the Pyrenees Mountains, and managing more than 3 million hectares of forests. It sees global warming as a threat to biodiversity. WWF France decided to challenge the electricity industry because it was the largest single source of carbon dioxide. Until recently, the government-owned Electricitié de France operated as a monopoly. However, European Union directives are forcing its privatization. Furthermore, nuclear plants, which do not release carbon dioxide, account for three-quarters of generation. WWF International opposes nuclear power, so the French affiliate feels obliged to follow but is less enthusiastic. Since most plants in the country were built during the 1970s, they are nearing the end of their lives. The government must decide how to replace them. Many can be refurbished so they can generate electricity for another 10 or 20 years. Moreover, nuclear plants are often inefficient, so another step is to improve efficiency.

In contrast to WWF's ambivalent attitude, Greenpeace France vigorously opposes nuclear power. The French office of this international group opened in 1977. In 1985 the world was outraged when French secret service agents bombed a Greenpeace ship, the *Rainbow Warrior*, in the harbor of Auckland, New Zealand. The ship was in the South Pacific to monitor and protest the French military detonation of an atomic bomb on the island of Moruroa in French Polynesia. A photographer on board was drowned. Eventually, the government admitted its guilt and paid $8 million to Greenpeace International. Greenpeace France has 110,000 members.

The Friends of the Earth founded a French affiliate in 1971. Another group established at that time was Pollution Non. During the 1970s, these were the only national-level organizations concentrating on the environment. Later, Greenpeace established a French affiliate, targeting nuclear energy and weapons in particular. The League for the Protection of Birds now has 33,000 members and has affiliated with Bird Life International. An antinuclear group, the Association for Protection against Radiation, began in 1962.

Citizen groups often have a quasi-governmental role. For example, the 1976 Nature Act provided for land reserves, now more than 100, many managed by private hunting associations. Environmentalists find themselves in conflict with hunters, who got official recognition under a 1964 law coordinating hunting associations. They are organized as the ACCA (registered municipal hunting associations) with authority to set the rules and issue hunting licenses. Many lack safety training in firearms. Dozens are killed every year. Hunting is allowed nearly everywhere on private property, whether or not the owner objects. Game wardens in effect work for the hunting association. The season extends from July to February. The National Hunting Office in the environmental ministry is largely staffed with hunters, and follows the will of the ACCA. To please the hunters, the hunting office has experimented with captive breeding of animals to be released into the wild. They were overly successful with hybrid boars which, once set free, proved ferocious and damaged forests and farms.[8]

Besides hunters, legislation provided for official status for many citizen associations that sign an agreement, thereby giving them access and legitimating them. By 1991 the number of enrolled groups was 1,434. They are represented on various councils at the national, regional and local levels. Twenty environmentalists sit on the High Committee on the Environment. Enrolled associations may receive government subsidies. The largest amount of the money (about a fifth) goes to France Nature Environnement.

As in other Western democracies, business groups are active politically. The largest is the Movement of French Enterprises (MEDEF), established in 1998 from the former Council of Employers. MEDEF's interests cover a broad range of topics such as taxation and employment. The environment is only one of its many issues. Regarding global warming, its official position is to say that the greenhouse effect is a serious problem, but in fact, it is unenthusiastic about controls. The big steel company, Arcelor, makes the public relations claim that it seeks Sustainable Development by protecting the environment, achieving profitable growth, and being "a model of corporate social responsibility." In spite of its governmental ownership, Electricitié de France lobbies the government, acting as an interest group.

Since the 1970s, many French citizens have strongly opposed nuclear power, whether in the form of weapons or electric generating plants. In 1974 the conservative government announced its plans to generate 70% of electricity from the atom. People demonstrated against new plants in the Gironde, Flamanville and Alsace. Two years later the proposal to build the first fast breeder reactor, the Super Phenix, at Malville sparked a demonstration by 15,000 people. Six other big demonstrations had little effect on the government plan. Only one facility was canceled. The government was quite determined, seeing nuclear power as a route to independence from foreign oil supplies, and connected it to the defense policy of an independent nuclear weapon strike force. Furthermore, the utility, Electricité de France, was a government corporation. The French polity is highly centralized, depends on experts, and has a long tradition of planning. In the 1981 presidential election, the Socialist candidate François Mitterand promised to hold a referendum on nuclear energy, but after his victory decided against it. He did cancel one plant and slowed the pace of the program, but by then Electricité de France already had overcapacity. Eventually France generated 77% of its electricity from the atom (plus 13% from falling water). It has a total of fifty-nine reactors. Radioactive waste is sent to reprocessing plants at La Hague and Marcoule. Highly radioactive waste is vitrified (sealed in glass), and stored at La Hague in the Rhone Valley for several decades waiting for permanent geological disposal in deep clay or granite. No permanent sites have been selected yet. In spite of criticism, the atom continues to enjoy strong governmental support. Protests continue, to little effect. In 2004 activists lay on the railroad tracks to block a shipment of nuclear waste en route to the reprocessing plant at La Hague. One was killed when the train failed to stop. On Easter Sunday 2006 at Cherbourg, 20,000 protesters rallied against the decision to construct a new reactor.

Industrial pollution is regulated by licenses for each factory or installation. This dates to the 1810 law, with amendments in 1917, stressing health and safety. By 1976 this was outdated due to rapid industrialization in the preceding 30 years, thus the law that year added environmental controls. Larger installations required an environmental impact study, while smaller ones needed to follow regular standards. Although the French government claims near absolute authority, in practice it negotiates with the owners on reasonable levels of compliance. The licenses are enforced by inspectors detailed to the environmental ministry on a day-to-day basis, but actually employed by the industry ministry, consequently, they were less strict. Once discovered, violations must be proven according to rigid legal procedures, hence, the industry is less likely to be convicted. Finally, even when finding the industry guilty, courts often reduce fines and penalties.[9]

Upon assuming the presidency in 2012 François Hollande, a Socialist, set a course more favorable to the environment than his predecessor. He would close the nuclear plant in Alsace, the oldest one in France.

This fulfilled a campaign pledge, and reflected safety concerns after the Japanese melt down in Fukushima after the tsunami. He also continued a ban on fracking for natural gas. Third, he recommended a 40% cut in European Union carbon dioxide emissions by 2030 and a 60% reduction by 2040. Hollande called for a new treaty to replace the Kyoto Protocol.

The European Union has strong policies to protect the environment. Unlike the individual countries analyzed in this book, the EU is a federation of sovereign countries. Its importance is twofold: (1) as a transition between being an international collection of nations to becoming a single government, and (2) for its strong influence in national policies to protect the natural environment.

The idea of a "United States of Europe" has been proposed multiple times. Its chief goal has been to end the recurring wars that had brought so much death and destruction to the Continent. The worst were the First and Second World Wars that pitted Germany against France, Britain, and Russia. In the first, 16 million soldiers and civilians died, and in the second, 60 million or more died in Europe. Many wars in the past centuries centered along the Rhine River with quarrels between the historic enemies of Germany and France. After the war, wise leaders from these two countries decided the best way to start would be to foster economic cooperation.

In 1950 the French foreign minister Robert Schuman, proposed a European Coal and Steel Community as the centerpiece of a supranational organization. He said the goal was to "make war not only unthinkable but materially impossible." Without steel there could be no guns, munitions, tanks, or battleships. Because of the location of coal mines, iron ore, and water transportation, the steel industry was centered in a geographical area of northeast France, northwest Germany, and the Low Countries. (Ironically, this most polluting of all industries became the foundation for the environmentally conscious European Union.) The following year the five countries signed a treaty establishing the ECSC. As envisioned by the Schuman Plan, this created the High Authority (now the European Commission) and the Common Assembly (now the European Parliament). During the 1950s, the benefits of broader economic cooperation became apparent, so in 1957 the five countries, plus Italy, signed the Treaty of Rome. The key feature was a customs union among The Six. Goods could be transported and sold without tariffs and restrictions. This was an immediate achievement and promoted prosperity. The official name was the European Economic Community (EEC or later the EC), and the popular name was the Common Market. A parallel agreement in 1957 established the European Atomic Energy Commission (Euratom). At the time, most experts believed that a bright future lay ahead for the atom as a cheap and clean source of energy, not foreseeing the later environmental controversy.

The 1950s and 1960s were the era of the Economic Miracle, and few people worried about the environment, but this changed. Dangerous chemicals were an early concern for the EEC. Although the Treaty of Rome gave no authority to regulate air or water, it could be interpreted as covering chemicals in so far as guaranteeing a single market for these goods. It developed procedures for testing, recording, tracking, and disposing of hazardous materials, which promoted safety and protected the natural environment. These served as model regulations for countries such as the United States, for example.

The 1972 environmental summit in Stockholm brought attention to the risks of air and water pollution and prompted the Commission to issue its first Environment Action Program in 1973. This set forth a number of principles that have been adopted worldwide: prevention is better than remediation, prevention at the source, the polluter pays, integration among air, water and groundwater, and precaution.

Expanding the EC proved controversial. Originally, the United Kingdom chose not to participate because it would draw it away from its Empire, by then referred to as the Commonwealth. However, in 1963, once Common Market's success was apparent, the British applied to join, but the French president, Charles de Gaulle, vetoed this, believing it would dilute his country's power. Thus, the British were not admitted until 10 years later, after passions had cooled and de Gaulle had retired, then died. Denmark and Ireland joined at that time. Greece joined in 1981, Spain and Portugal joined in 1986, and Austria, Finland, and Sweden joined in 1995. Thus, the EC encompassed nearly all of Western Europe. Its members were all economically prosperous, adhered to the rule of law, and shared common democratic traditions.

The collapse of the Soviet domination of Eastern Europe in 1989 changed the situation dramatically, however. The Eastern countries wanted the economic advantages of their Western neighbors. Having been under Communism for 40 years or more, the European Union (as it was now called) was leery of the East's lack of a free market and its Communist legal system. Moreover, these countries had horrible air and water pollution from their old-fashioned and inefficient factories and mines. The EU required the Eastern countries to meet high standards for economic, legal, and democratic procedures. In 2004, it admitted eight new members: the Czech Republic, Estonia, Hungary, Latvia, Lithuania, Poland, Slovakia, and Slovenia. It also admitted Malta and Cyprus, small islands in the Mediterranean Sea. At that time Romania and Bulgaria were not considered ready but were admitted 3 years later. Croatia joined in 2013. Switzerland would be an ideal member, but it has chosen not to join. When Norway proposed joining, it citizens voted against it in a popular referendum. Turkey applied but has not been accepted, and many Europeans are opposed.

The legal basis of the EC remained unchanged from the Treaty of Rome until 1986 when the members signed the Single European Act with the purpose of deepening integration. The act strengthened the power of the European Parliament to discuss proposed laws and increased the areas in which the Council of Ministers could pass laws without a requirement of a unanimous vote. The original requirement for all countries to approve decisions unanimously proved more and more difficult as membership increased from 6 to 15.

The act added explicit authority regarding the environment. Part of the impetus was that the new members of Greece, Spain, and Portugal were weak in safeguards. On the other hand, the act specifies that the EEC can only intervene in environmental matters when this action can be attained better at EEC level than at the level of the individual country. This is called "subsidiarity." The European Community became the European Union in 1993 with the Treaty on European Union signed in Maastricht in the Netherlands.

The Council of Europe, previously called the Council of Ministers, may be described as the upper house in the EU legislature, the lower one being the Parliament. Its members directly represent the chief executives of the Member States; that is, they are appointed by the prime minister of Britain, the president of France, and so forth. They are not elected. The particular representatives for a session depend on the topic. For example, when discussing environmental policy, the people will be the 28 national ministers for environmental affairs.

This body is not to be confused with the European Council, which consists of the heads of state or of government (presidents or prime ministers) who meet at least twice a year. This semiannual session is usually concerned with big issues of foreign policy, an economic crisis, or admission of new states.

Leadership of the Council of Europe has been an evolving function. With only six countries originally, coordination was easier, but with each enlargement, it became more difficult. Unanimity became harder to achieve. Moreover, since 1957 the scope of the EEC-EU has grown. By analogy to the parliamentary systems of most democratic countries, the leader was to be a member of the legislature. Thus, the council president was to be like a prime minister. Yet the president did not have the authority that comes from a popular election based on political parties. Furthermore, the president could not secure his power from a majority in a parliament, presenting the issue of how he or she was to be chosen. The solution was a rotating presidency. The term of office is only 6 months, too short to establish authority or a comprehensive set of policies. Moreover, the council needed a way to choose its president, given the disparity in size of the member states from 82 million in Germany to 500,000 in Luxembourg. The solution was to do it by chance—casting lots.

The short time of leadership with the revolving presidency has occasionally promoted environmental issues. Because of the impossibility to accomplishing much in 6 months, some countries entitled to the presidency have focused on an environmental question as being easier to attain. For example, for the period of January through June 2013 the Irish presidency concentrated on this. Topics were to be the Seventh Environment Action Program, the Emissions Trading Scheme, and legislation on water, carbon dioxide emissions from cars and vans, and ship recycling. On the other hand, this does not always work. The previous year the Danish presidency made similar promises but ended up spending its time on the euro financial crisis.

The European Parliament plays the role of the lower house of the legislature. While originally members were appointed by their countries' governments, elections have been direct since 1979. There are 754 MEPs. The body has become a hotbed of environmentalism. Members organize themselves according to "groups," which are the equivalent of parties. The biggest are the Socialists and the Peoples Party, with two to three hundred members each. This latter is center right on the political spectrum. The Greens–EFA are midsized with about 50 members. For many years its head has been Daniel Cohn-Bendit, a fiery advocate nicknamed Danny the Red both for his radical politics and his red hair. Although representing a German constituency, he was born in France, where his parents had fled to escape Hitler. He returned to Germany for secondary school, then went back to France for university, where he joined an anarchist group. In 1968, he was a leader in the student uprising against the Gaullist government. Another group supporting the environment is the European United Left–Nordic Green Left. The Socialist group often supports the environment. The parliament has its official Standing Committee on Environment, Public Health and Food Safety to handle pending legislation. The parliament meets in Strasbourg, its official seat, and in Brussels. The founders in the 1940s and 1950s believed Strasbourg would be a symbol of peace and unity since this city on the Rhine River had been fought over so many times in the past.

The EU has numerous administrative departments or ministries, known as directorates, to implement its programs. Collectively, they are known as the commission, employing a total of 24,000. Like the other directorates general, the DG Environment strives to ensure that member states adhere to EU law. It investigates complaints and can take legal action. It often represents the EU at international meetings. Unlike the bureaucratic implementation of laws typical of most governments, the commission is not required to be exact in its implementation. Most EU legislation takes the form of "directives." These are not identical to laws found in national governments. They are weaker and more flexible. According to Article 288 of the Treaty of European Union, a directive is general, leaving the member state to choose the form and methods. They are binding on the member state in terms of the results to be achieved, but not the exact wording. Some say that the directives are more like suggestions. They are passed by the council and parliament. Often they were originally proposed by the commission. Alternatively, the EU may issue "regulations," which are binding. These are becoming more common with each passing year. The fact that the EU directorates based in Brussels can issue regulations binding on ordinary citizens and businesses sometimes annoys them. It seems so far away and not connected to their own parliament and agencies. They refer to this as a "democracy deficit."

Within the commission, the DG Environment is one of 40 and is often outgunned by bigger ones such as DG Industry, DG Economics, or DG Energy. In 2010 climate issues were split off into a new DG Climate Action. This bureau leads international negotiations on climate, helps the Union deal with the consequences of climate change and to meet its targets for 2020, and develops and implements the Emissions Trading System. The commission offices are located in Brussels. A separate bureau, the European Environmental Agency, was established in 1993 in order to develop data. It is a technical agency with little policy role, having its headquarters in Copenhagen.

Many nongovernmental interest groups are based in Brussels in order to influence the EU headquarters. The biggest is the European Environmental Bureau (EEB), which is comprehensive. Established in 1974, it is a federation of 140 national groups such as France Nature Environnement, the Royal Society for the Protection of Birds, and the German Grune Liga (Green League). In turn many of these groups are federations themselves. Other comprehensive interest groups in Brussels include Friends of the Earth, WWF, and Greenpeace. Climate Network Europe and Bird Life are more focused. All except Greenpeace have received some funding for their maintenance from the EU Commission, and their members are often employed temporarily by the commission as experts.

Global warming has emerged as a scientific and political issue at the same time as the EU has evolved and become more integrated. Indeed, it has been the most important environmental issue. Geographically, the continent is under grave threat from warming. According to traditional oceanography, the Gulf Stream–North Atlantic Drift moves warmth from the tropics to keep the winter temperatures moderate, and its disruption would make London and Copenhagen as cold as Montreal and Calgary. They have a lot to lose. Europeans both as individual countries and as the EC participated in the 1988 Toronto Conference, where they strongly backed an international treaty. Prior to the 1992 Rio de Janeiro Earth Summit, the EC coordinated a bargaining position. The various countries competed for greenness by proposing reductions in greenhouse gases (based on the year 1990). France bid a 15% reduction, Britain bid 20%, and Germany bid 25%. They also proposed reductions based on the continent as a whole, whereby countries with low emissions like Portugal could transfer their surplus "hot air" to high emissions countries like Belgium. The Framework Convention on Climate Change signed at Rio did not list specific targets, but as negotiations moved forward the Europeans lowered their promises. At Kyoto the EU agreed to an 8% reduction. During the negotiations leading up to Rio, the Europeans wanted to have it both ways. They wanted to vote as 12 countries, plus an extra vote for the EU.

Even these modest quotas proved too much. The EU and most members did not actually ratify the Kyoto Protocol for several years. Finally, the approach of the 10th anniversary of the Rio Summit, to be celebrated with another summit, this time in Johannesburg, South Africa, prompted the union and most members to ratify the protocol. This was cosmetic, and the Europeans did not actually meet their targets. Indeed, all but Sweden exceeded them. Spain and Italy were emitting 40% more instead of reducing 8%. The prime minister of the United Kingdom said he had changed his thinking and that no country would be willing to cut its growth or consumption substantially,[10] and the chancellor of Germany said she did not want to hurt industry. The parties to the Framework Convention have met annually to monitor and move forward on climate change, but these became less and less productive. In 2009 the parties decided to rally support at a session in Copenhagen. Close to 115 presidents, prime ministers, and kings attended. More than 40,000 people, representing governments, nongovernmental organizations, religious groups, and news reporters, were there. The results were disastrous. Major conflicts opened between the Europeans and the Americans and the industrial world and China. Many leaders just went home early.

Water has been another major issue for the EU. Early programs focused on particular problems: pollution, availability, surface water, groundwater, and so forth. Obviously, water flows from one country to another. The Rhine and Danube rivers are examples. For a long time, the European Community addressed water piecemeal. In 1975 the Surface Water Directive focused on rivers, lakes, and reservoirs used for drinking. In 1976 the Bathing Waters Directive required member states to identify and safeguard marine and fresh bathing sites for compliance. Beaches were to be free from sewage, for example. This effort garnered a lot of favorable publicity from ordinary citizens. That same year, the Dangerous Substances Directive required member states to regulate hazardous chemical discharges. Directives protecting fish, shellfish, groundwater, and drinking water, and controlling urban waste followed. All these programs depended on the underlying work of the various countries.

In 2000 the EU issued a unified Water Framework Directive. It was intended to replace a fragmentary, top-down approach with a comprehensive approach. The framework expanded the scope to safeguard all waters, set standards to be met by certain deadlines, based the program on river basins, and encouraged citizen participation. The scope now included aquatic ecology and specific habitats as well as water for drinking and bathing. Standards have two elements: "good ecological status" and "good chemical status." River basins that are well managed include the Rhine, the Maas, and the Schelde. Citizen participation is good for two reasons. The first is that the decisions involve balancing the interests of various groups. The economic analysis requirement is intended to provide a rational basis for this, but it is essential that the process is open to the scrutiny of those who will be affected. The second reason concerns enforceability. Greater transparency is intended to make it more obvious when violations occur. The directive calls for correct pricing for water to encourage conservation and to avoid subsidies that distort the market. The whole program is to be in operation by 2015 with milestones along the way.

At the 10-year mark, the European Environmental Bureau (EEB), the large citizen federation, published an assessment harshly critical of the framework. It reported that only 14 of 27 member states had written their River Basin Management Plans. Many countries had evaded cleaning up by giving exemptions to heavily polluted water bodies. The EEB found particular weaknesses in ending eutrophication, where agricultural runoff was a major problem.[11] Other assessments were more generous, believing the framework had made progress and that it should not be expected to solve pollution problems when the national governments were not enforcing their own laws.

Auto emissions have been a recurring issue, one that has juxtaposed the EC–EU origins in a common market for manufactured goods with a later concern with clean air. In 1970, the community issued its first directive on exhaust. This was in reaction to national regulations in Germany and in France that threatened continent-wide uniformity. These covered carbon monoxide and hydrocarbons, to which nitrogen oxides and particulates were soon added. From the perspective of sales, uniformity within the EEC-EC was essential. Manufacturers needed to be able to export to all countries on the continent, and were obligated by the Treaty of Rome to open their own domestic markets. Failure would have led to a trade war. Moreover, at this time, German public opinion was becoming alarmed at damage to the Black Forest from air pollution. The particular method of meeting air quality standards varied by country and by manufacturer. In Germany Mercedes-Benz, BMW, and Volkswagen built larger vehicles for which a catalytic converter would work best. In Italy, Fiat built smaller vehicles for which a clean-burning engine was cheaper. France and Britain likewise made smaller vehicles such as the Renault, Peugeot, and Leyland, and their public opinion was not so green.[12]

Automotive standards tend to be among the most detailed of any. The industry is huge, and any loopholes would be quickly exploited. Bureaucratic implementation comes from two directorates. The DG for Internal Markets and Industrial Affairs favors the manufacturers and the

DG Environment seeks cleaner air. The Motor Vehicle Emissions Group is a technical body with the purpose of working out the engineering side. It is staffed by government and industry experts.

Technical expertise was not enough. To resolve the disagreements, the parties met in Luxembourg in 1985 where they negotiated a compromise that set up three categories of small, medium, and large cars, with the most stringent standards for the large ones. The starting dates were postponed, and as a concession to environmental demands, more stringent standards were promised in the future. At the time, the EC required unanimous agreement in the Council of Ministers, and Denmark vetoed the compromise because it did not do enough. Fortunately, the Single European Act came into effect soon thereafter, and the proposal got enough votes under the new qualified majority. This was not the end, however. With more political maneuvering, a new, different Small Car Directive was issued in 1989.[13]

In recent years auto exhaust has been covered by the Framework Directive Automotive.[14] Under its provisions the commission has promulgated numerous detailed regulations on emissions, safety, and so forth. This moved EU rule making from the suggestion condition to the mandatory condition. With greater concern with greenhouse gases since the Kyoto Protocol, the EU has extended is scope into carbon dioxide emissions, quite different from the concern with carbon monoxide, nitrogen oxides, and particulates of the 1970s.

EU programs on water and auto exhaust illustration the "Monnet Method," which means that a series of small technical steps over many years will build integration. It is named for Jean Monnet, a French civil servant who worked closely with Robert Schuman in the 1950s to set up the Coal and Steel Community and then the Common Market. Monnet recognized that grand international treaties were important, of course, but he also believed in taking many small steps.[15] He compared it to riding a bicycle: riding forward maintains balance, but if the momentum stops, the bicycle will fall over.

Although environmental policy has been important to the EU, and the union has done much to promote it, there are many other aspects, some of which have not fared as well. The logic of a Common Market led to a common currency, the euro, which came into circulation in 2002. Not all member states agreed to use the euro, however. The United Kingdom maintained its own pound sterling, which was and continues to be one of the most important international currencies. Poland, the Czech Republic, and Romania have not been invited to join because their economies are not strong enough. At first, the euro appeared to be doing well, enjoying the backing of the strong German economy. But in 2009 the government of Greece found itself with a sovereign debt of 300 billion euros, far more than it could support. When the government imposed austerity programs of high unemployment, firing civil servants, reducing pensions, and raising prices, the Greek people rioted. Soon Ireland, Portugal, and Spain were also unable to pay their debts. The EU does not have a real central bank that can intervene. The euro crisis led to economic recession, with more unemployment and reduced prosperity. The hard times spread to Britain, dragging down its economy. In turn the British government toyed with leaving the Union.

CONCLUSION

The British frequently participated in demonstrations to support nature. Hikers and ramblers staged a mass trespass in 1932. In 1961, thousands marched against nuclear submarines in Holy Loch in Scotland, which later inspired the Danes. In 1971, protesters dumped nonreturnable Schweppes bottles in London. In France, the 1960 attempt by the government to dump atomic waste into the Mediterranean Sea caused protesters to sit on the tracks to block the train that carried the waste. Once more, nuclear electric plants and nuclear weapons can mobilize citizens better than other issues. Voters in both countries show support for Green Parties at a level of 5%–6%, but in the United Kingdom, the first-past-the-post method means none have won seats in Parliament. In France, they usually elect a few members of the assembly. In the European Parliament, the voters in multiple countries elect candidates of the Green Group. The method of proportional representation makes it possible to aggregate votes over a wide area.

Interest groups are ubiquitous in the United Kingdom. The Royal Society for the Protection of Birds has more than a million members. Friends of the Earth has 200,000 members. The National Trust (with a scope of historic buildings as well as nature) has more than three million. On the other side are the Confederation of British Industry, the Society of Motor Manufacturers and Traders, and the Country Land and Business Association. France Nature Environnement is huge, with many affiliates. Pollution Non began in the 1970s. International groups like Friends of Earth and WWF have French affiliates. In Brussels, European Environmental Bureau and Climate Network Europe join more general groups. In Britain, France, and the EU, interest groups often receive money from the government and supply personnel to staff official agencies. This does not happen in the United States.

Both the United Kingdom and France have parliaments elected on the first-past-the-post rule that makes it hard for small parties like Greens to win seats. They have never won any in Westminster. They have, however, occasionally won in France, holding 12 out of 577 recently. The situation is different in the European Parliament, which uses proportional representation. The Green Group (Party) routinely has about 50 seats.

The French constitution provides for a strong president, modeled in part on the United States. On the other hand, it also has a prime minister who sits in the assembly, and ministers appointed from the assembly or the senate. In the United Kingdom, the prime minister and his or her ministers sit in parliament. Both France and Britain are unitary, unlike the federations of the United States and Germany. Implementation of national laws is not filtered through a lower level. The effect of these differences of structure on environmental laws and regulations is not apparent. The European Union, of course, is not a single country (at least yet). Nevertheless, it does have a strong bureaucracy with directorates that impose their will directly on citizens and business firms.

Britain and France often lead the diplomatic agenda, with sponsorship of conferences and strong ties to the United Nations. Across the spectrum, both countries have dominated diplomacy for centuries. Furthermore, the talent and strength of British and French scientists allow them to lead. For example, the first empirical measurements of the Ozone Hole came from the British Antarctic expedition, and Sir John Houghton chaired the technical portion of the Intergovernmental Panel on Climate Change. The European Union, itself an evolving form of diplomacy, diffuses air pollution standards such as the harmonization of auto exhaust emissions.

France and Britain have been fully aware of events elsewhere. The Environmental Decade affected them throughout the 1970s. EU programs like standards on air and water spread across the continent. Although in the 1970s the United Kingdom was tarred with the label of "laggard," that was too harsh. British laws on air and water pollution were copied by the United States. Its scientists led by discovering the Ozone Hole and in chairing the Intergovernmental Panel on Climate Change. French science has been influential for two centuries. Sixty years ago,

Jacques Cousteau invented and popularized underwater exploration. When President Pompidou established the Ministry of the Environment and Protection of Nature in 1971, it was a model for the rest of Europe.

NOTES

1. Gilbert White, "Letter LXXVII to the Honourable Daines Barrington," May 20, 1777. *Natural History of Selborne* (London: Macmillan, 1887), p. 191.
2. Council for National Parks "History of the Parks." Web.
3. William Wordsworth, "I Wandered Lonely as a Cloud" in *Literature and Nature,* ed. Bridget Keegan and James C. McKusick (Upper Saddle River, N.J.: Prentice Hall, 2001), p. 454.
4. Interview with Philip Booth, Institute of Economic Affairs, April 2, 2004.
5. Derek Burke, "GM Foods and Crops," *EMBO Reports,* 2004 (5): 432.
6. Theophile Gautier, "The Flower That Makes the Spring," Read Book On-line, Web.
7. Richard H. Grove, *Green Imperialism* (Cambridge, U.K.: Cambridge University Press, 1995), pp. 168–263.
8. Joseph Szarka, *The Shaping of Environmental Policy in France* (New York: Berghahn, 2002), pp. 133, 34.
9. Szarka, *The Shaping of Environmental Policy in France,* pp. 148–152.
10. Gwynne Dyer, "Global Accord on Emissions Still a Crisis Away," *Toledo Blade,* Dec. 6, 2005.
11. European Environmental Bureau, *10 Years of the Water: Framework Directive: a Toothless Tiger,* Brussels, 2010, Web.
12. Henning Arp, Technical Regulation and Politics," in *Environmental Policy in the European Union,* ed. Andrew Jordan (Sterling, Va.: Earthscan, 2002), p. 265.
13. Arp, "Technical Regulation and Politics," p. 268.
14. Directive 2007/46/EC.
15. Albert Wade, "European Environmental Policy by Stealth," in *Environmental Policy in the European Union,* ed. Andrew Jordan (Sterling, Va.: Earthscan, 2002), p. 330.

5

Canada and Australia

Canada and Australia share many aspects of their environmental politics and history with the United States. They are former British colonies with democratic governments based on the two-party system and subject to similar influences from science, literature, and art. Canada shares the same continent and has had parallel development in agriculture and industry. Australia is "that other America on the other side of the Pacific."[1]

Canada: The Canadian coast of North America was discovered in 1497 by John Cabot, sailing for England. This was only 5 years after Columbus's discovery of the New World. Landing on the Gaspé Peninsula in 1524, Jacques Cartier claimed Canada for France. Permanent settlement did not occur until 1605 when the Sieur de Monts and Samuel de Champlain established Port Royal in Acadia (now Annapolis Royal in Nova Scotia). Three years later a trading post was established in Quebec. Settlement was slow, with fewer than 300 colonists arriving between 1608 and 1640. The focus was on fishing and trading fur. On numerous occasions, the British attacked the French. In 1713 the Peace of Utrecht gave them Acadia, the Hudson Bay area, Newfoundland, and Labrador. In 1690 Henry Kelsey explored northern Saskatchewan, starting from York Factory on Hudson Bay. Another Hudson Bay Company trader, Samuel Hearne, reached the Arctic Ocean in 1771. Meanwhile, the French had explored west to the foothills of the Rocky Mountains. Other Frenchmen like Pere Jacques Marquette and Robert Sieur de la Salle, turned south to explore the present-day United States. With the conquest of Quebec City in 1759, Britain became the permanent master of Canada. In 1789 Alexander Mackenzie reached the Arctic Ocean along the river that bears his name, and in 1793, he reached the Pacific Ocean over the Rocky Mountains. By 1778 James Cook, George Vancouver, and other English naval captains had explored and claimed present-day British Columbia.

The Europeans encountered native peoples whose ancestors had migrated to Canada from Asia via the Bering land bridge prior to 13,000 BC. The eastern woodland Indians both fought the colonists and cooperated with them in the fur trade. With their hunting, gathering, and a little farming, their impact on the land was slight. In the Arctic the Inuits (Eskimos) had arrived much more recently, around AD 1000. Likewise, the Inuit impact on the land was slight.

In area, Canada is the second largest in the world. Although cold weather limits agriculture, the country exports much wheat. Only 4% of the land is arable. In terms of geology, half of the country consists of the Canadian Shield, which is rich in minerals like iron, copper, and nickel but is delicate in terms of exposure to acid rain. Oil and natural gas are plentiful in Alberta. Farther west, the Rocky and Coastal mountains offer spectacular scenery. The temperate rain forests of the Pacific Coast have some of the highest species diversity in the world and support a large timber industry. Almost the entire population lives in the south, within a hundred miles of the US border. To the north, the land is forested, with the trees dwindling to tundra toward the Arctic.

Even today the mountains and remote areas support many animals like bears, wolves, and eagles extinct elsewhere. The fur trade was responsible for much of the country's early development. The Grand Banks off the coast of Newfoundland was the most abundant fishery in the world. Historically, access there was contested by the English, French, Portuguese, and Spanish. The Peace of Utrecht regulated the fishery, making it the earliest example of a natural resource conflict resolved by an international treaty. In 1868, the newly created national government passed the Fisheries Act. Besides fish, the Grand Banks was home to the Great Auk. This big bird was flightless, but an expert swimmer and diver, with a range from the St. Lawrence Gulf to Iceland. Hunting drove it to extinction in 1844.

The Romantic Movement came late to Canada. The few early poets tended to rather slavishly imitate the British. A major tenet of the movement was nationalism, but Canada was late to become a nation. In 1832 Major John Richardson published *Wacousta*, a novel of the Pontiac conspiracy. Richardson was considered the father of Canadian fiction. Charles Sangster published *St. Lawrence and the Saguenay, and other Poems* in

1856. Canadians read British authors like Wordsworth and Lord Byron, French ones like Jean Jacques Rousseau, and American ones like James Fenimore Cooper, Ralph Waldo Emerson, and Henry David Thoreau. Audubon visited in the 1830s, and Muir also came. The Romantic tradition in nature was perpetuated into the 20th century by A. S. Belaney, who published under the pseudonym of Grey Owl. Actually born in England, he pretended he was a native Canadian, the son of a Scottish father and an Apache mother. He married an Iroquois woman. Grey Owl, who worked as a trapper and a park ranger and authored four popular books and many magazine articles on the wilderness.

Early 19th-century painting followed European themes and subjects, but by about 1830 Peter Rindisbacher began painting Indians and buffalo near his frontier home in the Red River Colony. Later Paul Kane, inspired by the American work of George Catlin, painted western Canadian scenes. During a wilderness trip in 1846–48 with fur traders from Ontario to Fort Vancouver, he sketched native peoples and scenery, producing a hundred canvases upon his return. William G. R. Hind worked as an artist for a scientific expedition exploring Labrador and, in 1862, joined prospectors traveling to British Columbian gold fields.

References to nature in the national anthem, "O Canada," composed in 1880 for the National Congress of French Canadians, were slight, mentioning only "leaves of red and gold." A later version sang:

> O Canada! in praise of thee we sing;
> From echoing hills our anthems proudly ring.
> With fertile plains and mountains grand, With lakes and rivers clear,
> Eternal beauty, thou dost stand, Throughout the changing year.

The present version, adopted in 1980, has dropped the references to nature. On the other hand, the flag, adopted in 1965, features a maple leaf, one of the few nations in the world to give such prominence to a natural symbol.

In 1885 the federal government established Banff National Park, and 2 years later parliament passed the Rocky Mountains Park Act. The example of its neighbor to the south in establishing Yellowstone Park was a major influence. Indeed, some of the language of the law was copied word for word from the US law establishing Yellowstone Park. The first bird sanctuary was founded in Saskatchewan in 1887. By then the number of bison were down to only 2000 animals. In 1911 the national government established a park agency.

Scientific study of nature dates to 1697 when the Royal Physician for New France, Michel Sarrazin, arrived in Quebec, where he collected plants for a herbarium and sent reports back to Paris. A 1749 expedition by Pehr Kalm and J. F. Gaultier provided 200 species to Swedish botanist Carolus Linnaeus, constituting most of his Canadian material. Arriving from France in 1785, Andre Michaux studied trees. In the mid-19th century, William J. Hooker organized amateur botanists to assemble collections. The Botanical Society of Canada was founded in 1860, but did not endure long. The Botanical Club of Halifax lasted from 1891 to 1910.

While botany was largely a field for amateurs, the government supported geology. In 1842 William Logan was appointed to survey the United Province of Canada, thus establishing the Geological Survey of Canada. In 1856 Elkanah Billings became a full-time paleontologist for the agency (although an amateur). Toward the end of the century, the Geological Survey was operating in Manitoba and the Northwest Territories. In 1874 G. M. Dawson announced the discovery of the dinosaur fauna of Alberta and Saskatchewan. In the early 20th century, the agency cooperated with oil wildcatters by analyzing microfossils in the well cuttings. Canadian participation in the International Polar Year of 1882–83 was minimal. A team of German scientists explored and observed at Baffin Island, and a British team was stationed at Great Slave Lake.

Three treaties in the early twentieth century broke new ground for the two countries sharing the North American continent. The 1909 Boundary Waters Treaty guaranteed clean water in rivers crossing the border, as well as cooperation on the Great Lakes, and established the International Joint Commission. In 1911 Canada signed the North Pacific Fur Seal Treaty. That year it also established its forest reserves, and set up a Commission on Conservation to investigate natural resources (as well as town planning and public health). The 1918 Migratory Bird Protection Convention was a treaty to protect birds. A 1939 law regulated pesticides. Rapid urbanization after 1945 required more municipal water and sewer systems.

The Audubon Society was established in 1948, one more example of how bird-watchers are early leaders in citizen groups. Now called Nature Canada, it has 40,000 members and 350 affiliated organizations. It seeks to protect plants, animals and habitat. Endangered species are a special concern. Its education programs aim at children.

In the 1950s Canadians began to ask the degree to which their country would remain merely a primitive source of timber, oil, copper, and iron ore, instead of becoming a modern industrial country. Later several events stimulated popular concern. In 1969 at Placentia Bay, Newfoundland, fluoride effluent from a plant that produced phosphorus for metal finishing killed tens of thousands of fish. Only a few months later the oil tanker *Arrow* ran aground on Cerberus Rock in Chedabucto Bay, Nova Scotia. As the ship broke up over the following days of stormy weather, half its cargo of 108,000 barrels leaked out. At the same time, scientists discovered high levels of mercury in the fish in the Great Lakes. The 1973 energy crisis caused severe shortages in the eastern provinces at the same time as it rewarded oil rich Alberta. Responding to public demands for environmental protection, Parliament passed the Water Act in 1970 and the Clean Air Act in 1971. In the late 1970s, Canadians became aware that sulfur dioxide and nitrogen oxides from US factories and electric power plants were blowing north across the border to cause acid rain and smog. They put pressure on the Americans to control the problem.

Government: France lost its Canadian colony permanently in the Treaty of Paris of 1763. The British Quebec Act of 1774 guaranteed the French inhabitants their civil, legal, linguistic, and religious rights. At the time very few English speakers lived in the colony. This changed at the end of the American Revolution when the Loyalists arrived. These were residents of the Thirteen Colonies who had remained loyal to Britain. Those deported by land went to western Quebec and those deported by sea went to Nova Scotia. The new arrivals, English speaking and Protestant, clashed with the Canadians, French speaking, and Catholic. To resolve the conflict, the British Parliament passed the Constitution Act in 1791 that divided the territory into Upper and Lower Canada, present-day Ontario and Quebec. By 1849 those two colonies, as well as the Maritimes (Nova Scotia, New Brunswick, Prince Edward Island, and Newfoundland), were granted responsible government on internal matters. Great Britain continued to control its foreign relations for many years.

By the early 1860s at least three factors showed the need for unity. The American Civil War was raging, and many feared that once it was over, the Union army of a million men might invade Canada. The United States had tried it twice before in 1775 and 1813. Conflict between the French and English continued. And a railroad was needed to the Pacific. Representatives from all provinces met in Charlottetown in 1864 to initiate negotiations for unification, and 3 years later the British Parliament made it official in the North American Act. In 1869 the new federation acquired the extensive territory of the Hudson Bay Company. The powers of the national government are less than found in the United States. The provinces retained their authority over minerals, water, land, and forests as well as property, civil rights, and education.

The new federation needed a new capital city. Ottawa was a logical site, on the boundary between Quebec and Ontario, the border between the French and the English. Ten years earlier, the small lumber town had been designated as a compromise location for the capital for the combined province of Upper and Lower Canada, then designated West and East. The site is on the Ottawa River at Chaudières Falls. The river had been the chief route to the west for explorers and fur traders. The neo-gothic style of the Parliament building echoed the British Parliament. The City Beautiful Movement influenced the city in erecting imposing government buildings, avenues, and parks.

At the national level, the most important governmental agency is Environment Canada, established in 1970. Its name reflects a Canadian method of bilingualism for agencies with their names being nearly identical in English and French. Its major divisions are the Environmental Protection Service responsible for air pollution control, the Conservation Service responsible for water, and the Meteorological Service. It has five regional divisions: Atlantic, Quebec, Ontario, Prairie, and the Pacific. With 4,700 employees, the agency enforces the laws, controls dangerous chemicals, gives scientific advice, and funds local programs. It also protects species at risk and handles global warming matters. The Minister of the Environment sits in the cabinet.

Parks Canada, under the jurisdiction of the same minister, manages the 41 national parks, in addition to a number of historic sites. The largest is Wood Buffalo Park, which is bigger than Switzerland. Two of the most famous are Banff and Jasper in the Rocky Mountains. All three are UNESCO World Heritage Sites. The newest is Ukkusiksalik Park in Nunavut, a semi-autonomous Native People territory carved out of the Northwest Territories in 1999. Several parks cooperate with American parks across the border. Waterton Lakes in Alberta adjoins Glacier Park in Montana, Kluane in the Yukon adjoins Wrangell–Saint Elias in Alaska, and Ivvavik in the Yukon adjoins the Arctic National Wildlife Refuge in Alaska.

Natural Resources Canada is the agency concerned with natural resources, water power, energy, minerals, metals, and forests. The Forest Service and sectors for earth sciences, minerals and energy are its major divisions. The ministry is responsible for survey, water power regulation, oil and gas regulation, and mining.

The division of governmental power between the federal and provincial levels is a frequent source of controversy. Compared to the United States, the system is more decentralized. Provincial governments control public lands, and they own gigantic electric systems like Quebec Hydro and Ontario Hydro. Municipalities control land use planning. The federal level has narrower authority: the seacoasts, fisheries, shipping and native people. In addition, the provinces all have their own agencies. In Ontario the Ministry of the Environment sets the standards for pollutants, issues certificates for industrial facilities, oversees pesticides, and cleans up after spills. Other ministries in the province concerned with protection are those for natural resources, agriculture, municipal affairs, health, energy and transportation. In Quebec the Ministry of Sustainable Development, the Environment and Parks is the key agency, and in British Columbia it is the Ministry of Environment. The environmental ministers of the 10 provinces meet at least annually in their Council, joined by the federal minister and ministers from the territories. The council works by consensus, under the assumption that voting, bargaining, and majority rule is not consensus.

Canadian national government follows the Westminster system copied from the British. The prime minister and his cabinet are selected by parliament by the party (or coalition of parties) that has a majority. The House of Commons is far more powerful than the Senate, which is not elected and does little. The environmental ministers are elected members of Commons. For most of its history, Canada had a two-party system: the Liberals and the (old) Conservatives. This is a consequence of the electoral system of single member districts. Victory goes to the "first past the post." Occasionally, a third party has won enough votes to become the balance of power. At the time, Parliament passed the law establishing Environment Canada in 1970, three political parties were represented: the Liberals, the Conservatives, and the small New Democrats. All supported environmental programs, differing mostly on style.

A major change in the two-party system occurred suddenly in the 1988 election when the Conservative Party totally collapsed, going from a majority of 169 out of 295 to only two in 1993. The Liberals won 177 seats. Two new parties were the Reform and the Bloc Québécois. The latter was only from that province and advocated greater autonomy or perhaps independence. The Liberals won again in 1997 and 2000. In 2004 the Liberals failed to gain a majority but continued to govern with a minority. A new Green Party ran candidates for all 308 seats, but did not win any, although it got 4.3% of the vote. Four years earlier it got less than 1%. Parliament took a turn to the right in 2006 when the Conservative Party won 124 seats in Commons, giving it more than the Liberals with 103. This gave it control of the government with a new prime minister, Stephen Harper. Unfortunately for the Conservatives, however, they did not have an absolute majority, and hence had to try to govern with a minority. Neither of the two small parties, the Bloc Québécois or the New Democrats, were willing to enter a coalition for two reasons. Coalitions are rare in Canada, and in any case, the two small parties are ideologically at the opposite pole from the Conservatives. Harper called another election in 2008, hoping to get an absolute majority. This time he won more seats, 143, but still did not get the majority.

The 2011 election was very favorable for the Conservatives, giving it an absolute majority of 166 seats out of 308. The once dominant Liberals won only 34 seats, and the New Democratic Party became the official opposition with 103 seats. The Bloc Québécois nearly disappeared with only four seats. One Green Party member won election. Stephen Harper was at last clearly in charge.

The Conservative Party Platform contains a number of planks favoring the environment. It brags of having created eight new protected areas, expanded Nahanni Park to six times its previous size, and cleaned up rivers and lakes. It describes its climate policy as supporting the Copenhagen Accords of 2009, but many consider this voluntary agreement a step backward. The party promotes the oil sands, which require much energy to mine and refine, adding excessive greenhouse gas. It has acquired the nickname of "the world's dirtiest fuel." Harper has sought to export crude from the sands to the United States and to China. That will go via the new Keystone XL Pipeline crossing the border in Montana, then over the Ogalala Aquifer south to refineries in Texas. Crude bound for China will flow to a new port in Kitimat in northern British Columbia, a site many consider environmentally fragile.

Harper represents a riding (district) in Calgary, Alberta, the center of the oil industry. His father had been employed by the Imperial Oil Company, and he began his own career in the mail room of the company's office in Edmonton. Later he worked on computers and took a degree in economics from the University of Calgary. He began his political career in high school with the Liberal Party, but left it because he disagreed with its National Energy Program. He then joined the Reform Party, winning a seat in Parliament in 1993. Harper found differences with his new party, however, and resigned his seat in 1997. He wanted more autonomy for Alberta, proposing a "firewall" to keep the rest of Canada from draining its wealth from oil and gas to other provinces. He advocated conservative social positions, including parents' right to use corporal punishment on their children. In 2002 he was elected once more to Parliament with a new party, the Canadian Alliance, which soon merged with the Conservative Party. And he was elected the leader. Harper had a penchant for insulting people, saying Quebec had too many privileges, and that the Atlantic provinces were trapped in a culture of defeat, and had a "can't do" attitude.

All four parties in Parliament claim to favor environmental protection. The New Democratic Party wants a vigorous program on greenhouse gases, more renewable energy and Green Bonds to finance sustainable energy. It proposes a cap-and-trade system for greenhouse gases aiming for a level 80% below the 1990 emissions by 2050. Also it promises to help Canadian communities deal with the unfolding impacts of a warming planet, anticipating the country's northern geography will make it especially vulnerable. The Liberals promise to protect the environment, encourage sustainable energy and return to a scientific basis for climate change. The Bloc Québécois wants to protect the St. Lawrence River, combat blue algae in lakes, lessen dependence on petroleum, and use cap-and-trade to reduce global warming. The Policy Declaration of the Conservatives states that "the quality of the environment is a vital part of our heritage to be protected by each generation for the next."[2] In fact, this latter seems largely lip service, in light of their recent actions.

In the 2011 election, Harper claimed he was pro-environmental, including renewing an existing pledge to support the Kyoto Protocol with a 17% reduction in greenhouse gases by 2020, but this was the weakest of the three major parties. Once in office, Harper backed away. In June the parties to the treaty met in Bonn, Germany, to plan a Second Commitment Period. The 1997 commitments were scheduled to end, and the parties wanted new commitments until 2020. Canada announced it would not agree to binding limits. Russia and Japan also said they would not participate either.

Canada has a wide range of environmental groups. Many started as affiliates of US organizations. The big ones have chapters in many provinces and head offices in Ottawa. The Wildlife Federation claims 300,000 members and supporters. Organized in 1962, it promoted the endangered species program. The World Wildlife Fund, founded in 1967, has more than 50,000 members. It is concerned with over-fishing, endangered species at home, and international trade in species like tigers and sea turtles. With

40,000 members, Nature Canada began in 1948 as the Audubon Society, changing its name in 1971. Endangered species have been a special concern. Friends of the Earth, with 10,000 members, is a branch of the international organization. The Sierra Club has been active in Canada since 1963, and it established a national office in 1989. The Parks and Wilderness Society, begun in 1963, concentrates on protecting big, wild ecosystems in parks, refuges, and wilderness areas. It is proud of having conserved more than 100 million acres of wild places.

The most noteworthy group is Greenpeace, now grown to be the biggest environmental organization in the world. In 1971 a few people from Vancouver, British Columbia, organized to protest a US nuclear bomb test in Amchitka, an island in the Aleutian chain of Alaska. Some had been active in the peace movement against the US war in Vietnam, some had experience trying to save whales, and still others were members in a new Sierra Club chapter. They chartered a fishing boat, re-christened it *Greenpeace*, and sailed for Alaska. The name reflected a joining of the environmental and peace movements. The US Coast Guard arrested the crew and sent them away, but the bomb test was canceled. Emboldened by their success, the next year the group decided to challenge French nuclear testing in the South Pacific. The ship sailed into the forbidden safety zone near the blast site and launched little Zodiac boats to harass the French naval ships. As they sailed across the ocean, they became beguiled by the whales and sea life they encountered. In 1975 the *Greenpeace* sailed to fight illegal whaling, confronting Russian ships in the Pacific. The following year, the organization first demonstrated against the slaughter of seals in Labrador. Soon the Greenpeace movement spread to California, Hawaii, England, France, and Germany. Today, the international organization has 2.8 million supporters and affiliates in 40 countries. The Canadian organization campaigns to save forests, stop genetic engineering, and prevent climate change as well as protect the oceans. It maintains a fleet of six seagoing boats.

In 1977 Paul Watson, one of the most radical members of Greenpeace, broke away to found his own organization, the Sea Shepherd Conservation Society, named for its boat, the *Sea Shepherd*. Its goal is protection of marine mammals. The society contends it is only enforcing the regulations of the International Whaling Commission, which has no police authority of its own. One technique is to publicize the violations with photographs and videotape. It often has news reporters sail aboard its vessels to document the violations. Other techniques are violent, including harassment and ramming of illegal ships. In 1979, the *Sea Shepherd* located and rammed the pirate whaler *Sierra* at sea. This then led to the arrest of the crews of two other pirate whalers in South Africa. The next year the *Sea Shepherd* was involved in the sinking of two illegal Spanish whaling ships that had flagrantly exceeded whale quotas. In 1986 the *Sea Shepherd* was implicated in sinking two Icelandic whalers in the harbor at Reykjavik. Captain Watson has been arrested on a number of occasions but never convicted of a crime. The society works to defend fur seals in Canada, Norway, and South Africa, turtles, sharks, and sea cucumbers in the Galápagos Islands, and dolphins off Japan.

Industry has interests that often conflict with the environmental groups. The Canadian Electricity Association, founded in 1891, represents the electric utilities, which burn a lot of coal. While pledging to pollute as little as possible, the association urges efficiency, flexibility, and market-based solutions. Coal Association members include producers, coal-using utilities, railroads, and suppliers. The Mining Association covers minerals other than coal for companies engaged in exploration, mining, smelting, and refining. The association pledges to work with the government to develop effective, efficient, and equitable measures to protect the environment based on sound science. Moreover, it promises to reclaim mines according to site-specific criteria in a planned and timely manner. The Forestry Association mixes industry and a few members from the environmental side. It advocates sustainable development and wise use. The Chemical Producers Association represents more than 65 manufacturers across the country, which collectively produce more than 90% of all chemicals. It actively lobbies parliament.

Issues: In 1971 Robert Bourassa, the premier of Quebec, announced the gigantic James Bay hydroelectric project at a provincial Liberal Party conference. Its purpose was to develop the Quebec economy, which had remained stagnant while Ontario and the West were prospering. Between 1944 and 1963 the provincial government had taken over private utilities to form Hydro-Quebec, with the goal of spurring industrial development. The project tied into the government's desire to strengthen the French culture and language. Collectively, the changes in Quebec of modernization and assertion had earned the sobriquet of the Quiet Revolution. The negative features of the early 1960s were a series of kidnappings and bombings by extreme Quebec nationalists.

The project involved damming eight rivers draining into James Bay, at a cost of US $20 billion. It was to generate 16,000 megawatts, submerge

135,000 square miles of valleys, and bring roads to virgin forests and taiga. The power would be the equivalent of three times the power station at Niagara Falls. Although ambitious, the project was not cost-effective, even according to engineering studies at the time. And these studies did not consider the environmental impact. Most of the Cree Indians living in the region opposed the project as disruptive to their culture. Besides the damage to nature, the project was generating more electricity than it could sell. Much was exported to the United States, but even that market became saturated. The two difficulties combined to cause the government to suspend further construction in 1994.

Air pollution is a major problem throughout Canada. Its energy consumption per capita is the highest in the world, even higher than the United States, and more than twice Russia, Britain, France, Germany, and other industrial countries. Four factors explain this. First, Canada produces abundant oil and natural gas so it tends to be cheap. Second, distances are great for auto and airplane travel. Third, the need for space heating is great. And fourth, it favors a lifestyle of urban sprawl and big automobiles and trucks. Most air pollution comes from automobiles, with Ontario producing the greatest amount by far. The country also has much heavy industry like petroleum refining and metal smelting. Recently, it has begun to produce oil from the tar sands in Alberta, which uses a lot of energy and produces much pollution.

Controlling air pollution is a function shared by the national and provincial governments. The national level in Ottawa establishes nonbinding guidelines for ambient air based on science, called National Air Quality Objectives. The provinces have the option of adopting them as binding. Although the national-level Environmental Protection Act allows the minister to declare a substance toxic, he has not done so. Because the national law does not authorize enforcement, an alternative path has been to have the Council of Environmental Ministers develop programs. In 1990 the Council approved a Management Plan to address ozone that causes smog. This was done in consultation with industry and environmental groups. Unfortunately, this was not effective, so in 1997 the national government proposed a Phase 2 Federal Smog Management Plan. The next year the Council adopted the Canada Wide Accord on Environmental Harmonization. Legal critics have challenged this as exceeding the authority of the council and being unconstitutional. Environmental critics believe it has not moved very fast or been very effective. Moreover, Quebec did not sign the accord, although it has participated in parallel implementation.

Most discussions of air pollution soon point the finger at the neighbor to the south. For example, Windsor, Ontario, suffers from smog that blows across the Detroit River. More generally, pollution from the US Midwest afflicts most of eastern Canada. Indeed, it afflicts the eastern United States. One avenue for complaints is under the 1991 Canada–Air Quality Agreement regarding the study and control of transborder air pollutants. Another avenue is the North American Free Trade Association (NAFTA) Commission on Environmental Cooperation.

In northern Alberta, the environment is damaged by mining the tar sands along the Athabasca River. In total, 82,000 acres of forest and wetland have been disturbed and only 13,000 acres have been restored. Tar sands, more politely known as oil sands, are essentially asphalt—petroleum tar mixed with sand that can only be exploited by digging and heating. Two tons of sand yield one barrel of oil. Collectively, however, the quantity is stupendous. Potentially, the region holds 1.6 trillion barrels of oil, compared to 260 billion barrels in Saudi Arabia. Unfortunately, only 300 billion barrels can be recovered economically with current prices and technology. But both of these can change in future years. A price of $20 per barrel or more makes the projects profitable, and in 2013 the price was $100 a barrel. In order to get deeper deposits, engineers are experimenting with injecting steam and air. Both of these require a lot of energy. Present methods of strip mining also require a lot of energy. The oil sands use around 1 billion cubic feet of natural gas per day, around 40% of Alberta's total usage. In the future it can come from the MacKenzie River Delta 800 miles to the north. All this will release a lot of carbon into the atmosphere, making it hard for Canada to meet its quota under the Kyoto Protocol.

Environmental groups oppose developing the tar sands. It will damage the delicate northern forests and wetlands, which are breeding grounds for millions of birds, and where bogs filter water. The huge volume of water needed for the process threatens the Athabasca River. The emissions of sulfur dioxide and nitrogen oxide will increase levels of acid rain and destroy lake fish. The Pembina Institute has complained that "We're using natural gas, which is the cleanest fossil fuel, to wash sand and make a dirtier fuel. It's like using caviar to make fake crabmeat." Responding to the government of Alberta's proposed Mineable Oil Sands Strategy, the director of the Sierra Club of Canada said, "The real purpose of the Strategy appears to be to create a regulation-free zone to give the companies the freest hand to increase oil production from the tar sands as quickly as possible."[3]

The government of Alberta owns 81% of the province's oil, natural gas, and mineral resources, and each citizen—man, woman, or child—has received a check for $400 in royalties. The province gets a third of its revenues from royalties. The longtime premier, Ralph Klein, used the money to build his political base. Nicknamed "King Ralph," he was a flamboyant Conservative who frequently has quarreled with the Liberal national prime ministers, Jean Chretien and Paul Martin.

In the 1970s, Canadians realized some of their lakes were sterile because acid in the water was killing the plants and fish. The problem was particularly bad near Sudbury, Ontario, and more generally throughout Quebec. A total of 14,000 lakes were acidic. The cause was acid rain and snow that drained into the lakes, while other acid fell dry or in fog. For the most part, it was sulfuric acid, although nitric acid was also common. The dual mystery was the source of the acid, and why one lake could be afflicted and not others. Except for those near nickel smelters in Sudbury, the lakes were remote from industry. Scientists eventually demonstrated that the acid had traveled long distances. Much came from the United States from coal burned in the Ohio Valley, emitted high into the air where the sulfur combined with oxygen to form the acid, then deposited in rain, snow, fog, or powder in the north-country where the soil lacked buffers to neutralize the acid. US emissions of sulfur dioxide are six times as great as Canadian emissions. While not all falls on Canada, much of it does. Other acid came from closer to home from automobile exhaust. The soil of the Canadian Shield, which contains the oldest rock on the planet, tends to be thin and worn. When acid rain fell on soil to the south with more natural buffers, alkalis neutralized it so the damage was less.

Based on better scientific information, the government demanded the United States control its pollution. At first the United States denied responsibility, but when scientific evidence demonstrated the problem, the two governments first agreed to monitor the air and coordinate their research, then as the cause became clearer, to limit emissions. In 1991 the two countries signed the Air Quality Agreement. Reduction of acid on both sides of the border improved the situation. By 1995 sulfur dioxide emissions in eastern Canada were down by 54% compared to 1980. The West suffers less because of fewer cities and industries, as well as more alkaline soils.

Controversy arose in 1998 regarding withdrawing water from the Great Lakes. The Nova Group, a company based in Sault Ste-Marie, Ontario, asked for a permit to withdraw water for beverages to be sold in Asia. At first, the national government granted permission, but in the face of outraged citizens, the provincial government claimed that it had juris-diction and denied permission. Ontario prevailed in the legal dispute. Although the amount was small, people worried that exporting a little water for beverages would lead to tapping the Great Lakes for munici-pal supplies in the United States, and even big canals or pipelines carry-ing water to irrigate the West. Diversion comes under the jurisdiction of the International Joint Commission set up by the Boundary Waters Treaty. In 2001 Canada and the United States amended the treaty to give the national government the authority to prohibit bulk water removal. Moreover, all provinces now have developed laws or regulations to cover the problem. However, little agreement exists north or south of the border as to what constitutes reasonable withdrawal for municipal or agricultural use. Quebec and Ontario joined eight US states in 1985 to sign the Great Lakes Charter, and in 2001 amended it to strengthen it, especially regard-ing water removal.

The Arctic remains nearly pristine. This land of tundra and ice has only a few inhabitants, chiefly Inuits (Eskimos). In 1999 Canada established a semiautonomous government called Nunavut. The territory stretches from the northern border of Ontario and Hudson Bay toward the North Pole, covering 700,000 square miles, and constitutes nearly one-fifth of Canada. The population density is only one person per 27 square miles. The area to the west, about equal in size, remains part of the Northwest Territory. Although remote, the Arctic suffers from deposition of toxic pollutants blown from the south. Warming global temperatures affect the region disproportionately. Already sea ice is receding, and the entire Arctic Ocean may be ice free in the summer in a few decades. The fall freeze-up is later, and the spring thaw is earlier. The delta of the Mackenzie River has extensive reserves of natural gas, and when these are tapped, the Northwest will change. About 1974 the United States proposed an oil pipeline from the North Slope of Alaska to Chicago. Although never built, recent proposals call for transporting natural gas from the Delta to Ontario or Alberta. More than 30 years ago the threat of a pipeline caused environmentalists to organize the Canadian Arctic Resources Committee. Geologists have found that the warming is melting the permafrost tundra, which in turn releases methane, which is a greenhouse gas so the cycle will be exacerbated.

The abundant fishery of the Grand Banks in the Atlantic began to suffer decline in the 1970s. In 1974 the government imposed Total Allowable Catches for each stock. This helped temporarily, but by 1992 the government had to impose a complete moratorium. The limits and moratorium devastated the economy of the fishermen. The government gave them $4 billion in financial aid. In 1999 fishing was again permitted, but after 4 years the moratorium had to be reinstated. Part of the Grand Banks is within the 200-mile territorial limits declared in 1977 and part is in international waters. These are subject to cooperation under the Northwest Atlantic Fisheries Organization. Success has been mixed, with the decline of cod, but increases in shellfish.

Canada has often played a role in international environmental issues. As a midsized developed country, it has tried to specialize in its contributions to international affairs, and this is one area. (Another was military peace keeping for the United Nations.) In 1987 it played a key role in controlling damage to the ozone layer caused by CFCs. These chemicals found in Freon eventually floated up to the stratosphere where they destroyed the natural ozone layer that protected plants and animals from the destructive forces of ultraviolet radiation. Canada sponsored an international conference in Montreal, where 24 industrial countries agreed to a detailed program to limit CFC production, known as the Montreal Protocol. It was considered a great success.

With respect to global warming, the Canadians wanted to repeat their diplomatic achievement. In 1988 they convened a conference in Toronto at which the 300 participants voiced their agreement with the scientific consensus on the greenhouse effect, and set out the three-part proposal of a 20% reduction in emissions by 2005, a comprehensive treaty, and a fund to compensate the developing countries. Although the targets were lessened, the basic tripartite form became the basis for the eventual Kyoto Protocol. Canada faces the risk of great environmental changes. Melting the Arctic Ocean ice and the Greenland icecap would modify its climate immediately. On the positive side, warmer temperatures would moderate its severe winters and allow wheat and corn to be grown at more northern latitudes.

The Toronto proposal became the basis for the Framework Convention on Climate Change signed by 160 countries at the Earth Summit in Rio de Janeiro in 1992. In the election the following year, the Liberal Party under Prime Minister Jean Chretien promised that "environmental security through sustainable development will be a cornerstone of Canadian foreign policy."[4] To set an example, he said Canada would aim to cut carbon dioxide emissions by 20% from 1988 levels by the year 2005. In fact, little came of this promise. Chretien toyed with a carbon tax, but dropped it. Environmentalists pointed out that the petroleum industry got $3.2 billion a year in tax concessions and incentives. In the 1997 election, Chretien continued to talk about controlling greenhouse gases but offered nothing specific.

That November Canada signed the Kyoto Protocol committing itself to reduce carbon emissions by 8% by the year 2010, and to aid Third World countries with money and technical help. After the conference, the next step was ratification, but Chretien dithered, talking of implementing the protocol but doing little. After meeting with provincial leaders, their joint decision was to study the problem for another 2 years. The most vigorous opposition came from the Alberta premier, Ralph Klein.

Prime Minister Chretien was in for worse treatment when he took Team Canada to Moscow in February 2002. This was the name of the trade and diplomatic mission with the provincial premiers. At a news conference, Chretien was asked about the Kyoto agreement. As he began to answer that federal government remained totally committed, Alberta Premier "King Ralph" pushed forward to the microphone, pulled a letter from his suit jacket, and read it. The letter, which had secretly been signed by 9 of the 10 premiers at a recent meeting in Vancouver, demanded a unified North American position on global warming and told Chretien that the federal government should not ratify the protocol. Because President Bush had previously said the United States would not ratify it, this seemed likely to doom the protocol from ever garnering ratification by countries emitting 55% of the greenhouse gases, a provision necessary for the protocol to enter into force. The letter listed nine provincial conditions on global warming, including reiteration of provincial control of natural resources, a pledge of provincial–federal consultation, and a shift from regulation to conservation and education. Chretien left the room in anger and embarrassment for having been so rudely ambushed in a foreign country by his countrymen. So much for Team Canada. Eventually, in December 2002 Canada ratified the Kyoto Protocol.

David Suzuki typifies mainstream environmental support for the Kyoto Protocol, considering it one of the most pressing problems Canada faces. Suzuki has been active as an ecologist and geneticist since the 1960s. Born of Japanese descent in British Columbia in 1936, he loved hiking, fishing, and camping with his father. In 1942 he was forced to move to an internment camp when the government expelled ethnic Japanese from the West Coast. At the end of World War II, his family had to resettle in the east. After earning a PhD in genetics, he began a long career at the University of British Colombia. Suzuki became concerned that the public did not understand scientific and ecological issues. He wrote books to popularize the problems, including many for children, and appeared on television and radio. His radio broadcasts stimulated so much response that in 1990 he organized the David Suzuki Foundation. Besides climate change, the foundation concentrates on forests and oceans.

Maurice Strong is another man with a long and influential career as an environmentalist. Born in Oak Lake, Manitoba, in 1929, his family suffered during the Great Depression. After completing high school at the age of 15, he worked for the Hudson Bay Company as a fur trader in Chesterfield Inlet in the Northwest Territories, where he learned the Eskimo language. At 17 he formed his own mining exploration company. In the late 1940s, he worked for the fledgling United Nations. This whetted his appetite for international organizations, but his lack of a university degree barred him from promotion. He moved to Calgary, where he became a mining and oil stock analyst. Still restless, he and his bride traveled the world, spending time in Kenya, where he learned to speak Swahili. By the age of 25 he was back in Canada, where he worked for the Dome Petroleum Company, eventually becoming vice president. In 1962 Strong was hired as head of the giant Power Corporation of Canada. Three years later he became the director-general of the Canadian International Development Agency.[5] His dynamism, UN experience, language ability, and Canada's status as a midsized diplomatic power made him a natural choice to head the Stockholm conference in 1972. Twenty years later he headed the Earth Summit in Rio de Janeiro.

Australia was not discovered by Europeans until the 17th century and was barely explored until Captain James Cook visited Botany Bay in 1770. His name for the bay reflected the scientific mission of his voyage. Sailing north, he accidentally discovered the Great Barrier Reef by running his ship aground on it and nearly perishing. Only 17 years later (and with amazing confidence since there had been no further visits), the British government sent a fleet of eleven ships to colonize the continent. The pioneers were largely convicts from English jails. Settling in present-day Sydney, the new colonists struggled. They were not farmers but city people, and the soil was poor. An early environmental problem was to keep the water in the Tank Stream safe for drinking. In 1805 the governor decreed that people who polluted the creek would have their house torn down.

At that time about 350,000 Aborigines inhabited the entire continent, descended from ancestors who immigrated from Asia 40,000 years ago. At the time of European contact, up to 600 different tribes existed, speaking 200 languages. They were hunters and gatherers. Although virtually none of them practiced agriculture, they had affected the landscape by fire. They routinely set fire to the grass and scrub bushes in order to encourage new growth that attracted animals they hunted. White settlement pushed the Aborigines out of the fertile land, and disease took its toll.

Unlike North America, most of Australia was unsuited for agriculture. The entire interior is extremely dry with only a few inches of rainfall a year. Moreover, the precipitation is not seasonal, so farmers cannot count on rain each spring or each winter, but experience great variation from year to year. A wet year may be followed by another wet one, or more likely by four or five dry years. Scientists believe the weather may be related to the El Niño patterns. The only area good for farming is a boomerang-shaped crescent along the southeast. The extreme north has tropical conditions and heavy rainfall, but the soil is poor. Although conditions do not favor agriculture, the country is rich in minerals. It has abundant coal, gold, alumina, and iron ore. Much of its 19th-century history revolved around gold rushes, and Melbourne is still a banking center based on gold mining a century ago. Australia is the biggest coal exporter in the world.

The animals are unlike the rest of the world. Marsupials dominate. At the time of European settlement, the only placental mammals were bats that had flown in from Indonesia, and feral dogs, called dingoes, which the Aborigines had brought in their original migration. With the continent isolated from the rest of the world, marsupials have evolved to occupy all ecological niches. Kangaroos and wallabies are herbivores, and Tasmanian devils are carnivores. The now extinct Tasmanian wolf occupied the place at the top of the food chain. Australia is the only home of the platypus and the echidna of the primitive monotreme order. Many plants are unique, also. The continent has hundreds of species of eucalypts and acacia, like the golden wattle.

The colonists soon decided that the native animals and plants were inferior and began introducing European ones. Some were livestock for farming like sheep and cattle, which at least could be justified on the basis of establishing profitable farms, but the settlers introduced songbirds like sparrows, robins, and starlings just so their homes could seem more like England. One of the worst ideas was to introduce rabbits, which soon bred like rabbits, overrunning the countryside. They were introduced by a wealthy landowner who wanted to hunt them. In 1859 he turned two dozen rabbits loose on his estate in Victoria, and soon their descendants inhabited nearly the entire continent. They had no predators because the native ones—the dingo and the Tasmanian wolf—were already being shot and kept in check by sheep ranchers.

Farmers did not always accept the fragility of the land, in spite of wise governmental policies. In 1865 the Surveyor General of the colony of South Australia, George Goyder, charted a line to delineate areas with adequate rainfall for growing wheat from areas that were too arid. Settlement was not permitted north of the line. Several years of above average precipitation prompted farmers to establish farms beyond Goyder's Line. Then in 1880, droughts began that caused total crop failure. Farms and towns had to be abandoned, and people lost all their wealth.

Australia was influenced by European and North American trends. As early as the 1830s, John Gould was painting birds in Van Diemen's Land and the Swan River Valley, eventually published as *Birds of Australia*. The colonists were influenced by British Romantic poets and by American writers like Henry David Thoreau. A group calling themselves the Woodlanders named their retreat Walden Hut. Scientific societies were founded. The first was the Philosophical Society of Australasia, established in New South Wales in 1821. By 1857 the Zoological Society of Victoria was meeting. The Royal Society of New South Wales was founded in 1866. One member, William Clark, addressed the society on the disastrous effects of forest clearance. Another member, Eccleston du Faur, a surveyor for the government, became chairman of the Geography Section and promoted environmental approaches to understanding climate patterns. He proposed an expedition to travel to Antarctica to study how the polar icecap influenced Australian weather.[6] The predecessor of Birds Australia was founded in 1903 as the Royal Australasian Ornithologists Union.

R. M. Collins, who came from a wealthy sheep-raising family, took a world tour, and in 1878 visited California, where he learned of Yellowstone National Park and of the proposal to establish another one at Yosemite. Upon his return he was elected to Parliament and later to the presidency of the Queensland branch of the Royal Geographical Society. Collins proposed a national park in the McPherson Range in the southeast highlands of Queensland, and although this met with local opposition, the Queensland parliament did pass legislation in 1906 that created two other parks. Finally, in 1915, the McPherson Range became Lamington National Park.[7] In New South Wales, the Royal National Park, encompassing

18,000 acres, was dedicated in 1879. (The designation "national" referred to its importance rather than ownership. It was and continues to be owned by New South Wales.) Another tie to California was the introduction of the Monterrey Pine, known as *Pinus radiata*, in 1876. The tree adapted well to dry conditions, especially in South Australia, and quickly grew tall and straight making it ideal for lumber. In a reciprocal fashion, Californians imported the eucalyptus trees, which were soon planted everywhere, becoming an ecological pest in many areas.[8]

By the turn of the 20th century, Australians were taking a positive attitude toward their Quiet Continent. Other nicknames were the Happy Country, the Lucky Country, and the Antipodes. Dorothea Mackeller composed one of its most popular poems.[9]

> I love a sunburnt country, A land of sweeping plains,
> Of ragged mountain ranges, Of droughts and flooding rains.
> I love her far horizons, I love her jewel-sea,
> Her beauty and her terror, The wide brown land for me.

Government: Australia was not organized into a single nation as a federal Commonwealth until 1901. Prior to then, the six colonies were governed independently of one another. The government was primarily copied from Britain, and referred to as the Westminster System. Parliament, consisting of two houses, elected a prime minister and cabinet ministers from the party with the majority. Yet it also copied some features from the United States, such as the term *states* rather than *provinces*, and Senate and House of Representatives rather than the House of Lords and House of Commons. The High Court is similar to the American Supreme Court. Wags call the hybrid the Washminster System.

Again, like the United States, Australia selected an entirely new site for the national capital: Canberra. Like Washington, D.C., Canberra has long avenues meeting at traffic circles, and many parks and monuments that fit the natural topography. Built in a remote valley, beginning in 1913, and designed by an American landscape architect, the capital incorporates the principles of the City Beautiful Movement. Capital Hill dominates the city, crowned by the New Parliament House with a giant flag flying over it.

At the national level, the chief agency is the Department of Environment and Heritage. Major divisions are Parks, Meteorology, Resources, Wildlife and Marine. Others are the Antarctic Division, the Great Barrier Reef Authority, and the Greenhouse Office. Established in 1971 as the Department of the Environment, Aborigines, and the Arts, it has had varying names and functions since then. Two other important departments are Agriculture, Fisheries and Forestry and Industry, Tourism and Resources.

The federal structure of the commonwealth means that each of the six states has its own agencies, such as the Department of Environment and Conservation of New South Wales or the Environmental Protection Authority of South Australia. Prior to the 1970s the states passed laws on sewage, clean water, irrigation, forests, parks, mining, fisheries, and so forth. The federal level did not enter the field until 1974.

More like Canada and less like the United States, the states retained much authority over land, mining, forests, and fisheries. This is because the federal Commonwealth was imposed on the existing six colony-states. The Constitution copies the American one by enumerating the specific powers of the national government and leaving all the rest to the states. This resulted in a shortage of authority for the commonwealth as environmental issues arose during the 20th century. Two ways around this were to use the power to conduct external affairs and the power to regulate trade and commerce. Its external affairs authority was the basis for the Sea Dumping Act of 1981 and the Seas and Submerged Lands case in 1975. It was also the authority for the Great Barrier Reef Park Act of 1975 and World Heritage Properties Conservation Act of 1983. Commonwealth authority to regulate trade and commerce was the basis for the Impact of Proposals Act of 1974 and the Endangered Species Protection Act of 1982. In 1999 Parliament replaced these with the comprehensive Environment Protection and Biodiversity Conservation Act. This clarifies the scope and triggering of an Environmental Impact Assessment.

Because the constitution is vague about federal relationships and the environment was not foreseen as an issue in 1901, the prime minister, the premiers of the six states and two territories, and the head of the local government association met in Brisbane in 1992 to sign the Intergovernmental Agreement on the Environment, laying out the relationship. In fact, this agreement is still vague, affirming the existing balance, and setting forth goals and procedures. The entire Constitution of 1901 is often criticized for vagueness. It has been described as a constitution that does not really tell how the government is constituted. There is no explanation of how a political party holding a majority is entitled to form a government, and it says that the executive function is to be exercised by the governor general, in reality a figurehead.

Forestry was an area reserved for the states in the 1901 Constitution. Most of them encouraged settlement and logging with no regard for conservation. In the 1920s the Queensland Department of Lands made plans to open rain forests in the north to settlement. The head of the Forestry Board, E. H. F. Swain, opposed this, arguing that the Crown lands should be held in trust. Furthermore, he began a program of replanting. The outcome was an investigation by a royal commission that concluded that "Queensland needs no forestry science for present requirements," and "There is abundance and enough timber for all."[10]

Like Britain and the United States, Australia has a two-party system, Labor versus the Liberals, with the proviso that the Liberals are in a permanent coalition with the small National Party. Labor is the oldest party, having been established in several of the colonies prior to federation. Moreover, it was the first labor party in the world to actually govern a nation when it took power in 1904. Its main opposition over the years has been the Liberal Party, which governed from 1949 to 1972, and several times since. To achieve a majority in Parliament, the Liberals formed a coalition with the Country Party (now called the National Party). This was not a logical combination because the Liberals were promarket and antigovernment intervention while the Country Party wanted government intervention on behalf of farmers. Opposition to Labor united them. In 1975 the Country Party changed its name to the National Party in a bid to attract nonrural votes. The Liberals are, in fact, the more conservative party compared to Labor, and have advocated free-market policies such as deregulation since the 1980s. The Liberal–National coalition came to power under the leadership of John Howard by defeating Labor in the 1996 election. Yet while the Liberals have controlled the Commonwealth level, all six states had Labor governments. Voting is compulsory, enforced by a $50 income tax credit, which is said to encourage middle-of-the-road voters to go to the polls, strengthening moderate policies.

Labor won the 2007 federal election with 83 seats to 65 for the Liberal-National coalition. The new prime minister was Kevin Rudd, who immediately signed the Kyoto Protocol, an action Howard had refused to take. Rudd also apologized to the aboriginal people for their mistreatment. His personal popularity faded quickly, however, and he lost party leadership 3 years later to Julia Gillard, prompting another federal election. This produced a muddled situation. Labor and the Liberal–National coalition each won 72 seats in the House of Representatives, four short of a majority. Three independents and the sole Green Party representative backed Labor, enabling it to form a minority government. In the Senate, Labor had only 31 seats compared to 34 for the coalition, but support from nine Green senators allowed it to prevail in selected votes.

Rudd's time as prime minister was brief. In June 2010 his own Labor Party turned against him for a variety of reasons, including dislike of his leadership style. Many believed he could not win the next election. The party voted to replace him with Julia Gillard, his deputy prime minister. Gillard called a snap election two months later that resulted in a "hung parliament." In other words, neither Labor nor the Liberal–National coalition had enough votes in the House of Representatives to form a majority. Gillard was able to secure the support of one Green MP and three independents to form a minority government. In the Senate six Green Party senators gave it enough votes.

The situation reversed dramatically three months later when Rudd won back the Labor Party leadership, and became the prime minister once again. Gillard had called an early election and polling data showed she was likely to lose. Part of her problem was that the carbon tax her party had passed earned the ire of heavy industry, and seemed likely to raise prices to consumers. Carbon dioxide emissions would be taxed at $25 per ton. Business groups claimed it would hurt the economy, and few people shared Labor's concern with reducing global warming.

Victory in the September, 2013, election went to the Liberal–National party coalition led by Tony Abbott, who became the new prime minister. His coalition took 88 seats in the House of Representatives against 57 for Labor. Voter distaste for the carbon tax appeared decisive, and Abbott pledged to scrap it. He had earlier announced that he did not believe the science behind global warming. Abbot was personally very conservative, and blatantly favored business and industry.

For the past two or three decades, the major parties have claimed that they were pro-environmental. Labor promised to ratify the Kyoto Protocol, set targets to reduce energy consumption, protect rivers and coasts, and phase out plastic shopping bags. It said it would support World Heritage listing of suitable areas of Cape York. From 1983 and 1990 when Bob Hawke was prime minister, the government was the most favorable of any period. It blocked hydroelectric dams in Tasmania, protected forests in Tasmania, Queensland, and Victoria, stopped a mine at Coronation Hill in the Kakadu National Park Conservation Zone, and blocked a pulp mill in Tasmania. The economic prosperity during the period allowed the Labor Party not to be overly concerned with the working class and to respond more to the middle class.[11]

Until recently, the Liberals pointed with pride to their accomplishments in taking a comprehensive approach, establishing parks, and improving water quality. They maintained that their approach to reducing greenhouse gases is superior to the Kyoto Protocol method. The Nationals pledge to protect the environment and conserve its unique beauty. As befits the former Country Party, they argue that "farmers ... have always recognized the need to be good stewards of our land and water resources," and seek "arrangements for stable, well-defined water allocation." They want to "secure the resource base of Australia's primary industries."[12] While Labor continues to advocate for the environment, the Liberals and the Nationals no longer do so. Their attacks particularly focus on the carbon tax, which both Coalition parties oppose.

A small Green Party has existed since 1992. Although its representatives and senators became pivotal to Labor control in the hung parliament after the 2010 election, over the long term the electoral system does not give much opportunity to small parties with diffuse support like the Greens. Moreover Labor's positive attitude toward the environment has preempted room for a big green party. In 1984 the Labor Party voted to approve a uranium mine. Opponents from the peace movement, in existence since the 1950s and active in protesting the Vietnam War, countered by organizing the National Disarmament Party, eventually supporting the Green Party. Present-day Greens continue to be antiwar and antinuclear. Recently, the Green Party had nine senators and one representative.

At the federal level, the Labor government elected in 1972 and headed by Gough Whitlam, sought to protect the environment. Three years earlier the party platform first offered detailed proposals to protect natural flora, fauna, and landscapes, to preserve the Great Barrier Reef, to ban DDT, and to conserve the land against loss, drought, overstocking, or erosion. In 1974 Parliament passed the Environmental Protection (Impact of Proposals) Act. The next year it passed the National Parks and Wildlife Conservation Act, and later the Nuclear Codes. Automobiles were required to have catalytic converters.

Much of the authority over mining and forests belonged to the states rather than the Commonwealth government. For example, in 1984 the federal government was afraid to force the Queensland government to nominate the Daintree rain forest as a World Heritage Site. The states have a full array of environmental laws. For instance, New South Wales has provisions on soil conservation, clean air, clean water, waste disposal, hazardous chemicals, ozone, threatened species, and many other items.

At this time Australia was influenced by global events like the *Club of Rome Report*, the Stockholm Summit, and activity in the United States and

Europe. Three international arrangements played a part. First was the evolution of the International Union for the Conservation of Nature (IUCN), a mixed private–governmental organization that Australia joined in 1974 after its participation at Stockholm. Its interest in protecting endangered species was a logical match with Australia with its many marsupials. The second was the World Heritage Convention, which Australia signed in 1974 and became one of the first countries to ratify it. The third was the Convention on International Trade in Endangered Species (CITES), which was fathered by the IUCN. At the time, the commonwealth government rather arbitrarily imposed a ban on exporting kangaroo products, which angered the states. In fact, most of the kangaroo population is thriving.

As in Europe and North America, interest groups play an important role in politics. The Australian Conservation Foundation was established in 1964 with an elite cast. Prince Philip of England had suggested it on a visit when he noted that no countrywide organization existed. In the beginning, its focus was more on animals and parks than on air and water pollution. Early leadership positions went to the governor general, the chief justice, and even Prince Philip himself. It was weak at the local level. In the 1970s, Friends of the Earth challenged it with active local branches. Greenpeace was also ready to take direct, symbolic action. Nevertheless, the foundation held its position as the leading group, enjoying good access to government decision makers. It received grants from the commonwealth government of up to $150,000 annually, and for a number of years was the only ecological group so funded. Since its beginning, the foundation has opposed mining the Great Barrier Reef, promoted national parks in Tasmania, Queensland, and the Northern Territory, advocated the moratorium on commercial whaling, and opposed the Franklin Dam. It supported Australia signing the World Heritage Convention in 1974. The foundation lobbies parliament, meets with farmers and takes its message to the corporate board rooms.

The Australian branch of the World Wildlife Fund was established in 1978. It now has nearly 80,000 members and a paid staff of 80. Its headquarters is in Sydney, with regional offices in Canberra, Melbourne, Darwin, Brisbane, and Perth. Besides protecting animals, its priorities are oceans, rivers, forests, and grasslands. WWF has supported a plan by the state of Queensland to reduce commercial fishing in the Great Barrier Reef Park. This involves establishing protected zones, setting quotas, and buying back commercial licenses. The organization pointed out that tourism for the reef contributed $3.2 billion to the economy, while commercial fishing contributed $90 million, less than a third as much. WWF sees itself as more active than the Conservation Society.

The Wilderness Society was established in 1976 as an outgrowth of the campaign against the Lake Pedder dam. It was originally the Tasmanian Wilderness Society but expanded to the mainland to work to protect the wet tropical forest at Daintree on the Queensland coast. In the federal election of 1987, the Labor Party agreed to list the forest as a World Heritage site in order to stop logging. Ties between the Party and the Society were strong. Some observers credit the margin of victory for Labor to its pro-environmental stance.[13]

Greenpeace came to Australia in 1977, a few years after its founding in Canada to protest the American nuclear test in Amchitka, Alaska. The Australian affiliate became concerned about the French nuclear testing in its colony of Moruroa in the South Pacific. Opposition intensified when the French secret service bombed the Greenpeace ship, the *Rainbow Warrior,* in the harbor of Auckland, New Zealand, killing one man on board. Back in Australia, the group campaigned against uranium mining. Greenpeace vigorously supports the Kyoto Protocol and advocates phasing out fossil fuels to replace them with solar, wind, and water power.

Business interests are powerful in Australia. Their main organization is the Business Council of Australia, an association of chief executives of the biggest corporations organized in 1983. It believes the country is not paying enough attention to economic growth, especially exports, and that water and electricity are not managed efficiently. The Australian Chamber of Commerce and Industry is the peak council of business associations indirectly representing 350,000 businesses. It advocates self-regulation, a minimum role for the federal government, and technological innovation. The mining industry is strong, too. The Australian Coal Association promises that its members will restore the land and that electric generators will minimize air pollution. Coal exports are worth $50 billion, more than any other commodity. Other exports are gold, iron ore, aluminum ores, nickel, copper, and zinc. The total mineral exports amount to 200 million metric tons, more than four times the comparable American figure. Although the market for uranium is depressed, the continent has the largest reserves in the world. All this mining is hard on the land.

Two think tanks stand on opposite sides of environmental issues. The Institute of Public Affairs, established in 1943, is a conservative think tank advocating free enterprise. To ensure adequate water supply, it promotes developing a market for buying and selling water as a commodity.

The institute questions the creation of the Pilliga-Goonoo National Park, arguing that 150 years ago the thick cypress forest was grassland and that the cypress was suppressed by Aborigine fires. It notes that establishing a park will decimate the logging industry and suggests a better method would be mixed use. The institute maintains that the scientific case for global warming has not been proved and that the costs of trying to control it would be too high.

The Australia Institute, established in 1994, counters that probusiness groups give too much priority to a narrow definition of economic efficiency over community, environmental, and ethical considerations. It opposes the waste of consumerism, believes the government is not doing enough to protect biodiversity, and favors controlling greenhouse gas emissions. Besides its ecological views, the institute supports health care, income redistribution, and gay rights.

Issues: Besides official governmental action, the 1970s were notable for private actions, notably the Green Bans, whereby environmentalists cooperated with trade unions to stop construction of buildings or projects that threatened neighborhoods or natural sites. The Builders Laborers Federation became radicalized with the election of a reform ticket. Under its new leadership, the union simply refused to build undesirable projects. An early success was saving Kelly's Bush, a natural area in the Sydney suburb of Hunter's Hill. The local municipality had approved constructing a number of high-rise apartments. Local housewives enlisted the cooperation of the Builders Union.[14] The consequence was to halt construction.

The Great Barrier Reef is one of the natural wonders of the world. Extending 1,200 miles along the northeast coast, the reef is unique in the world for its delicate marine life. It is composed of more than 2,800 individual reefs and is 400 feet thick in places. Four hundred types of coral, 1,500 species of fish, and 30 species of whales and dolphins are found there. The threat first became apparent in the 1960s. At first the danger was from overeager tourists and shell collectors. Scuba diving was becoming popular, and the divers damaged the coral. Then a mining company proposed to dig out limestone from the reef for fertilizer. The Preservation Society was able to block this, but another threat appeared when the state government leased 20 million hectares for oil exploration.

During the 1950s, the commonwealth (i.e., national) government had done nothing to protect the reef. After Australia signed the United Nations Convention on the Continental Shelf in 1958, it had a legal basis, and enacted the Continental Shelf (Living Natural Resources) Act but did little more. Meanwhile, the Queensland government actively promoted development. After the Japex-Ampol company chartered an oil drilling ship and it set sail from Texas, the prime minister was able to block the exploration. Parallel royal commissions at the national and state levels reported on the dangers to the Great Barrier Reef, leading in 1975 to the creation of the National Park.[15] Management is joint between the national and state levels. The act established a Great Barrier Reef Marine Park Authority with primary responsibility. The State of Queensland Parks and Wildlife Service manage on a day-to-day basis. A zoning plan prepared in 1981 provides for multiple use, and has been considered successful.[16] Its categories range from general to protective. The preservation zone is to be undisturbed except for scientific research, while the general zone allows fishing, shipping, and trawling. Mining, oil drilling, and spear fishing are never allowed in the park. In 1993 the park authority imposed a management charge of $3.50 per tourist, which met opposition at first but is now accepted.

Two early threats to the Australian environment were in Tasmania. This island state off the southeast coast has a reputation for natural beauty, but also for isolation from the political mainstream. Lake Pedder is a glacial lake with a spectacular beach of pink quartz sand three kilometers long and nearly one kilometer wide. In 1955 it became the heart of a new national park. Then in 1967 the Hydro Electric Commission proposed to build a dam that would destroy the lake. To preserve it, the Lake Pedder Action Committee organized. Despite its efforts and petitions, the Tasmanian parliament did not stop the project. The attorney general refused to accept a petition because it was "in conflict with government policy."[16] Mainland environmentalists demonstrated against the project in Melbourne, where eight protesters were arrested. Neither Tasmanian political party showed much sympathy for protecting Lake Pedder. The state government refused an offer by the commonwealth government to fund an alternative project. One consequence was that in the 1972 state election, the opponents organized the United Tasmanian Group, the world's first green party. In spite of its efforts, the dam was built, raising the water level by fifteen meters.

A decade later, environmentalists were stronger when construction of the Franklin River Dam in Tasmania sparked protests. Over the Christmas–New Year season in 1982–83, the National South West Coalition blockaded the site, taking advantage of the slow news period to gain publicity. The dam became an issue in the federal election 2 months later when the Labor candidate, Bob Hawke, promised to help the environmentalists.

After the Labor victory, it promptly passed the World Heritage Properties Conservation Act that ended the dam proposal. Developers challenged this as usurping the power of the states, but the High Court ruled that the Commonwealth government had the authority, at least in part, because the law was based on an international treaty.

In 1992 the High Court shocked the country in its *Mabo* decision on Aboriginal land rights. Contrary to the assumption of the previous two centuries, the court ruled that the country had not been an empty piece of real estate when Captain Cook claimed it for Britain in 1770. Treaties and acts of the colonies, states, and commonwealth may or may not have extinguished Aboriginal title to the property, the court announced. One factor in making the determination was the extent to which Aborigines had maintained their connection with a piece of land. The High Court had created a chaotic situation in which title to much of the land was in limbo and could be challenged in legal proceedings. The decision said that if title had been granted, such as by sale to a farmer, it was valid, but this left many questions, such as whether a lease for grazing conferred title. To address the problem, the Commonwealth Parliament passed the Native Title Act of 1993, which provided procedures. In fact, these have proved expensive and difficult to use to establish title. Private owners and state and local governments have vigorously opposed native claims.

Several parks are managed jointly by the Aborigines and the Common-wealth. One of the most controversial has been Kakadu National Park on Van Diemen Gulf in the Northern Territory. This large, little-disturbed area encompasses the floodplain and mangrove swamps of the Alligator Rivers. It has 1,600 plant species, over one-quarter of the country's mam-mals, about one-third of the total bird fauna and freshwater fish species, and 15% of Australia reptile and amphibian species. Moreover, the park has Aboriginal archaeological remains and rock art. Just about the same time as its natural importance was first recognized in 1969, prospectors discovered uranium deposits there. The Northern Territory established a wildlife sanctuary and listed it as a World Heritage Site under the interna-tional convention. The United Nations Educational and Scientific Organi-zation lists places of particular value. Also at this time, the Commonwealth assumed authority over Aboriginal affairs from the states. The region was important to their culture, and eventually they became jointly responsible for managing the area. In 1976 the prime minister announced both the establishment of the park and that mining would begin. When the World Heritage pointed out the danger of mining and toyed with listing it as in danger, the commonwealth government objected that that was interfering in a domestic issue. Mining was limited, however, due to the low price of uranium on the international market. While it did not officially defy the World Heritage Center, the Commonwealth government under John Howard ignored its duty to implement the convention.[18]

Uluru National Park, also on the World Heritage List, has been a flash point for tension between Aborigines and whites. Uluru is the massive stone monolith that rises a thousand feet high out of the desert scrub in the Red Center, a thousand miles from the populated southeast coast. As sunlight plays across it, the rock changes from red to purple to blue. Its English name is Ayers Rock. Aborigines consider it sacred, the focus of their spiritual origins. In 1985 legal title was handed back to the Aborigines, who manage it jointly with non-Aborigines. Visitors hear a mixed message, that climbing is allowed, but please do not do it, and that photography is allowed but not here or here.

The Daintree forest on the northeast coast of Queensland was the center of conflict between the timber industry and environmentalists during the 1980s. This is a rare remnant of the tropical rain forest that once covered much of the continent in ancient time. In spite of citizen demonstrations, the Queensland government built a road from the Daintree River north to Cooktown. The primitive track was poorly constructed, leading to erosion and washouts, but it gave access to cut the trees commercially. In the 1987 federal election campaign, Labor promised to list the area as a World Heritage site, which it did upon winning. In turn the Queensland government challenged the listing in the High Court. Then in the state election the following year the Labor Party won, and withdrew the legal challenge, thus protecting the park.

The Commonwealth has continued to expand protection. In 2012 it established the Coral Sea Marine Reserve in the area off shore from the Great Barrier Reef. The area of almost one million square kilometer will be managed for its biodiversity. All mining and oil drilling will be excluded. Commercial fishing will be restricted. The area is famous for its dive sites, including Osprey Reef with its impressive shark populations. During World War II the Battle of the Coral Sea between Japan and the Allies (Australia, Britain, and the United States) 5 months after the attack on Pearl Harbor was the first one the Allies did not lose. Like the United States, Australia is extending its protection of nature into the oceans as sites on land are used up.

At the 1992 Earth Summit at Rio, Australia signed the Framework Convention on Climate Change. But the treaty was vague and awaited details. As the parties negotiated the protocol eventually was signed at Kyoto, Australia had some second thoughts. Perhaps limiting greenhouse gases would cramp its industry. Business groups were negative and environmental groups were positive. Opponents got help from the United States. The ultra-conservative American Frontiers of Freedom Institute, based in Washington, DC, cosponsored a conference in Canberra that sought to derail the Kyoto negotiations. The Business Council, the Minerals Council, and the Aluminum Council said that the government should only sign a climate change protocol if all countries would accept the "differentiation" model. Surprisingly, the Labor Party, now in opposition, also announced that it supported key aspects of the policy. Despite all the criticism from Europe and others abroad and the environmentalists at home, once at Kyoto the new Australian demands were accommodated. Its quota was increased to a positive 8%. In other words, while everyone else was making reductions, Australia was entitled to an increase. Moreover, it could count increases in its forests as credits for carbon sinks and participate in emissions trading.

Like virtually every government around the world, Australia was shocked when President Bush announced his outright rejection of the Kyoto Protocol. Nevertheless, this dramatic action offered a way out for the Howard government, which promptly announced it would join the United States in rejecting the protocol. The prime minister said it would be "silly" to ratify it without the biggest emitter in the world. At the time it seemed possible that other industrial countries like Canada would join in refusing to sign the protocol. Howard seemed to enjoy his status as the US partner in rejecting Kyoto. Two years later he contributed troops to invade Iraq with the Americans, further strengthening the trans-Pacific bond. When his successor as prime minister, Kevin Rudd, immediately signed the protocol upon being sworn in, it seemed like a new day for controlling global warming worldwide, but over the next few years, support waned from its European champions and the efforts fell from favor.

Horrible wildfires throughout the county in the first two months of 2009 seemed to confirm the danger of global warming. The death toll reached 210. The fires followed extreme drought. Australia is often prone to years and years of drought, but this was worse than ever. On February 7, labeled Black Saturday, temperatures reached 46 degrees Celsius (115°F) and winds were over 100 kilometers an hour. Four hundred different fires broke out. People died while trying to evacuate and died while huddled in their homes. Fires afflicted towns as well as farms and ranches. Although scientists are loath to blame any single occurrence on climate change, the connection here seemed obvious to ordinary Australians.

Air pollution is less of a problem for Australia than for most countries. It has fewer sources of pollution, a smaller population, and winds from the oceans and the interior blow it away. Nevertheless, the problem exists in Melbourne, Sydney, Brisbane, and other large cities during the summer and fall, which on average have 20 days of smog exceeding 10 particles per hundred million. Automobile exhaust is the chief culprit. Since 1986 new autos have been required to have catalytic converters, and lead has been banned in the gasoline. Most cities have outlawed incinerators. Industrial pollution has been a problem. For example, the government determined that the lead smelter in Port Pirie was damaging the brains of the children, so required drastic cuts in emissions. The Commonwealth passed the Air Quality Monitoring Act in 1976 under the provisions of Section 96 of the Constitution regarding financial assistance to the states, not its trade and commerce authority in Section 51.

The availability of water is of great concern. In 2004 the governmental leaders from the national, state, and local levels signed the National Water Initiative that expanded a system of buying and selling water, strengthened planning and addressed over-allocated systems. Like the Intergovernmental Agreement of 1992, this was not done by legislation, but by a compact among the three levels under the auspices of the Council of Australian Governments. The council consists of the national prime minister, the six state premiers, and the president of the Local Government Association. Previously, it has addressed issues of environmental regulation, human embryos in medical research, counter-terrorism arrangements and restrictions on handguns. Its stance on the environment was to call for better delineation of responsibility between the national and state governments.

In the 1980s cotton farming expanded. One new region was along the Macquarie Marshes, a beautiful wetland in the Darling River in New South Wales, with a greater bird diversity even than Kakadu National Park. Many of the planters were Americans from California and Arizona. Except for the marshes, the region is quite arid. The cotton farmers soon came into conflict with the graziers who needed the water. Moreover, the fickle weather also threatened floods some years, so the dams needed to remain partially empty to fill up with the rare heavy rains. In the vicinity of the Namoi River, but away from irrigated land, the planters installed large, powerful pumps to draw up groundwater. The graziers could not compete using their old-fashioned windmills. The cotton growers organized the Namoi Water Users' Association, and later the graziers organized the Lower Namoi Riparian Occupiers Association.[19]

Water quality is largely under the jurisdiction of the states. This is appropriate since, with the exception of the Murray-Darling system, most rivers are short and within a single state. The six states are supposed to be guided by the National Water Quality Management Strategy issued in 1992. The standards were developed jointly with New Zealand. Salt deposition and algae blooms are the major problems.[20]

Tourism is a major industry, with more than three million overseas visitors each year. Although its impact on fragile eco-systems can be great, it does not always occupy an important place in the political debates. For example, little was said about tourism in establishing the Great Barrier Reef or the Kakadu Parks. While it is often touted as not injuring the natural setting like mining or timbering does, in fact it can cause damage. Visitors stay in hotels built on sensitive land, consume 10 times as much water for their showers and swimming pools as local people, and arrive in jet airplanes that pollute the air. The industry is cyclical, depending on the economic prosperity of Japan, Europe, and North American. Conversely, extractive industries like mining and timbering can ruin the tourist potential of a place. Marine sanctuaries are not compatible with offshore fisheries. Most Aborigines do not like tourists because they intrude on their lives. Mining is less of a problem, providing the mineral reserves are not proscribed. Roads built for timber cutting may allow access to visitors, or may destroy a virgin forest.[21]

The Ecotourism Association of Australia was established in 1991 as a peak association, with members from travel agencies, hotels, and government agencies. It offers Eco Certification for companies, resorts, and sites, a program it claims is the first in the world. The association defines nature tourism as ecologically sustainable tourism with a primary focus on natural areas. The organization intends to foster environmental, cultural, and social understanding, appreciation, and conservation. The association also certifies individuals as Eco Guides.

CONCLUSION

Canadians and Australians participate directly and by voting. The 1969 poisoning of fish at Placentia Bay and the oil spill from the tanker *Arrow* on Cerberus Rock in Chedabucto Bay outraged tens of thousands of Canadians.

In Australia the 1967 proposal by the Hydro Electric Commission to dam Lake Pedder sparked demonstrations in Tasmania and on the mainland. The Green Bans in the 1970s in Sydney were spontaneous stopping of construction in natural areas. A decade later Tasmania was again the center of demonstrations, this time opposing the Franklin River Dam.

Canadians and Australians belong to many nature groups: Nature Canada began in 1948, and Greenpeace began in 1971. Many like WWF, the Wilderness Society, and the Sierra Club are branches of international groups. The Australian Conservation Foundation dates to 1964. Like Canada many are branches of international groups: WWF, the Wilderness Society, and Greenpeace.

Australia has two political parties much like the United States and Great Britain (noting that the Liberals are in permanent coalition with the Nationals). Representatives in the House are elected by the first past the post system, making it hard for a Green Party to win. However, the Senate has the option of proportional representation, so Greens frequently have a few seats. These have twice made the difference in giving a few extra votes to Labor allowing it to form a government. Labor has consistently favored environmental protection. In the past the Liberals used to at least pay lip service, but no longer do. Canada used to have a two-party system of Liberals versus Conservatives, but this fell apart in 1988. Today, the Conservatives are in power, although this used to be as a minority. They pay lip service to the environment, but oppose serious climate change programs and enthusiastically mine the Athabasca tar sands.

Both Canada and Australia are federations, with greater authority for mining, water, and air are the province-state level compared to the United States or Germany. The 1998 dispute between Ontario and the national level on water exports by the Nova Corporation was intense, finally decided in favor of the province. In Australia the lack of clarity in the Constitution as to authority over pollution and natural resources led in 1992 to the Council of Australian Governments consisting of the national prime minister, the six state premiers, and the president of the Local Government Association, which signed the Intergovernmental Agreement. Canada has a Council consisting of the environmental ministers of the 10 provinces plus the federal minister which meets annually. Both Canada and Australia have similar parliaments based on the Westminster model. Heads of the cabinet-level ministers are drawn from parliament.

Canada has chosen diplomatic leadership in the environment as a major initiative. It sponsored the 1987 conference on the ozone layer, known as the Montreal Protocol. It sponsored the 1988 Toronto conference on global warming that set the pattern for the Framework Convention and the Kyoto Protocol. The 1909 Boundary Waters Treaty was the first to control water pollution and supply. The 1918 Migratory Bird Treaty, besides protecting birds, was the first time Canadian diplomats were allowed to play a part in negotiations. Previously, the British Foreign Office had handled the Dominion's international affairs. Australia, at least in part due to its remote location in the Antipodes, has been less active diplomatically. It did send a delegation to the Stockholm summit, generating concern at home. Lacking apparent authority under its constitution, it used adherence to the World Heritage Convention to legitimate protection for the Great Barrier Reef. Prime Minister Howard's outspoken rejection of the Kyoto Protocol isolated the commonwealth. Howard's successor, Kevin Rudd, was a career diplomat who won instant plaudits for immediately signing the Protocol.

Inspired by Yellowstone, both Canada and Australia established national parks: Banff and Royal, respectively. During the Environmental Decade they passed laws controlling air and water pollution. The Canadian group—Greenpeace—has grown to be the largest in the world. The first green party in the world—United Tasmanian Group—was one of Australia's contributions.

NOTES

1. Herman Melville, Quotation at the entrance of the Sydney Maritime Museum.
2. Conservative Party of Canada, *Policy Declaration*, National Convention, November 15, 2008.
3. Clifford Krauss, "In Canada's Wilderness, Measuring the Cost of Oil Profits," *New York Times,* Oct. 9, 2005; Sierra Club of Canada, "Oil Sands Strategy a Comprehensive Abdication of Government's Environmental Responsibilities," October 27, 2005, Web.
4. David Crane, "Chretien's Environmental Slide," *The Toronto Star,* October 23, 1997.
5. Wade Roland, *The Plot to Save the World* (Toronto: Clarke, Irwin, 1973), pp. 35–37.
6. Drew Hutton and Libby Connors, *A History of the Australian Environmental Movement* (Cambridge, UK: Cambridge University Press, 1999), p. 35.
7. Hutton and Connors, pp. 33–35.
8. Ian Tyrrell, *True Gardens of the Gods: Californian-Australian Environmental Reform 1860–1930* (Univ. of California Press, 1999), pp. 88–89, 56.
9. Dorothea Mackeller, "My Country," 1904.
10. Hutton and Connors, p. 54.
11. Nicholas Economou, "Backwards toward the Future: National Policy Making, Devolution and the Rise and Fall of the Environment," in *Australian Environmental Policy, 2* ed., Kenneth J. Walker and Kate Crowley (Sydney: University of New South Wales Press, 1999), pp. 67–68.

12. The Nationals, "Policies: Environment and Conservation," September 16, 2005, Web.
13. Timothy Doyle and Aynsley Kellow, *Environmental Politics and Policy Making in Australia* (South Melbourne: Macmillan, 1995), p. 127.
14. Richard J. Roddewig, *Green Bans: The Birth of Australian Environmental Politics* (Montclair, NJ: Allan, Osmun, 1978), p. 9.
15. James Bowen, "The Great Barrier Reef," in *Australian Environmental History*, ed. Stephen Dovers (Melbourne: Oxford Univ. Press, 1994), p. 253.
16. Hutton and Connors, p. 120.
17. Graeme Palin, "Kakadu National Park World Heritage Site," *Australian Geographical Studies* 42 (2004): 152–174.
18. Helen Wheately, "Land and Agriculture in Australia," in *The Face of the Earth*, ed. J. Donald Hughes (Armonk, N.Y.: M. E. Sharpe, 2000), pp. 135, 138–141.
19. Arthur and Jeannette Conacher, *Environmental Planning and Management in Australia* (South Melbourne: Oxford, 2000).
20. David Mercer, *A Question of Balance*, 2nd ed. (Sydney: Federation Press, 1995).

6

India and Brazil

India and Brazil are both developing countries, that is, former colonies that were not industrialized until the mid-20th century. Both are vibrant democracies, with rough and tumble politics based on many parties. Their populations are big: India has more than a billion people and Brazil has nearly 200 million. Many people are poor. Both have free markets, with a background of socialism, that is, government ownership of major industries, now largely abandoned. Their economies are big: $4.1 trillion for India and $2.2 trillion for Brazil. Pollution has accompanied the industrial development. Finally, both have remote regions of natural beauty and wildness.

India: As early as 8000 years ago the inhabitants of the Indian subcontinent first abandoned the natural life of hunting and gathering for life in villages. The Indus River civilization flourished from 2500 BC onward, making it nearly as ancient as Mesopotamia and Egypt and older than China. India has fertile plains in the river basins of the Indus, the Ganges, and the Brahmaputra, but it also has deserts and mountains. To the north, the Himalayas, the highest mountains in the world, form a barrier both to Arctic winds and to invading armies. The river valleys form a fertile belt across the middle with moderate temperatures in the winter. The southern third has mountains and deserts. Rainfall is sparse in the west and torrential in the east. Except in the mountains, the temperature is hot. Much farming depends on irrigation, and in some places flooding is a danger. Spectacular wildlife like tigers and elephants still lives in patches of the forests and mountains. Yet most of India has long been under cultivation, and natural areas are scarce.

The Indus River, which gave the subcontinent its name, has been mostly within the boundaries of Pakistan since the division of that country from India in 1947. Its source is in the Kailas Mountains in western Tibet, where it flows west across Jammu and Kashmir, India, then into Pakistan. Water for irrigation is disputed between the two countries. The Ganges River rises from the Gangotri glacier in the Himalayas in northeast India, and flows southeast to the Bay of Bengal in Bangladesh. This is the most densely populated part of the country and contributes much pollution. The Brahmaputra River rises in southwest Tibet and flows through northeast India to join with the Ganges River in central Bangladesh to form a vast delta. The interior south is arid, rainfall being blocked by mountains. The coastal littoral is moist and tropical, famous for growing spices. Each June monsoon rains bring water from the south to all parts to India. These monsoons are heavy, even violent. In September, the smaller northeast monsoon brings rain to the south.

Areas of what is now called India were first united as the Maurya Empire in the third century BC. The population was estimated at fifty million people, stratified as slaves, farmers, herdsmen, soldiers, and artisans. The government encouraged clearing the forests by remitting taxes. Wars were avoided, and the empire enjoyed a golden age. The government was benign and tolerant. Although Hinduism was widespread, the emperor personally favored Buddhism, with its pacifism and admonitions to not kill animals. After the Mauryan regime began to decline in 184 BC the empire fragmented into regional kingdoms. In AD 320 the Gupta dynasty established an empire, which in various forms lasted until after 467. Once more, a number of small kingdoms existed. Buddhism gave way to the older Hinduism. Following invasions from central Asia between the 10th and 12th centuries, much of north India came under the rule of the Delhi Sultanate and later the Mughal Empire. Although the rulers were Muslims, they were few in number, hence did not do much to impose their religion or culture on the native Indians. Under the rule of Akbar the Great, India enjoyed cultural and economic progress as well as religious harmony. The dynasty continued until the mid-18th century.

During the 17th and 18th centuries, as Portuguese, Dutch, English, and French ships explored the Indian coast and elsewhere around the Indian Ocean, they investigated the natural environment as well as navigation and commerce. The Portuguese first engaged in trade in Goa in 1510. All the Europeans reported on the wonders, natural and human, that they encountered. In 1666 the British Royal Society issued instructions for travelers on how to report scientific observations. Besides maps and trade items, the explorers brought back plants and animals, some dead and some alive. The Dutch cultivated exotic plants at their botanical garden in Amsterdam (for a while employing Carolus Linnaeus). In 1778 the British East India Company appointed a naturalist to reside at Madras. Company officials were concerned with the frequent famines that plagued India. One response was to establish a botanical garden in Calcutta to investigate cultivating new plants for food. Another was the recording and publication of meteorological observations in Madras, which include some of the earliest scientific documentation of El Niño on its Asian side. The company botanist, William Roxburgh, recorded the severe drought of 1787–91, now recognized to be connected to one of the most extreme El Niño episodes ever. His curiosity piqued, he examined the chronicles of the Rajah of Pittenpore, discovering records of a similar drought in 1685–87 and a less severe one in 1737.

Prior to European colonization, Indian princes had regulated forests preserves for their personal benefit in cutting timber and for hunting. Once the British East India Company established itself and undermined the traditional authority, both the British and the locals wanted to exploit the forests. The British particularly wanted to use the timber for shipbuilding. To a large extent, the company assumed control of the princely preserves and continued to manage them, earning handsome profits. Beginning in 1810 the company began systematic surveys of the subcontinent's forests. Protection was dismantled in 1823, however, and by 1847 the problems of deforestation were readily apparent. Peasants could not even find firewood. Colonial officials made the argument that lack of forests led to lack of water. The Bombay region established the Forest Department, later followed by a forest department in Madras. In 1878 the British promulgated a Forest Act that introduced scientific forestry on the European model, which in practice amounted to maximizing the amount of timber harvested. Traditional rights of villages to local woods nearly disappeared. During World War II, the demand for lumber for the British troops in the Middle East resulted in the greatest exploitation.

The ideas of Mohandas Gandhi, the leader in the campaign for independence from Britain, provide a model for sustainable development. Although Gandhi's direct purpose was not ecological, he strongly opposed industrialization. In 1928 he wrote "God forbid that India should ever take to industrialization after the manner of the West."[1] His vision was a nation of self-sufficient villages. He often said, "The world has enough for everybody's need, but not enough for everybody's greed."[2] Gandhi modeled his passive movement for independence, in part, on the American Henry David Thoreau, and in turn was a model for Martin Luther King's civil rights movement, which in turn inspired the environmental movement.

After India gained independence in 1947, the government moved in exactly the opposite direction, embarking on an ambitious program of industrialization based on state ownership. The model was the Soviet Union. The first premier, Jawaharlal Nehru, who served for 17 years, had fallen under the sway of Fabian Socialism during his student days in England and had gained a positive impression of the economic success of the Soviet Union during a visit in 1927. A series of Five Year Plans beginning in 1951 promoted the steel industry, which proved an economic as well as environmental failure. Massive dams were other favored projects. Nehru called dams the "Temples of Modern India." The largest was the Bhakra Dam, which rises 170 meters above the river level and irrigates 40,000 square kilometers. Critics used the term *gigantism* to describe the phenomenon. Although Nehru denied he was a socialist, the central government directed the major sectors of the economy, regulations covered even small businesses and farmers, and taxes were high. Foreign investment was discouraged.

These policies are often blamed for the country's poor rate of economic growth. Although many point to the Soviet Union as the model for Nehru's policies, another influence was the British Labour Party that governed the United Kingdom from 1945 to 1951, and was the impetus behind Indian independence. Besides gigantic dams and heavy industry like steel and cement, the Indian government discouraged imports, intervened in the financial markets, subsidized cottage industries and regulated business. The growth rate from independence to 1980 was only 3%, barely keeping up with the growing population. By 1991 this economic policy was reversed with the liberalization of markets, foreign investment, and the end of central planning. Today, the growth rate is 7%.

When the British granted independence to its Indian Raj (Empire) in 1947 it partitioned the subcontinent into two (eventually becoming three) countries. This was because the Muslims and Hindus could not reach agreement on a unified government. The areas of most concentrated Muslim population, now Pakistan and Bangladesh, became a single country known as Pakistan with an east and a west component. The negotiators agreed that people who wanted to migrate to join their coreligionists could do so. In fact, the migration was far greater than anticipated. Millions of people fled. Even worse, religious riots erupted as adherents of one religion attacked their former neighbors. Half a million were killed. Later, in 1974, tension developed between East and West Pakistan, leading to a revolt by those in the east. India favored them and assisted with troops. The eastern portion became the new country of Bangladesh.

India suffers from many environmental problems. The rapid population growth has overtaxed its resources. Poverty is intense. Water is not drinkable in many rural villages or city slums. Raw sewage and agricultural pesticides pollute the rivers. Air pollution comes from factories and automobiles. Coal-fired electric generating plants are inefficient. Forests are being cut down, and deserts are spreading.

The worst single tragedy occurred at the Union Carbide pesticide factory in Bhopal in 1984, when 40 tons of poison gas spilled out. With safety systems either malfunctioning or turned off, the fatal cloud soon dispersed over a city of half a million. In the first 3 days, 8,000 people died, mainly from cardiac and respiratory arrest. Eventually over 20,000 people died from the gas, and 120,000 became chronically ill. Tragic as the case may be, it is not really an environmental event, but an industrial accident caused by a malfunction at a factory. As such it is more like a coal mine accident. Typically, environmental pollution occurs over a long time and in small quantities. Air pollution, for example, is a continuing release of small amounts of chemicals from the routine production of a factory or driving a motor vehicle. The means to control air pollution are quite different from the means to avoid industrial accidents.

India also suffers from the environmental problems of its neighbor Bangladesh. Overpopulation and lack of farmland force migration of poor people seeking land and jobs. Due to its extremely low elevation above sea level, Bangladesh is often flooded, and with the prospect of global warming the future holds more danger. India makes legal immigration nearly impossible. In recent years it has been building a barbed wire fence three meters high to keep the Bangladeshis out. The wall extends nearly 3,000 kilometers along the shared border.

The threat of global warming is vague and in the distant future, hence India paid little attention. This changed briefly in 2002 when the annual Conference of the Parties for the Kyoto Protocol was scheduled for New Delhi. Playing host stimulated Indian scientists and officials to mobilize, which they would not have done otherwise. This was only the second time the parties had met in a developing county. The government proposed and won approval for the Delhi Ministerial Declaration saying in more detail that the industrial countries would give money to the developing countries.

The industrialization of India in the 20th century contrasts with the religious and social values of its people tracing back 4000 years. Hindus, who make up 80% of the population, believe in a religion concerned with the proper relation between the self, the gods, and nature. The soul is reincarnated, often as an animal; hence, a person should respect animals, and especially not kill them. Hinduism sees the universe as undergoing an eternally repeated cycle of creation, preservation, and dissolution, represented by the trinity of Brahma the creator, Vishnu the preserver, and Shiva the destroyer as aspects of the Supreme Being. While this might seem ideally compatible with ecology, it also has elements of fatalism that discourage working to protect the environment.

Indian society is stratified into a caste system, meaning groupings based on birth that determine a person's social place, marriage, occupation (much less today), living arrangements, and so forth. This system of hereditary assignments dates back to prehistoric times. The four major groupings are the Brahmins (teachers, scholars, and priests), the kshatriyas (kings and military), the vaishyas (farmers and traders), and shudras (artisans and servants). In turn, these groups are subdivided into many castes. The lowest of the low are the *dalits*, once called untouchables, because if a higher status person touched one, he would be defiled and have to undergo ritual purification. Dalits have risen politically and economically, but many still hold jobs like sweeping streets and cleaning sewers and can be extremely poor.

Today, the caste system is much reduced and found mostly in rural areas. The Indian Constitution of 1950 outlawed it. (Yet even now virtually all marriages are within the same caste.) The leaders of the independence movement and early period through the 1970s like Mohandas Gandhi and Nehru were staunchly opposed to the caste system. Members of the lowest castes are now classified as Scheduled Castes and given preference for government jobs and for education that are reserved for them. But since the 1980s some politicians have exploited it. A number of political parties have a caste appeal. Recently, many ordinary Indians have held public demonstrations to protest the reservation of places for the Scheduled Castes.

There is disagreement over the extent to which the caste system is a product of the Hindu religion. While the two have been intertwined for thousands of years, religious leaders point out that there is little theological basis.

It is barely mentioned in sacred scripture. They claim it is merely cultural. Furthermore, Muslims living in India adhere to a parallel caste system. Christians also have not completely abandoned their original castes.

Government: India is a parliamentary democracy with institutions copied directly from the former colonial power of Great Britain. The bicameral Parliament consists of the Council of States of 250 members elected by the state and territorial assemblies, and the People's Assembly of 545 members elected by the people directly. The president, holding a largely ceremonial position like the queen of England's, is chosen by an electoral college consisting of both houses of the parliament plus the legislatures of the states. The prime minister is elected by parliamentary members of the majority party. In turn, he selects his cabinet from his party. The republic is federal with 28 states and seven territories.

While India has many political parties, the biggest, oldest, and most powerful is the Congress Party. Founded in 1885, it took up the cause of independence in the early 20th century. It became a mass organization with millions supporting its opposition to the British. The 1920s saw the rise of Mahatma Gandhi, who advocated simple living and rural self-sufficiency. Wearing only the most basic of village cotton garments, he promoted cottage industries like spinning and weaving and led a protest against the tax on salt. He insisted on nonviolence and persuasion through civil disobedience. His young protégé was Jawaharlal Nehru. After independence in 1947 Nehru became prime minister, remaining in power until his death in 1964. (Gandhi was assassinated in 1948.) Under Nehru the Congress party embraced socialism and did not favor either the Hindu or Muslim religions. During the Cold War, the foreign policy steered a neutral course between the Western block and the Communist block. Nehru often spoke of his admiration for Soviet economic policies.

The Congress Party remained in power continuously until 1977. Following Nehru's death it elected the mild-mannered Lal Bahadur Shastri, who died 2 years later. At this point the party turned to Indira Gandhi, daughter of Nehru (and no relation to Mohandas Gandhi). She thus became the second of four family members to head the party, moving toward an unofficial dynasty. The Congress Party soon split, and Mrs. Gandhi headed the dominant left-wing faction. She campaigned against poverty and favored the Soviet Union in foreign policy. Mrs. Gandhi became increasingly authoritarian and took to rigging elections. When confronted with opposition in parliament and in the courts in June 1975, she ordered a State of National Emergency and ruled by decree. She lifted the state of emergency in March 1977 and promptly suffered electoral defeat, forcing her to relinquish the post of prime minister. In 1980 she was back in power after the Congress Party won the parliamentary election. Her life ended violently in 1984 when she was assassinated by a Sikh member of her own bodyguard. The Sikhs are a religious and cultural group that suffered under her policies.

Once more turning to the Nehru–Gandhi dynasty, the Congress Party chose Indira's son Rajiv as leader. Congress won, and he became prime minister, serving from 1984 to 1989. He proved to be more moderate and democratic. Rajiv had not been interested in politics as a young man, and had a career as a commercial airline pilot. His brother Sanjay had been the heir apparent, and had served in government under his mother, but died in the crash of a private airplane in 1980. The Congress Party had lost the election in 1989, but the opposition was not strong and had to call a new election in 1991. Once more violence struck as Rajiv was assassinated while campaigning. Congress won the election and formed the government that lasted until 1996. The following years were difficult for the Congress Party, with disputed leadership and instances of bribery. The party abandoned its support for socialism and favored free-market policies. Once more the party turned to its dynasty, naming as its head Sonia Gandhi, the widow of Rajiv. It returned to power in the 2004 election. Because Sonia was an Italian woman whom Rajiv had married while a young airline pilot, she was denied holding the position of prime minister, although she continued to head the party. Manmohan Singh was chosen instead. In 2009 he won again, leading a coalition called the United Progressive Alliance dominated by the Congress Party. About 714 million citizens voted, making it the biggest election in the world.

India has many other parties. Those operating at the national level include the Bhartiya Janata Party, the Bahujan Samaj Party, the Samajwadi Party, and two Communist parties. Additionally, many parties operate only at the state or local level. They often form partnerships with other parties to win seats in parliament. In the national parliament coalitions, minor parties have won control of parliament a few times. Although the Congress Party has declined, it is still the biggest.

The Indian civil service is famous worldwide for its expertise and efficiency. The British organized it in the early 19th century, and it served as a model for the British civil service at home and for the United States. Of course, during the colonial period, Englishmen held the top positions. After independence the new Indian government continued it. The elite of only about 5000, now called the Administrative Service, gives direction. The total number of central government employees, called Central Public Services, is 17 million. In addition, the states have their own civil service systems.

The chief agency is the Ministry of Environment and Forests, which is responsible for planning, promoting, coordinating, and implementating programs, such as pollution control, wildlife surveys, and reforestation. In accordance with the federal structure of the government, the national Central Pollution Control Board sets discharge and ambient standards for pollutants and coordinates the state agencies. The State Pollution Control Boards then implement the laws. The major laws are the Water (Prevention and Control of Pollution) Act of 1974, the Air (Prevention and Control of Pollution) Act of 1981, and the Environment (Protection) Act of 1986. Although the standards are supposed to be the same everywhere, certain states have a reputation for lax enforcement. These laws were copied from Britain and the United States.

Interest groups are active in the Indian democracy. Of course, business and industry are well represented, but so are labor unions. One of the biggest is the Federation of Indian Chambers of Commerce. Religious groups are strong. One of the oldest environmental groups is the Bombay Natural History Society, more than 125 years old. The Sálim Ali Centre for Ornithology was established in the Western Ghats because it is a hotspot of biodiversity. A number of groups labeled nongovernmental organizations are, in fact, sponsored by government agencies, thus being a paradox of a governmental nongovernmental organization. The Centre for Environment Education, founded in 1966, is an example. There are many examples of grassroots efforts. The State of Kerala in the southwest has a reputation for supporting the ordinary citizen. (It has often had a Communist government.) In 1953 a development project in cooperation with Norway introduced mechanized trawlers to increase the catch of fish. This proved so successful that the boats depleted the fish close to shore that supplied the local fishermen. They also destroyed the spawning grounds. The local catch declined by a third. In-shore fishermen organized cooperatives and a union to fight the trawlers. They held mass rallies, blocked roads and railways, and sabotaged the trawlers. This led to a national trade union, the National Fishworkers Federation in 1978. Eventually, they were able to persuade the state and national governments to outlaw mechanized trawlers.[3]

When in 1973 the government sold a forest sector of ash trees in the state of Uttar Pradesh in the Himalayas to a sporting goods company to make tennis rackets, it was too much for the residents. They had suffered for years from floods due to deforestation. The local people demonstrated by going into the forest and literally hugging the trees the loggers were trying to cut down. They gained the name Chipko (to hug). The movement spread, but the government continued to sell trees. One of the leaders went on a hunger fast. Thousands demonstrated against the tree harvest. Finally, Prime Minister Indira Gandhi met personally with leaders and promised a 15-year moratorium in Uttar Pradesh. Elsewhere groups protested by hugging trees. Some saw the movement as embodying the ideals and techniques of Mohandas Gandhi, even claiming to literally see his spirit in the forest.[4]

WWF India, an affiliate of the international group, focuses on big animals. It estimates that there are 1100–1700 wild Bengal tigers scattered throughout the country from the Himalayas to the mountains of the Western Ghats and from the forests of Rajasthan to the seven states of the northeast. The chief danger is loss of habitat, but poaching is a serious threat, too. Hunters kill them for their skins and for traditional Chinese medicine. Their ground-up bones supposedly enhance male sexual performance. Wild elephants, numbering as many as 26,000, live many places. They eat 200–300 kilograms of vegetation a day, so need vast tracts of forest. When close to human habitation, they eat crops. The 1989 international ban on the ivory trade has decreased poaching, but it has not disappeared. Rhinoceroses, numbering about 2,500, live only in small areas nears Nepal, in north Bengal, in Assam, and in a few other isolated spots. Besides loss of habitat, a threat is poaching for their horns, which are used in traditional Asiatic medicine. They are among the world's most endangered species. WWF hopes to set up three or four new Protected Areas and establish breeding populations there

Greenpeace has a small presence in India. It campaigns to stop killing the olive ridley sea turtle along Orissa on the east coast. It recommends a return to traditional fishing instead of mechanized trawlers, reminiscent of the Kerala situation 30 years ago. Additionally, Greenpeace objects to the introduction of genetically modified crops. This is part of an international campaign. It objects that GM food may contain unknown health risks, that the food may be less nutritious, that the strain may spread to ordinary crops, that crops may fail, that the crop may harm beneficial insects, and that the Monsanto Corporation will profit unfairly.

Birth Control: The one-billion-plus people who live in India put a terrible burden on its environment, but the government is currently doing little to limit population growth. Its experiment with birth control in the 1970s was disastrous. In the impoverished countryside, peasants have desired many children to help with the chores when they are little and to provide for the aged parents when they are adults. Urban people consider a large family a sign of prosperity and seek to carry on the family lineage. Upon marriage, daughters go to live with and support the husband's family. Although dowries are theoretically illegal, tradition always demands it.

Immediately after independence, the government did little more than pay lip service to family planning. At the time of independence, population was about 335 million. At first the government did not consider more people a serious problem, but the 1961 census recorded 439 million. The growth rate increased from 1.3% annually to 2.0% in only 10 years. The government now recognized that it needed to take action. The first approach to birth control was sterilization, which was not particularly effective and generated backlash, even riots. Since then the population has continued to increase, now at the rate of 16 million a year, to a figure today of more than one billion. The hero of independence, Mahatma Gandhi said "celibacy is the best contraceptive." To demonstrate this, he would occasionally sleep naked with young women. Although the First Five-Year Plan, announced in 1951, established a committee to study the problem of population, little came of it.

In the 1970s the government attacked the problem. At first sterilization appeared to be the best form of contraception. It was permanent, cheap, and required no tracking of days of the month. It appeared to be the optimal solution for an underdeveloped country. Because the surgery was simpler for a male vasectomy than a female tubal ligation, men became the targets. The simpler technique for a laparoscopy was not available until later. Prime Minister Indira Gandhi took a personal interest and put her son, Sanjay, in charge. In spite of his reputation as a playboy and dilettante, Sanjay Gandhi took the danger of overpopulation seriously and consulted with experts. His solution depended heavily on sterilization. He organized vasectomy camps, recruiting men from the villages by the truckload. The patients received money. Yet problems soon surfaced. The surgery had a high failure rate. Many men were tricked, for instance, not understanding that the operation was permanent. Some were coerced, even kidnapped. The program tried to increase its statistical success by sterilizing old men who were unlikely to become fathers, and boys as young as 14 years old.

At the same time, the government faced a political crisis resulting in the 1975–77 state of emergency. The forced sterilizations were a major cause of it. Family planning had become one of the prime minister's Twenty Point

Program to be "implemented on a war footing." The government budgeted $200 million a year. The same officials who had proclaimed 4 years earlier at the World Population Conference in Bucharest that "development is the best contraceptive" now ordered "disincentives" for those who did not cooperate. Family planning was now obligatory and New Delhi ordered "harsh measures."[5] Finally, the outcry at Mrs. Gandhi's dictatorship drove her from office. Yet 3 years later, she surprised her enemies by winning reelection and returning as prime minister. This time she was more cautious about vasectomies and claimed they would be entirely voluntary. By now laparoscopy was available and became more popular.

Acting on the preference of sons to daughters became easier for parents with improved medical technology. With the introduction of sonogram machines that can determine the sex of the fetus in the womb, many families opt to abort girls. Some without modern medicine resort to female infanticide. The sex ratio has fallen to only 89 girls to 100 boys at birth. The typical woman willing to undergo sterilization already has four living children, of whom at least two are boys.

The Indian government issued a comprehensive plan in 2000 to "promote the small family norm" in order to bring fertility down to the replacement rate. Unlike China, this advocates a two-child family. Incentives include payments of 500 rupees to poor mothers who wait until age 19 to have their first child, who limit their children to two, and who are sterilized after only two children. Communities will be rewarded for achieving the small family norm. Contraceptives and abortions will be made more available. The plan recognizes the problem of abortion and infanticide of girls by paying a bonus for girls first or second in birth order.[6]

With its swelling population, growing economy, and environmental problems, India has some common features with Brazil. Both are democracies with vigorous market economies. By many measures, the South American country has the advantage. It has only a fifth the number of people and a per capita income twice as high. In the Amazon region (the size of Western Europe), large tracts of land are undeveloped.

Brazil was discovered by the Portuguese in 1500 as they raced the Spanish for colonies and for trade routes to India. The vast territory lacked the advanced Indian civilizations and material riches the Spaniards found in Mexico and Peru. Only a few native people lived there, scattered about the rain forest. They found no gold or silver. One commodity worth trading for was the brasil tree, a source of red dye and possessed of a hard wood, today used for violin bows. The native population perhaps numbered two to four million, who were peripatetic, with a little farming. They were warlike and some were cannibalistic.

The Portuguese began to cultivate sugar, which needed laborers. At first they tried to enslave the natives, but they escaped or died. Next they imported Black Africans, thus establishing slavery that lasted until 1888. A few Portuguese earned great wealth on the backs of the slaves. The first capital was at Sao Salvador da Bahia, on the northeast coast. Virtually no one settled the interior of the Amazon Basin. Two hundred years later prospectors discovered gold and diamonds in the southeast in the region named Minas Gerais (General Mines). Although the gold and diamonds were soon mined out, other minerals remain. The Portuguese moved the capital of the colony to Rio de Janeiro in 1763.

At the turn of the 19th century, Brazil was a large, prosperous colony ruled by a European elite and supported by millions of African slaves. In many aspects it operated autonomously from the mother country. To forestall quarrels between two powerful Roman Catholic nations, the Pope in 1494 had proclaimed a compromise that divided the world. Portugal would get the right to trade and colonize east of a north–south line through South America, extending 180° to the other side of the globe, and Spain would get the other half of the globe. This gave Portugal Brazil, Africa, India, and the Spice Islands (present-day Indonesia). Spain got the west of South America, the Pacific Ocean, and the Philippines. The Pope gave nothing to the Protestant nations of England and the Netherlands.

By the beginning of the 19th century, the fateful event was the rise of Napoleon Bonaparte in France. In 1807 he invaded the Iberian Peninsula, striking directly at Lisbon to end the country's alliance with Great Britain. The royal family fled, sailing to Rio, where King John VI set up his court. With the defeat of Napoleon, John returned to Lisbon, leaving his son Pedro (Peter) in charge. In 1822 Pedro declared Brazil was an independent nation, and took the title of emperor. This was done peacefully. In the same period, the Spanish colonies of South America were fighting for their independence and establishing republics. The example of the American Revolution of 1776–1783 inspired them. The empire continued under Pedro and later his son, Pedro II. Under both father and son, the empire had many features of a constitutional monarchy. Slavery was abolished in 1888. The following year a military coup d'etat overthrew Pedro II and claimed to be a republic. A series of military dictators ruled until 1930, a period referred to as the Old Republic.

With the encouragement of the emperor, Brazil attracted visits from European scientists, many writing of a tropical paradise, and others warning of exploitation. The German botanist Friedrich Phillip von Martius came in 1817, describing the plants in fifteen volumes. The French botanist Auguste Saint-Hilaire published long accounts in 1833, complaining that the land was being exploited for agriculture. Charles Darwin sailed there aboard the HMS *Beagle*. Alfred Russel Wallace, the co-discoverer of the theory of evolution, spent 4 years exploring the Rio Negro. The Swiss-American geologist and paleontologist Louis Agassiz led an expedition in the 1860s.

The flag, adopted in 1889 with the creation of the republic, symbolizes the rational positivism of the 19th century as well as the nation's natural wealth. The motto inscribed is *Ordem e Progresso* (Order and Progress). The green and gold colors represent the green forests and gold, the country's most valuable mineral. The stars represent the 27 states, arranged to display the Southern Cross.

Brazil is huge, occupying half of the South American continent, and about the size of the United States or China. The climate is mostly tropical but is temperate in the south. Mineral resources are bauxite, gold, iron ore, uranium, and petroleum. Timber is abundant, as is falling water for hydropower. The Amazon River basin occupies most of the country. Originating in the Andes Mountains of Peru, and extending a total of 6,400 kilometers, the river is the largest in the world in terms of water volume and second longest in length. During the rainy season, it floods its banks to cover three times as much land as during the dry season. At its mouth at the Atlantic Ocean, it is 200 kilometers wide. Oceangoing ships can navigate 3000 kilometers upstream. Much of its enormous drainage basin is in adjoining countries like Peru and Ecuador. The Amazon Basin is little settled and few roads exist. Their construction is difficult, nearly impossible, due to the flooding. Sugar and coffee have been major exports of Brazil.

The population is nearly 200 million and grows 2% annually. Most people live in big cities along the Atlantic Coast. The two biggest are São Paulo with 19 million and Rio with 11 million. Racially over half of the people are white, 6% are black, and 38% are mixed white and black. Less than 1% remains of the original native Indians. The country now takes pride in its lack of racial prejudice.

Sugar plantations began early in the colonial period, based on slave labor. Although mineral wealth was less than in the Spanish colonies of Mexico and Peru, some gold was discovered, followed by other minerals. World demand for coffee generated a boom in the middle of the 19th century. Plantations centered in the vicinity of São Paulo. The market collapsed due to overexpansion. Soon thereafter European and North American demand for rubber increased sharply with the invention of vulcanization. The source was a tree found scattered about the Amazon Basin. The Indians had known of it for years. Workers tapped the tree, that is, scratched the bark and waited a few hours for the latex to ooze out, then collected it into balls, which they transported to a river, hence to Manaus or Belem. The business was lucrative, attracting migration from the east coast. Manaus became one of the richest cities in the world with an opera house and private villas. Demand climbed even higher when the bicycle craze broke out about 1890, followed by automobiles a decade later. But the boom ended when British, French, and Dutch smuggled out seeds to establish plantations in their colonies in Malaya, Vietnam, and the East Indies. Unlike the situation in Brazil, the rubber tree had no natural enemies in southeast Asia, so huge plantations were safe.

A military coup in 1930 ended the Old Republic. The populist Getulio Vargas took power and remained in office for 15 years, sometimes as a dictator but sometimes as an elected president. He served as an elected president from 1951 to 1954. Others were elected before and after him in the democratic period 1945 to 1964, known as the New Republic. In 1964 the military took power again, but this time there was no pretense of populism. The army governed directly. After initial success, problems multiplied. The economy fell apart and guerilla warfare broke out. In 1985 the military gave up and voluntarily turned the country back to civilians.

Even during the period of military control, the government responded to the worldwide Environmental Decade. In 1974 it established the Special Secretariat of the Environment (SEMA). In 1981 Brazil passed the National Environmental Protection Act, modeled on the US law. Under its provisions, in 1985 it established the Federal Council for Environmental Quality (CONAMA), composed of national agencies, state agencies, and representatives of nongovernmental organizations. In the early 1980s, state governments in São Paulo and Parana initiated cleanup of heavy industries responsible for air and water pollution.[7]

Government: Brazil is a federal republic with a presidential system modeled on the United States. The president is elected by all the people for a

4-year term. He appoints his cabinet. The president is not a member of the legislature as in many European countries. The bicameral National Congress consists of a Senate and a Chamber of Deputies. The senators are elected by majority, and the deputies are elected by proportional representation. Voting is compulsory (like Australia). Many parties hold seats in both chambers. Leading ones are the Democratic Movement Party, the Workers Party, the Social Democracy Party, the Democrats, and the Progressive Party. A small Green Party holds 10 seats in the Chamber of Deputies, amounting to 4%.

The president from 2002 to 2010 was Luiz Inácio Lula da Silva of the Workers Party, which he helped found in 1980. He came from a poor family and rose to power in the metal workers union, eventually becoming its president. Over the years he shifted from his socialist ideology to a moderate one. While his election appeared to repudiate earlier pro-market policies of the government, in office the change was not too great. His successor, whom he handpicked, was Dilma Rousseff. Educated as an economist, Rousseff came from an upper-class household but had become a socialist as a young woman. She fought against the military dictatorship with Marxist groups and was arrested, tortured, and imprisoned for 2 years. After her release she became active in politics in the state of Rio Grande do Sul as a member of the Labor Party and served as secretary of the treasury and of energy. Later she became the national Minister of Energy for Lula, implementing his rural electrification program, Luz para Todos (Light for All).

The Constitution of 1988 has an entire section of six paragraphs on the right to "an ecologically balanced environment." The government must preserve the land and the generic patrimony and protect against the extinction of species. Mine operators must restore the land, and nuclear plants are to be regulated. The national government has control over unoccupied lands or those seized by the states through discriminatory actions. Impact studies are required.[8]

The Federal Republic has 26 states and a federal district for the capital of Brasilia. Its regions are politically diverse, a feature dating back to colonial times. During the Old Republic of 1889 to 1930, the national government served merely as a clearinghouse for the states. Since 1930 the power of the central government has increased. Rather than act autonomously, the states strive to gain goods and services of the Brasilia authorities.

Like Washington, DC, and Canberra, Australia, the capital of Brasilia is a new city situated in a central location and completely built from scratch. The intention was to foster development of the interior, an idea dating back to 1827 and embedded in the Constitution of 1891. Nothing was done for a long time and the capital remained in Rio de Janeiro. Planning for construction began in 1956, and the government officially moved in 1960. The city has wide boulevards and long, sweeping vistas. After a half century the city has faithfully preserved the architectural integrity of its original plan. It focuses on the Congress building with its two domes, one inverted, and its twin office towers. One is for the Senate and the other is for the House of Delegates. The capitol forms one side of the Plaza of the Three Powers (congress, president, and courts). To the west the ministry buildings stretch out in their dignified cubic pattern. Only two buildings vary in design: the hyperboloid white cathedral with its crown, and the exhibition hall with its big dome and two ramps. The city has no museums because the whole city is a museum, with the public invited to wander into all government offices, even the presidential palace. Wide boulevards and freeways move auto traffic smoothly.

The key agency is the Brazilian Institute of Environment and Renewable Natural Resources, called IBAMA for its acronym in Portuguese. The Chico Mendes Institute for the Conservation of Biodiversity, called ICMBIO, manages the conservation units. IBAMA's greatest challenge has been to control deforestation of the Amazon Basin. In 2011 it announced its Zero Deforestation campaign, deploying 600 of its officers to priority zones. To concentrate on the worst offenders, it announced it would ease cattle seizures from ranchers who cooperated, and would sign agreements with local municipalities to enforce the regulations. Not everyone applauded this, however. The Greenpeace Amazon Campaign warned that the local governments are more easily pressured by local elites, wood barons, or agribusiness. Many times these have used violence and intimidation to silence critics. Worse still, an amendment to the national Forest Code took away IBAMA's authority to act directly.

Many nonprofit groups exist. These include SOS Atlantic Forest, the Social Environmental Institute, the Pro-Nature Foundation, and the Amazon Working Group. WWF and the Nature Conservancy have branches. Selection of Rio de Janeiro for the 1992 Earth Summit put Brazil in the center of world attention. Two years earlier in anticipation of the conference, 50 nongovernmental organizations established the Brazilian Forum of NGOs. They began a series of eight regional meetings, and by the time of the summit, over a thousand groups existed. During the summit the NGOs participated actively and forged alliances with groups internationally. Afterward, however, their activity declined. Political attention was diverted by the crisis and eventual impeachment of President Collor de Mello due to corruption.

Democracy returns: In 1985 the military voluntarily ceded power back to civilians. The generals were frustrated, and the people hated them. The proximate cause was hyper-inflation caused by the gigantic debt. Brazil had the highest foreign debt of any developing country. A major reason was that the 1973 oil crisis raised the cost of petroleum so high, and the additional price increases in 1979 made it worse. To pay for energy Brazil borrowed from commercial banks in New York and London, and the World Bank. This sparked high inflation and economic stagnation. The people blamed the generals, so they quit.

José Sarney was the first democratic president after the military voluntarily ceded power. Environmental protection took a back seat due to the transition from military power, hyper-inflation, gigantic foreign debt, and corruption. The Sarney government had limited success. In 1990 he was followed by Fernando Affonso Collor de Mello, whose chief distinction was presiding over the 1992 Earth Summit. In fact he was thoroughly corrupt and was impeached a few months after the Summit concluded. His vice president, Itamar Franco, took over and gave authority to his economic minister, Fernando Henrique Cardoso, to fight the hyper-inflation. Cardoso abolished the old currency and for a while pegged the Brazilian currency to the US dollar. Amazingly this worked, ending 40 years of high inflation. This success earned Cardoso the presidential nomination in 1994. He won the election and was reelected in 1998. In 2002 Brazilian voters turned a bit to the left to elect the nominee of the Workers Party, Luiz Inácio Lula da Silva, and reelected him in 2006. In fact Lula governed as a centrist rather than a leftist.

When Sarney took over from the military in 1985 he did some things for the environment. The SEMA was reorganized into IBAMA. The major parties adopted proenvironmental planks in their platforms. At this time the deforestation of the Amazon Basin was at an all-time high. This came about because of a well-meaning policy begun about 1955 to move poor people out of the slums of São Paulo, Rio de Janeiro, and other overpopulated cities into the interior. The expectation was that they would be given land and become prosperous farmers. Since the founding of the country, visionaries had viewed the interior as a potential source of prosperity. To some extent it copied the US expansion into the midwest during the 19th century. The difference was that, whereas the North American heartland was suitable for agriculture, the Brazilian one was not. Once the forests were cut down, the soil proved infertile. The topsoil was shallow, and without the rain forest, quickly dried out. Flooding was extensive. At best the Amazonian soil was suitable for grazing cattle. It supported few crops. Sometimes the forest was not even harvested but simply burned for grazing.

A further problem was the need for cash by the central government. Foreign countries would pay cash for the trees, and banks loaned money to the government that could be repaid by these exports. In the 1970s, this even included intergovernmental organizations like the World Bank and the Inter-American Development Bank. Since then these banks have become aware of their damage and now require better environmental practices. The rate of destruction has slowed, although it has not stopped. Furthermore, much of the land did not go to small farmers but to big corporations. Burning the forest amounted to 25,000 square kilometers a year. Criticism came from Europe and North America, specifically from the WWF and the Environmental Defense Fund. At first Sarney lashed out at the foreign critics, but this was not convincing. Criticism was also homegrown from the Rubber Tappers National Council, the Union of Indians, and the Brazilian Association of Anthropologists

Many of the local people suffered from the deforestation as corporations and large landowners profited. Starting at only nine years old, Chico Mendes joined his family in tapping the wild rubber trees to collect their latex for sale, a way of life a hundred years old in the jungle. The rubber tappers hated the loggers and ranchers who destroyed the forests, and as a young man Mendes engaged in vandalism to intimidate them. He and his gang would confront them in the jungle, demanding they stop. With maturity he adopted legal means, and began to organize a trade union of tappers, the Xapuri Rural Workers Union. Later he organized a national meeting of rubber tappers. Tragically, two ranchers assassinated him in 1988.

One sidelight of the debt crisis was the invention of Debt for Nature Swaps in Brazil, as well as Costa Rica and other countries. Environmentalists from the North (Europe and North America) proposed exchanging some of the debt for ecological protection. In return for forgiving some loans, Brazil would place a certain acreage under protection. For example, a group like WWF, the Nature Conservancy, or Conservation International would buy $100 million of debts at a steep discount, perhaps for only $20 million, then the entire amount of $100 million would be used to protect a particular natural location, turning it into a park. Although the concept was beguiling, it did not live up to its initial promise. Less-developed countries feared loss of sovereignty, and the nature groups feared that over the years the agreements would be repudiated.

When the first oil crisis occurred in 1973, Brazil depended on imports for 80 percent of its fuel. Ethanol from sugarcane seemed like a good substitute. The country produced a lot of sugar, and a sharp slump in prices due to declining export demand had generated a temporary surplus. The National Alcohol Program decreed ethanol would be blended with gasoline at 24% by volume. The program was administered by Petrobras, the government-owned oil company. Taxis and government vehicles were powered 100% by ethanol. Taxi owners got tax rebates. New cars were subsidized. From 1983 to 1989, ethanol-fueled autos accounted for 90% of those sold. Sugar refineries got big subsidies. Unfortunately for the Alcohol Program, world oil prices decreased greatly in 1986, and at the same time, world sugar prices increased greatly. During the 1990s, the new economic policies of stabilization and privatization were incompatible with the Alcohol Program. Nevertheless, the government continued to require gasoline to contain 20% ethanol. The official rational is that this is good for the environment and that it helps the economy because the sugar is grown locally. Since 2002 manufacturers have offered flexible vehicles that can burn either gasoline or ethanol.

Petrobras has been the government-owned oil company with a monopoly on exploration, production, and refining since it was founded in 1953. Its environmental record was bad. In 2001 two explosions destroyed the P-36 oil platform in the ocean, killing 11 workers. Costing $350 million, it was the world's largest floating rig. Three hundred thousand gallons of crude oil leaked into the ocean. A year earlier 350,000 gallons had leaked into Guanabara Bay near Rio de Janeiro. The same year an even bigger leak occurred at a refinery near Curitiba, where a million gallons of oil poured into two rivers.

The Itaipú dam, on the border between Brazil and Paraguay on the Parana River, constructed between 1975 and 1991, was the largest in the world at the time. Its electricity makes up 20% of the supply for Brazil and 94% for Paraguay. Indeed, in its early years, it generated more than could be used. The dam is close to Iguacu Falls, considered one of the most spectacular waterfalls in the world, and often ranked with Niagara and Victoria falls. The dam required cooperation between the neighboring countries, which took many years to negotiate. A further diplomatic issue was that Argentina, only a few miles downstream, feared that in the event of a military conflict Brazil would open the gates to cause a flood. A treaty in 1979 made that illegal. The environmental damage has been significant. At the beginning of construction, no attention was paid, but then Brazil and Paraguay agreed to control logging and protect endangered species.

Far to the north in the Amazon Basin, the government intends to build a series of dams. The first will be Belo Monte on the Xingu River in the State of Para. It will be 6 kilometers long, and its capacity will be 11,000 megawatts, making it the third biggest after the Three Gorges and Itaipú. First proposed in the 1990s, the dam has angered environmentalists who blocked it three times with lawsuits. They say it will flood 500 square kilometers and displace 50,000 people, many of them indigenous Indians. They complain that the dam will be inefficient because for three or four months each years the water flow is low, and it will generate only 10% of its capacity. Other dams on the Amazon will have this deficiency because the river does not fall much in elevation once it leaves the Andes Mountains. Final approval came in 2010. It will be constructed by the state-owned Companhia Hidro Eletrica do Sao Francisco

Beginning in 2003 President Lula promoted rural electrification, called Light for All (Luz para Todas). It is coordinated by the Ministry of Energy and Mines and run by the huge government-controlled energy holding company, Eletrobras. Most is supplied by the grid using conventional fuels on wires strung across the countryside. Slender wires on thin poles from one small house to another are now a common sight along the Amazon River. Many regions are too remote, however, so the program is encouraging renewable energy like solar, wind, or small hydro. In some areas, natural gas may be suitable. The government will pay up to 85% of the cost.

The indigenous population of between two and four million at the time of European contact soon came under attack from disease, conquest, and enslavement. In 1570 King Sebastian I of Portugal decreed that the Indians not be enslaved, but many were anyway. In 1755 Indian slavery was permanently abolished. Interbreeding with Europeans generated a large mixed population, but the numbers of pure-blooded indigenous people has declined to half a million today, less than half of 1% of the total population. They are divided into 200 tribes inhabiting multiple sites. Some have no contact at all with the rest of the population while others have contact. The National Foundation for Indians (FUNAI) is charged with their protection. Since 1952 the government has established many reservations. For example, the Raposa Serra do Sol reservation stretches more than 1.7 million hectares along the Venezuelan border and is home to up to 20,000 Indians. The oldest one is Xingu National Park, established only in 1952. One of the largest tribes is the Yanomami, a people well studied by anthropologists and known for their fierceness.

Uncontacted Indians continue to dwell in remote parts of the country, often in areas protected as parks or reservations. FUNAI guesses there may be 30 or 40 groups, with sizes ranging from a few dozen to a few thousand. Its current policy is to avoid all contact and let the tribes continue as they are. Once FUNAI discovers an uncontacted tribe, it notes its presence and places it off limits to everyone, including medical workers, anthropologists, and missionaries.

All the Indians face pressure from settlers, oil explorers, and mine prospectors. In the 1980s, gold was discovered in the north, especially in Yanomami territory. Some Indians were callously chased off as miners illegally appropriated their land. Others contracted diseases like influenza, measles, and tuberculosis. Some were shot for interfering with the prospecting. Tens of thousands of non-Indians invaded to mine the gold. Mercury used to reduce the gold ore polluted the rivers and killed fish. Roads destroyed the rain forest. Elsewhere in Brazil, logging and farming has harmed the Indians.

While the policy of developing the interior since 1955 has harmed the Indians, they had suffered even more in the 19th century during the Rubber Boom. At first the rubber traders hired the Indians to tap the trees in the forest, but they could not supply enough latex so they imported people from the coast to become tappers. After the boom collapsed at the end of the 19th century, they stayed on as subsistence farmers along the banks of the rivers, growing bananas and corn. Although geographically dispersed across the entire basin, their primitive farming techniques did not cause much damage. The one hazard comes from farmers who make charcoal to sell to towns downstream. Although these people typically have Indian blood mixed with Portuguese and a little African, they speak Portuguese and do not share the indigenous Indian culture. The local term for them is *cabuco* or *cabulco*, meaning "copper colored."

The indigenous people did not receive government recognition and help until 1910 with the establishment of the Indian Protection Service (SPI). A leader was Candido Rondon, famous with many North Americans as the co-leader with former president Theodore Roosevelt in their exploration of the River of Doubt. Rondon was an Army officer who built telegraph lines in remote regions, thus making the acquaintance of the native people. His father was Portuguese and his mother was of the Bororo tribe so he had a special sympathy. Rondon was the first director of the SPI, but after his retirement, less dedicated officials and Army officers took it over, abandoning its ideals and leading to corruption. Often they saw their role as easing the Indians out of the way so timber and oil companies could take the land. Sometimes they resorted to murder. By 1967 this became too much even for the military junta that ruled at the time. It abolished the SPI and replaced it with FUNAI. The new agency was an improvement, but not perfect as Indians continued to suffer and find themselves dispossessed. On one hand, the government protects them, but at the same time, it continues to build roads, construct dams, and promote agribusiness.

Far to the south, the city of Curitiba claims the title of the world's greenest city. It has been an innovator since the 1970s, when it converted a busy downtown street into a pedestrian mall. The mayor, Jaime Lerner, feared merchants and automobile drivers would object, so he accomplished the transformation over a weekend. Because garbage collection was so bad in the slums—favelas—that the city offered rewards to residents who would bring trash to central pickup points. The narrow alleys made regular collection impossible, and impoverished residents were simply dumping it in nearby rivers and fields. The people got bus passes and football tickets. Fishermen were paid by the pound to fish for rubbish. The city set up recycling plants that employed homeless people and alcoholics. Floodplains were purchased and converted to parks with lakes that could absorb floodwater. Lerner tackled the need for mass transit. The first proposal was for a subway system, but this would have cost $100 million per kilometer. A light-rail system would cost only $10 million a kilometer, but the cheapest was buses. The mayor championed articulated buses running on dedicated lanes. Routes extend throughout the city so that no resident is farther than 400 meters from a stop.[9]

CONCLUSION

India has had some dramatic instances of popular demonstrations. The Chipko of Uttar Pradesh literally hugged the trees they were trying to protect. More generally India has a long tradition of protests and demonstrations, but these were usually tied to political goals like independence, and not to environmental issues. Indians are enthusiastic voters. With over 700 million eligible to cast a ballot, elections take weeks. Worldwide, environmentalists tend to come from the middle class, and many Indians are poor, hence they lack the income and education to participate so much. Brazil also is a vibrant democracy. People, even poor people, have a long history of protesting to protect their forests. Chico Mendes earned international fame as a poor rubber tapper who confronted loggers and ranchers who cut down the trees in the Amazon Basin.

India has many political parties, Congress being the biggest. Perhaps understandably for a country so poor, they do not place a high priority on environmental protection. It has a tiny Green Party. Likewise, Brazilian parties do not focus much on the environment. The Workers Party, which has held the presidency from 2003 on talked only vaguely about deforestation and greenhouse emissions.

Interest groups are ubiquitous in both countries. Some are small and homegrown such as the Bombay Natural History Society and the Sálim Ali Centre for Ornithology. Others are Indian branches of international groups like WWF. A number get financial help from the government. In Brazil, one of the smallest groups is the best known: Chico Mendes's Xapuri Rural Workers Union. Bigger ones are SOS Atlantic Forest and the Social Environmental Institute. WWF, the Nature Conservancy, and Friends of the Earth have Brazilian branches.

Both India and Brazil have a federal structure, like the United States, Germany, Canada, and Australia. Since India does not do much to protect the environment, this makes little difference. In Brazil, federalism has made enforcement of national regulations more difficult. In the Amazon Basin, the state-level enforcement has made it easier for the logging companies to exert their pressure.

The diplomatic agenda has brought attention to the environment. Preparation for the Rio de Janeiro Earth Summit stimulated interest. In anticipation of the conference, 50 nongovernmental organizations established the Brazilian Forum of NGOs. India also found a diplomatic conference to focus attention. Holding the 2002 Conference of the Parties for the Kyoto Protocol in New Delhi stimulated Indian scientists and officials to mobilize.

India and Brazil came later to environmental issues than the industrial countries did. Poverty and less-educated populations meant the Environmental Decade did not penetrate so soon. Yet these countries made their own contributions. The whole concept of mass demonstrations owes much to the Indian marches for independence. More narrowly, the term "tree hugger" came from the Chipko movement. The Amazon Basin has attracted attention from all over the industrial world.

NOTES

1. Ramachandra Guha. "Mahatma Gandhi and the Environmental Movement in India," in *Environmental Movements in Asia*, ed. Arne Kalland and Gerard Person (Surrey, U.K.: Curzon Press, 1998), p. 69.
2. Guha, "Mahatma Gandhi and the Environmental Movement."
3. Vikram K. Akula, "Grassroots Environmental Resistance in India," in *Ecological Resistance Movements,* ed. Bron Raymond Taylor (Albany: SUNY Press, 1995), pp. 139–140.
4. G. Narayana and John F. Kantner, *Doing the Needful: the Dilemma of India's Population Policy* (Boulder: Westview Press, 1992), p. 71.
5. Akula, "Grassroots Environmental Resistance," p. 133; Guha, "Mahatma Gandhi and the Environmental Movement," p. 65.
6. Indian Department of Family Welfare, *Population Policy*, 2000.
7. Eduardo J. Viola, "The Environmental Movement in Brazil," in *Latin American Environmental Policy in International Perspective,* ed. Gordon J. MacDonald, Daniel L. Nielson, and Marc A. Stern (Boulder, Colo.: Westview Press, 1997), pp. 93–94.
8. Constitution of Brazil, 1988, Title VIII Chapter VI Article 225.
9. Mike Power, "Common Sense and the City: Jaime Lerner, Brazil's Green Revolutionary," *Guardian*, Nov. 5, 2009, Web.

7

Kenya and Costa Rica

Kenya and Costa Rica are comparatively small, developing tropical countries both enjoying reputations as natural paradises. Both are popular destinations for eco-tourism. In terms of economic development, they are emerging, with GDPs of $66 billion and $51 billion, respectively. They differ, however, in geographical size and population. Kenya has ten times the size and ten times the number of people. Costa Rica has a vibrant democracy, whereas Kenya has the official forms of democracy, but a history of conflict.

Kenya is an environmental paradise, and at the same time, a typical developing country with dirty air and water. The country is famed for its wildlife, making it a destination for travelers from all over the world. Its mountains and plains are home to vast herds of zebras, gazelles, and wildebeests. Lions stalk them as prey. Elephants, giraffes, and rhinos graze nearby. In the distance Mount Kenya and Kilimanjaro rise above them. Its famous national parks seem to be Edens. Yet life in the slums of Nairobi or Mombasa or Kisumu is far from paradise, with smog, polluted water, and poverty. Population has grown greatly, 2.5% annually, to over 40 million. The average woman has four children, making it one of the most fecund countries in the world, yet lower than several others in Africa. In its politics, Kenya is stable compared to others in Africa. Since its independence in 1963, it has not suffered a successful coup or a revolution. With one major exception, violence has been slight. Economically, it has been prosperous, at least compared to others on the continent. Its per capita income is $1,600 with a growth rate of 4%. Tribally and ethnically, it is diverse. Governmentally, it is the product of its colonial structure. In short, it is typical of sub-Saharan Africa.

Located on the Indian Ocean and stretching over 1000 kilometers west to Lake Victoria, Kenya is the same size as Spain. In the center of the country and sitting directly on the equator, Mount Kenya reaches 5,200 meters, the second tallest in Africa. It is a dormant volcano, and has a few small glaciers. Just a few kilometers south of the border with Tanzania, Mount Kilimanjaro reaches 5,905 meters, the tallest in Africa. Its volcanic origin gives it a distinctive cone, topped with permanent snow fields and glaciers, now threatened by global warming. These mountains have unique biospheres at their high altitudes. Alongside the Indian Ocean, the land is tropical with heavy rain producing dense jungle. Heading west, the country consists of broad savanna with scattered mountains. It is hot and arid. These plains are home to the millions of wild animals. Tsavo Park, one of the biggest in the world, is here. Lack of rainfall makes agriculture difficult. As the elevation increases toward the Highlands, the climate becomes cooler and moister. This land is good for farming, and was the region where most whites settled. A bit farther west is the Great Rift Valley. This gigantic fault between two tectonic plates extends throughout Africa and far north as Lebanon. In places steep rock cliffs of the valley are thousands of feet high. The valley is 50 miles across. The floor is suitable for farming and pasture. Farther north the Rift Valley becomes too dry to support farming. Lakes Victoria and Turkana (formerly called Rudolf) are there. The Nile River starts there. To the west, Kenya adjoins Uganda, to the north it adjoins Ethiopia, and to the northwest it adjoins South Sudan. Its southeastern boundary is the Indian Ocean, and to its northeast, Somalia.

Human settlement dates back as far as the human race, and indeed farther. Archaeological excavations at Lake Turkana have found proto-humans who lived two to three million years ago. Fossils of modern humans date back 200,000 years, and support the theory that *Homo sapiens* originated in Kenya, before spreading to the Middle East, Europe, and beyond. The concept is labeled "out of Africa." A recent interpretation, *biophilia*, maintains that all humans have retained a racial memory of their East African origin, continuing as the fondness people have for the landscape of grass-covered plains, water holes, and scattered trees like the acacia. People innately prefer this landscape to forests.[1]

The present inhabitants divide into about half a dozen ethnic and linguistic groups. Cushite tribes from Ethiopia arrived about two thousand years ago. In 500 BC Nilotic immigrants came, also from Ethiopia. Luo people came in the 15th century AD, and the Maasai arrived about 200 years ago. Bantu-speaking settlers, from the west, came only a century or so ago. Somalis, a Cushite people, continue to infiltrate into the northeast to this day. Experts list up to 50 tribes. The largest are the Kikuyu with 23% of the population, followed by the Luhya, the Luo, the Kalenjin, and several more. The population is 83% Christian and 11% Muslim.

The first non-Africans to arrive were Arab traders who appeared along the coast about AD 700, seeking ivory, animal pelts, and slaves. In this period slaves were exported as far away as Iraq and India. Some merchants settled in Mombasa and Malindi, as well as Zanzibar in present-day Tanzania, and Mogadishu in Somalia. By the 14th century a lingua franca had emerged—Swahili—from the Arabic, Bantu, Persian, and Indian tongues. (Today, it is, with English, one of the two official languages of Kenya.) In 1498 the Portuguese explorer Vasco da Gama arrived at Malindi, en route to India. During the next century the Portuguese conquered sea ports and built permanent forts. Fort Jesus still stands at the entrance to Mombasa. The Portuguese did not send settlers; instead, they sent only a few soldiers to man their fortifications. In 1696 the Arabs and local allies began a successful 33 month siege of Fort Jesus, and by 1720 chased the Portuguese out of East Africa. Even during the periods of Portuguese dominance, their impact was slight. Arab merchants continued to live and trade as permanent residents of the coastal cities. In 1840 the Sultan of Oman moved his capital from the Arabian Peninsula to Zanzibar to enjoy a better climate and trading advantages.

British colonization came late. During the nineteenth century, they showed little interest in East Africa until 1885 when the Germans demanded that the Sultan in Zanzibar cede territory on the mainland. When he refused, the Imperial German navy sailed up with five warships, forcing him to capitulate. With the new German colony of Tanganyika being established, the British negotiated an agreement so they would get control the region to the north as a Protectorate. The Sultan got nothing. After the Germans began building a railroad from Dar-es-Salaam to Lake Victoria, the British in 1896 began laying tracks for a competing line, reaching the lake 5 years later. Workers came from India. In the first months of construction in the Tsavo plains, two lions stalked and ate workers, dragging them from their tents at night. Estimates of the number of victims range from 35 to 135. The workers fled. Eventually, hunters were able to find and kill the lions. The city of Nairobi was founded where the grade of the rails grew steeper at the Highlands, necessitating switching engines. In the early years, there was little cargo for the railway to carry, but a solution appeared. If white farmers could be enticed to settle, their crops could be transported to Mombasa on the Indian Ocean for ships. Cash crops were coffee, tea, and flax. In 1902 a Crown Lands Ordinance provided that "empty lands" could be seized and given to whites. Of course, the lands were not empty, for the indigenous Africans had small farmsteads, or used the land to pasture their cattle, although perhaps only a month or two a year in the case of nomads like the Maasai. Four years later the Master and Servant Ordinance regularized the labor contracts. Only at this point did agriculture begin to put pressure on the environment. Prior to colonization, population density was low. Nomads moved their cattle about so the grass could recover. Native farmers cultivated only a few acres. The African population then was about two million, and the whites were only 20,000.

By 1945 the white population was about 60,000, and the British Colonial Office had granted them limited self-governance in a Legislative Council. Africans, with a population of six million, had only one representative. Instead, Africans were granted Local Native Councils, headed by tribal chiefs, who were not allowed to organize nationwide. The oppression fell particularly hard on the Kikuyu tribe because their home was the Highlands that the whites found so appealing for farms. Since 1920 dis-posed Africans had been forced to move to the cities because little land was available for farming and herding. One such migrant was Johnson Kamau, who organized the Young Kikuyu Association in 1924. He changed his name to Jomo Kenyatta. The group was banned during World War II, but it reorganized as the Kenya African Union (KAU), and tried to find alliances with other tribes. In 1951 the KAU presented to colonial secre-tary with demands for more money for education, more jobs in the civil service, an end to racial discrimination, and eight seats on the Legislative Council. At the time only, two Africans served.[2]

Indians, called Asians, who first came to build the railroad, soon moved into jobs as small merchants, and in the lower ranks of the civil service and the railway. By 1950 there were slightly more of them than whites. The British gave them five seats on the Legislative Council (compared to eleven for whites). Racial relations with Africans were often bad. For example, Indians often owned the only store in an African village and were accused of charging high prices.

By 1950 Africans had established a terrorist movement, the Mau Mau. The organization was secret and required members to take an oath to expel the whites, killing them if necessary. They attacked them on their farms and in ambushes. They also attacked fellow Africans who did not support their movement. Traitors were tortured and killed. Most members were

Kikuyu, but men from other tribes joined. The war caused the British governor to declare a state of emergency that lasted until 1960. Jomo Kenyatta and twenty-five leaders of the KAU were arrested and imprisoned. They claimed there was no connection between their party and the Mau Mau. Tens of thousands of Africans were placed in concentration camps to prevent them giving assistance to the terrorists. The Mau Mau withdrew to the safety of the forests, such as those near Mount Kenya where the Royal Air Force attacked them with heavy bombers. Eventually, the British recognized that independence as an African-run government was inevitable. There were millions of native Kenyans and only 80,000 whites.[3] Moreover, the United Kingdom was granting independence to other colonies like Ghana, Nigeria, India, and Pakistan. In the phrase popular at the time, the Winds of Change were blowing. The British increased representation on the Legislative Council to fourteen Africans compared to fourteen Whites. They re-legalized the KAU, which soon reorganized as the Kenyan African National Union (KANU).

Independence came in 1963. The British had set up a parliamentary system copied after Westminster. Kenyatta was the first prime minister. Within a year the new government switched to a republican structure with Kenyatta as the president. An opposition party emerged, the Kenya People's Union, which the KANU immediately tried to suppress. Another opposition party, the Kenya African Democratic Union, met the same fate. By 1968 Kenya was effectively a one-party state. KANU was dominated primarily by the Kikuyu, and secondarily by the Luo tribe. When Jomo Kenyatta died in 1979, Daniel Arap Moi, his vice president, succeeded him. This occurred even though he was not a Kikuyu, but a Kalejin. Moi consolidate his power within the KANU. In 1982 the KANU officially became the only legal party by amendment of the Constitution. That August some Air Force officers attempted a coup d'etat, but were put down. The government became increasingly authoritarian, and corruption became endemic.

By 1991 KANU power was under pressure. Many people resented the lack of freedom. Church leaders spoke out against it. The collapse of Communism in Eastern Europe and Russia offered a model of democracy. More ominously, popular demonstrations and riots in the western provinces demanded land reform. In December of that year, the KANU leadership recommended change; in the following year Parliament amended the Constitution to provide for multiple parties. Elections in 1992 were split among four candidates with Moi winning with 36% of the vote. The opposition could not unite and ethnic riots continued. The situation caused international and direct foreign aid programs to reduce grants, and tourist spending declined. President Moi proclaimed an election in December 1997. Again, the opposition could not unite, and Moi won 40% of the votes, well ahead of his four rivals. In Parliament KANU won a narrow majority against nine other parties.[4] To ensure control it invited a few minor parties into its coalition. The problem he faced, and one present still, is that parties are based on tribes, resulting in great fragmentation. There are 150 different parties. As might be expected, environmental protection has low priority.

In 2002 the opposition parties formed the National Rainbow Coalition, nominating Mwai Kibaki for president. He won with 62%. Problems arose by 2006 when two corruption scandals erupted. Then another one flared up about money laundering and tax evasion by cabinet members. The 2007 election brought about a further crisis. The official Electoral Commission declared Kibaki was reelected, but the vote was rigged in many places. Supporters of the other candidate, Raila Odinga, rioted, and 1,300 people died. Former United Nations Secretary General Kofi Annan arbitrated an agreement to share power, and Parliament amended the Constitution. As a compromise, a new office of prime minister was created, and Odinga appointed to it. A new coalition government promised to reform elections, redistribute land and root out corruption. The 2013 election was hard fought, but did not result in the extensive bloodshed of four years earlier. The winner was Uhuru Kenyatta, formerly the deputy prime minister and the son of the founder, Jomo Kenyatta. Unfortunately, the new president was facing charges before the International Criminal Court in The Hague that he had used his family fortune to bankroll death squads during the riots in the previous election.

After the 2007 election a Power Sharing Agreement had resulted in a new Constitution approved by the voters in 2010. This provided that the executive consisted of the president and the prime minister, who jointly appoint cabinet members from the National Assembly. The cabinet includes multiple parties according the agreement. The National Assembly has 210 members elected from single-member districts, plus 12 more nominated by the various parties. The judiciary consists of a court of appeal, a high court, and magistrate courts. When fully implemented, the agreement provides for a second legislative chamber and a supreme court. Dating back to the British colonial period, Kenya has had a unitary form, but the agreement gave it some federal features. There are seven provinces with a total of 140 rural districts. The president appoints the district commissioners.

There are 47 counties, each electing its own governor. The structure is in flux awaiting implementation of the new Constitution.

With respect to the environment, the key ministries are Forestry and Wildlife, Environment and Minerals, and Water. Within the Forestry and Wildlife Ministry, the Wildlife Service, which dates back to colonial programs, is responsible for the parks and game. Other bureaus cover forests. Like the rest of the bureaucracy, these ministries adhered to the model of the British civil service. In theory at least, the civil servants were hired and promoted for their competency. Employees entered at the junior level and could look forward to a life-long career. They were supposed to be politically neutral, following the directions of their minister who was a Member of Parliament. They were to be unbiased and not play favorites. There was a Permanent Secretary who was a civil servant who headed the bureaucracy, providing expertise and continuity. As with all agencies, it proved difficult to maintain neutrality and honesty.

Traditional life did not place a heavy burden on the land. Farming was primitive, and much of the countryside was used for nomadic grazing. People lived in harmony with nature. The first exploitation came from Arab traders who sent expeditions into the interior for slaves and ivory. They would kill elephants, and force the newly enslaved victims to carry the tusks to the coast for export. Early in the 20th century, British, Europeans, and American hunters began to come for the big game. In 1909, former president Theodore Roosevelt landed in Mombasa to begin a year-long safari. He had just left the White House and wanted some adventure.[5] Besides shooting, the expedition sought scientific data and specimens for museums. They took many photographs, and even motion pictures.

Africans, of course, had always hunted, mostly for the pot but also to defend their herds from predation, and to keep animals out of their small farms. Using arrows, they shot dikdik, bushbuck, and bush pig. Even prior to colonization, tribes like the Kamba hunted elephants for their ivory and rhinos for their horns to trade with Arab merchants on the coast. They were able to kill an elephant with poison arrows. Except the ivory and horn, subsistence hunting had little effect on the natural environment.

Sport hunting was different. As soon as the whites arrived, they pursued big game. Colonial officials and Highland settlers began to shoot lions, elephants, and rhinos. The British, Europeans, and Americans shot huge numbers of game for trophies, and occasionally as part of scientific exploration. Roosevelt sent specimens back to the Smithsonian Institution. By the 1920s settlers had increased in number, and they killed to protect their imported livestock as well as for sport. Besides shooting, their cultivation of tea, coffee, and flax removed habitat for animals. Finally, government got into the function of "game control." The colonial Game Department killed thousands of animals to prevent damage to crops, livestock, and fences by hunting on Crown Lands. Hunting on private lands was under the control of the settlers. During this period of the "White Hunter," Africans began to find employment as guides, trackers, and gun bearers. The Game Department routinized its operation with white wardens and rangers, and Africans in subordinate positions. The department required licenses, and the fees were able to support half its expenses. Taking ivory or rhino horn required a special fee. "Vermin" could be shot on sight. This category included zebras, baboons, and at one time, lions. In addition to regulating big game, the department protected the settlers' farms. It poisoned small animals, a function usually performed by its African employees. The department officially recognized a role of game preservation. Poachers smuggled ivory, horn, and leopard skins out via the Italian colony of Somalia. This led first to a treaty with Italy, and in 1933 to the international Convention on the Preservation of Wildlife negotiated in London (a predecessor of the Convention on International Trade in Endangered Species). The department paid little attention to hunting by Africans.[6]

An early Game Department employee was George Adamson, whose wife Joy won international fame when she raised a lion cub, Elsa, then returned her to freedom. Her book and movie *Born Free* publicized Kenyan wildlife. In the 1930s Kenya had enjoyed literary renown in Europe and America. Ernest Hemingway published *The Snows of Kilimanjaro* in 1936. Isak Dinesen published *Out of Africa* in 1937, telling of her life establishing a coffee plantation. Louis and Mary Leakey wrote frequently, starting in 1931, of their archaeological digs discovering ancient humans. Louis was born in Kenya of missionary parents, and as a boy joined the Kikuyu tribe.

In the late 1930s the colonial government added another dimension: parks. The model was the national park system in the United States. Other countries in the British Empire, like Canada and Australia, had national parks by then. A Kenya-born settler, Melvyn Cowie, took the initiative. Crown Lands and game reserves were organized as parks. Although World War II delayed implementation, the first was created in 1945 outside of Nairobi on the Athi Plains within sight of the capital city. It is home to the black rhino as well as lions, giraffes, and gazelles. During the 1930s it had been designated a game reserve, where hunting was not allowed, although farming and grazing were allowed. People who lived there, chiefly the pastoral Maasai, were removed. Tsavo, established in 1948, is one of the largest parks in the world, so large that it is divided in two for administration. Game includes elephants, lions, leopards, cape buffalos, and hippos. Mount Kenya National Park was established in 1949. The mountain has distinct biospheres as the altitude increases. In all there are 18 national parks and 11 game reserves. Right from the beginning the parks were oriented toward foreign tourists.

Cowie and others believed separating the parks from the Game Department was necessary to fend off pressure for farming and mining. Administratively the Parks were controlled by an independent Board of Trustees.[7]

In the 1950s poaching for ivory became more of a problem. The elephant population was declining, especially in Tsavo. The hunters there were the Waata and the Kamba bowmen. Rangers rarely could find them making a kill, so they adopted three strategies. First was a network of informers. Second was to raid their villages and hideouts, where they kept the ivory, and third was to recruit the poachers as park employees.[8]

With independence in 1963, the Game and Parks departments staff shifted from white control to African control, like all the government departments. Whites were eased out of their jobs to be replaced by Africans. Often a British permanent secretary would stay on for a number of years to run the bureaucracy while the minister would be appointed by the new prime minister or president. Kenya is often pointed to as an example of a smooth transition compared to other sub-Saharan countries. In 1976 the Game Department and Kenya National Parks were merged to form the Wildlife Conservation and Management District, and in 1990 was renamed the Kenya Wildlife Service.

Independence did not end the problem of poaching, however. Between 1976 and 1988, the population of elephants declined by 85% and the population of rhinos declined by 97%. The Convention on International Trade in Endangered Species (CITES) voted to impose a worldwide ban on selling or buying ivory, which was an immediate success. With no market, poaching declined, and the population rebounded. This had its own problems. With the human population increasing, more people lived near parks and reserves. Elephants wandered onto farms, destroying crops and smashing fences. People were injured. In 1991 the Wildlife Service began to pay farmers to tolerate animal damage in return for a 25% cut of the gate receipts from the nearby park. Funds went for schools, medical clinics, water supplies, roads, and so forth. Tourism was at an all-time high, so money was available. Unfortunately, the Wildlife Service lost popular support due to accusations of favoritism and corruption.[9] A further difficulty was that the elephant population rebounded too much. Elephants became more common after hunting was outlawed in 1973. Food was insufficient. They began to destroy all the plants in the parks. They even uprooted baobab trees to get the water stored inside. Poaching continues to be widespread. Elephant overpopulation is less a problem than in southern Africa.

The Maasai have frequently been on the forefront of conflicts over land. In 1911 the British signed a treaty with the tribe's nominal leader ceding the rich grasslands of Nairobi and Laikipiak. The Maasai were forced onto arid reserves, which could not support their cattle as well. In 1945 the government declared many of their reserves to be national parks and expelled the Maasai and their livestock. These pastoralists do not eat meat from wild game and their flocks did not eat the same plants as the wildlife, so they had been a compatible match. After independence, the World Bank funded the Livestock Development Project to convert their rangelands to Western-style commercial beef farming. Traditional communal land tenure was abolished, and the Maasai were given legal title to group ranches in 1968. The program was a fiasco. The ranches were not compatible with the existing tribal boundaries, the elected boards did not match the real tribal leadership, and the people wanted to continue their freedom to move about. In 1989 the government abolished the program and subdivided the land for individual ownership. This further destroyed traditional leadership. It caused exploitation of the land because the old system of nomadism had allowed time for grass to regrow. Maasai were able to sell their land for a profit to other tribes, but this left them without grazing territory. Today, more outsiders live in the sectors than Maasai. Further pressure comes from foreign nature groups that oppose grazing in the national parks.[10]

The Maasai Mara Game Reserve in the southwest has been a prime attraction for half a century. In 1961 the Game Department and the Maasai people agreed to develop the reserve cooperatively, with the formation of the Narok County Council. A core area was set aside for the animals, but nearby they built access roads and leased land for hotels. The Council appointed a warden and hired staff. The Maasai people were to share the revenues from the leases and gate fees. Other parts of the reserve could be leased by the tribes for hunting and photography. When Kenya banned hunting in 1977 income went down. Over the years complaints have emerged about corruption, claiming that powerful politicians in the

Narok Country Council or the national government have skimmed the revenue. People are also concerned that non-Maasai have moved in, and that the market for native handicrafts has been exploited.[11]

The Maasai Mara Reserve embodies the best, but nearly all tourism in Kenya is ecotourism. This dates back more than a century, when the colony became famous for shooting big game. Today the shooting is done with a camera. The visitors aim for the Big Five: lion, elephant, buffalo, leopard, and rhinoceros. Huge herds of zebras, giraffes, wildebeests, gazelles, hippopotamuses, and ostriches roam freely. Some tourists come to climb Mount Kenya and Kilimanjaro. Some come for the beaches, but it is a long flight from Europe. In all half a million visitors come annually to visit 54 national parks and reserves. Hunters with guns go elsewhere to South Africa, Namibia, or Zimbabwe. Game hunting was outlawed in reserves in 1972, and everywhere in 1987. The average tourist on a game reserve safari spends $4,400 and the average tourist at the coast spends $1,900.[12]

WWF has been involved in Kenya since 1962 when it purchased land to protect flamingos on Lake Nakuru. This led to establishing the black rhino sanctuary there, at the height of the poaching crisis. The International Union for Conservation of Nature has been in Kenya since the 1980s involved in projects on wildlife protection and preserving forests. Its project in the Garba Tula district seeks to return people to a pastoral way of life. For centuries nomads with their cattle enjoyed a symbiotic relationship and did not suffer unduly from droughts. If rainfall was sparse, the tribes moved with their herds. More recently their rights to pastures have been taken away and the land converted to farming, which was not sustainable.

Population growth has put pressure on the land and animals. Independence sparked an explosion. From 1969 (the first good census numbers) to 1989 the number of people doubled. The rate of increase peaked at nearly 4% in 1982, and remains high at 2.6%. Its present size is 41 million, compared to 10 million at independence in 1963. Much of the growth is in cities like Nairobi, but some is rural. This is not just natural increase of families already living there but is also interprovincial immigration by distant tribes eager to establish farms, for instance in the Rift Valley province. The more economically advanced regions have entered the so-called demographic transition of lower mortality due to modern medicine and sanitation with the high birth rate of traditional society. Less advanced regions continue to have the high death rates of traditional society, hence less population growth. The topic of population is controversial because the political forces are strongly based on tribes. Even the numbers measured in a census are controversial.

Kenya was one of the first developing countries to adopt a policy of limiting population. The average number of children for a woman was 8.1 in the late 1960s. This fell to 4.0 in 2012. Surveys report 39% of the women used birth control. The country has been hit hard by the AIDS epidemic. Life expectancy has fallen to 53 years from 59 years in the 1980s. The infection rate is 6.3%, placing it as one of the highest in the world, yet not as high as its neighbors in southern Africa. The infection rate has declined a bit since the high point of 2000, due to sex education and awareness. Moreover, many of the victims have died.

With a population of three million, the capital of Nairobi generates half of the country's GDP and provides a quarter of the jobs. The air is polluted from industry and automobiles. Less than half of the households have drinking water piped in. Its rivers and streams are choked with uncollected garbage and sewer overflows. It generates 1,500 tons of solid waste every day, of which 40% is not collected.[13] Similar problems are found in big cities like Mombasa and Kisumu. Indoor air pollution is a problem everywhere, in rural as well as urban homes. Cooking is generally fueled by wood, charcoal, or dung. In developing countries like Kenya, the World Health Organization estimates it accounts for a 3% to 4% decrease in life expectancy.[14] Women and young children are exposed most.

In 1977 Wangari Maathai founded the Green Belt Movement to address some of these problems. This paid poor women a few shillings to plant trees that would provide fuel and prevent erosion. Eventually, her program planted more than thirty million trees in Kenya and elsewhere. Professionally, Dr. Maathai taught veterinary science. Politically, she served as a member of parliament and as an assistant minister for environmental issues. Earlier during a protest against building a huge skyscraper in one of central Nairobi's few parks, she had been beaten unconscious by the police. At another protest, she was tear-gassed. In the mid-1960s as a young woman, she had studied biology at the University of Pittsburgh, where she had become aware of the citizen movement to clean up the city's air pollution. In 2004 she became the first African woman to win the Noble Prize.

Nairobi was selected to be the headquarters of the United National Environmental Program. The choice was intended to recognize the country's outstanding natural setting, and as a gesture to sub-Saharan Africa.

Kenya suffered smaller episode of unrest leading up to the 2013 presidential vote. Tribal rivalry was once more an issue, but this time land ownership had moved to the forefront. The Kalenjin people believe that the Kikuyu took much of their land in the Rift Valley, dating back to the British colonial government. They and others believe that land titles continue to be manipulated as political rewards. A new National Land Commission, which is supposed to resolve injustices, faces a nearly impossible task due to conflicting and unclear ownership. Observers suggest that the politicians are using land as an emotional topic to inflame partisanship.

Costa Rica is an environmental paradise, with soaring mountains, active volcanoes, tropical rain forests, and beautiful beaches on both the Atlantic and Pacific coasts. Moreover, it comes close to being a political paradise also. Since 1948 it has had a stable democratic government, has abolished its army, and enjoys economic prosperity. Its combination of mountains, middle-class prosperity, and democracy has earned it the nickname of the Switzerland of Central America. Additionally, it has the highest literacy rate and lowest rate of infant mortality in the region. In recent years, it has developed medical tourism. Hospitals and clinics offer high-quality surgery for joint replacement, cosmetic procedures, dental care, and weight loss at a fraction of the cost in the United States. Electronics is now a big industry.

The small nation borders Panama to the south and Nicaragua to the north. It is a bit larger than Switzerland. Its population is 4.6 million, about the size of Ireland. The people are 94% white, 3% black, and 1% indigenous. The white category includes mestizos of mixed Spanish and indigenous blood. Away from the coastal plains, the terrain is very mountainous, rising to 3,800 meters at Cerro Chirripo. More than a hundred peaks have volcanic origins, and a half-dozen are active volcanoes. The interior has many valleys, whose high elevation provides a cool climate. The Ticos, as the people are known, brag that they enjoy eternal springtime. A quarter of the land is protected as parks, forest reserves, wildlife refuges, and native people's reservations. This is a higher percentage than any other country. It has 850 species of birds, 280 species of mammals, 220 species of reptiles, and 1,200 species of orchids

Columbus arrived on the Caribbean side at present-day Puerto Limon in 1502. He noted the lush vegetation and prosperous indigenous people, bestowing the name of Costa Rica, "rich coast." He was fooled by gold pendants some of them wore. Unfortunately for Spanish greed, this jewelry was the only gold in the region, obtained over many generations of searching streambeds and from trade with distant sources in Mexico. Early attempts to farm tobacco and cocoa for export ended in failure. The joke became that Columbus should have named it Costa Pobre—poor coast. With nothing to export, few Spanish settlers came. The rugged terrain, lack of navigable rivers, and the hostility of the natives were further barriers to colonization. The locals withdrew to the highlands to escape Spanish attempts to force them to work on plantations and mines. Many died of European diseases. Intermarriage produced the mestizos that form the majority today. Ticos are proud that they have so much European blood. Due to the colony's poverty, the Spanish did not impose the harsh feudal domination common in the rest of the New World. In the 16th and 17th centuries, many people owned their own small farms. The colonial overlords based in Guatemala were remote and paid little attention. Settlers were relatively free to govern themselves. Municipal councils governed cities, including the capital.

Independence came in 1821 with little effort. The Napoleonic Wars had made it nearly impossible for Spain to have contact with the New World. Spain was allied with France so the British Royal Navy prevented ships sailing from the Peninsula to the colonies. Furthermore, Army officers and civilian officials were needed in Europe. In Mexico and South America the local elites declared their independence from Spain. Even after Napoleon was defeated in 1815, the Mother Country could not immediately reassert control. The Spanish army sent to reconquer Mexico was constantly attacked, and back in Madrid a coup d'etat weakened its resolve. Mexico became independent in 1821, and Costa Rica simply declared its own independence. There was no fighting on its soil.

Ticos brag of their emerging democracy of the 19th century with yeoman farmers and urban merchants and artisans. Rural laborers were well paid. The coffee crop, introduced about 1740, was typically grown by small farmers. That idyllic picture is partly a myth. Coffee was also cultivated on big estates as well as family farms. The large growers came to dominate the export trade. Wealthy investors from home and abroad invested in railroads. Foreign fruit companies established banana plantations, for example, the United Fruit Company. Income disparities increased. The rural elite and big city merchants dominated the government. An army was created and grew large.

In 1823 the other former colonies on the isthmus combined into the Central American Federated Republic, and Costa Rica joined them. The federation witnessed intense internal conflict, extending to open warfare, between the Liberal and Conservative members of the elite. The former were the merchants and the latter were the landowners. The Conservatives vigorously supported the Catholic Church. Fortunately, the worst fighting took place outside Costa Rica. In 1838 Costa Rica withdrew from the federation. The rest of the 19th century was unstable with a series of military dictatorships alternating with short periods of civilian rule.[15]

By the early 20th century, education was more available, and workers were organizing into unions. Many of the leaders were Communists. A unified General Confederation of Workers was created in 1913. The worldwide Great Depression caused a collapse of banana exports, resulting in much unemployment. A 1934 strike against the United Fruit Company was successful. Democratic institutions were strengthened early in the century. In the 1909 election President Gonzalez Viquez had permitted an opposition candidate to run. Four years later the constitution was amended to permit direct election of the president. The military seized power in 1917, but 2 years later, its failure to improve the economy led it to hand power back to civilians. Elections during the 1930s continued to be contentious and even violent. Voting fraud was common.

In 1948 a six-week civil war broke out. After losing the presidential vote, the conservatives refused to cede power, but the rebels defeated both the army and their union allies. The National Liberation junta, led by José Figueres, took power, and the following year promulgated a new constitution. It established the Supreme Electoral Tribunal. Electoral fraud was eliminated, women gained the franchise, and turnout reached 80%. The military was abolished. The reformers organized themselves into the National Liberation Party. Trade union power was fragmented, and the Communists lost influence. The politicians proved willing to transfer power if they lost. Cities grew and the economy prospered. The middle class grew.

The government is modeled on the United States. Voters directly elect a president for a term of 4 years. The unicameral Legislative Assembly has 57 seats, with members elected by direct, popular vote to serve 4-year terms. There is a Supreme Court. The leading parties are the National Liberation Party and the Citizen's Action Party, both moderate. The Ministry of the Environment and Energy is responsible for water, forests, climate change, geology, and energy.

Toward the end of the 19th century, exploration for a canal from the Atlantic to the Pacific drew foreign scientists to survey possible routes across Nicaragua, Costa Rica, and Panama. A number of them stayed to investigate its abundant birds and flowers. German naturalists Moritz Wagner and Karl Scherzer wrote extensively. The Danish botanist Anders Sandre Oersted studied plants. The British scientist William Moore Gabb investigated the geology, and the Lithuanian Joseph Warscewicz collected birds. The German Alexander von Frantzius came and stayed to teach natural history. The country's new National Geographic Institute was the focus for research. This scientific effort was far in advance of other Latin American countries. The institute forged close connections to the Smithsonian Institution in Washington, DC. Later the institute came under the supervision of the Costa Rican National Museum. The National School of Agriculture, established in 1926, promoted farming practices to prevent erosion, to avoid burning the land, and to protect forests. A modern national university was not established until 1940. Earlier a small one sponsored by the Catholic Church had existed, but it was abolished in 1888 because the government was anticlerical, and because secondary schools were inadequate to prepare matriculants.

Early in the 20th century, the government took steps to protect nature. In 1909 it passed the Fire Law to control burning forests. In 1913 it enacted a law to protect the area around the Poas Volcano. Also that year a law declared a 600-foot swath of land along the coast and an 800-foot swath along riverbanks to be safeguarded. In 1923 two laws regulated water. One prohibited dumping effluents from sewers, dairies, and slaughterhouses into rivers, and the other regulated watersheds. In 1930 the government hired forest guards and organized them under supervision of a forestry chief. Later the Law on Vacant Lands established preserves around the Poas and Irazu volcanoes and on both sides of the Cordillera Central. This also gave the government ownership of vacant lands. Unfortunately, implementation was weak. In 1940 Costa Rican delegates traveled to Washington, DC, where they signed the Convention on Nature Protection and Wildlife Preservation in the Western Hemisphere.[16]

Progress was erratic during the 1950s and 1960s. The 1953 Soil and Water Conservation Law authorized soil studies. That year President José Figueres appointed a commission to study tourism. The commissioners traveled to Peru, Mexico, Argentina, and the United States to learn about parks. A 1958 law regulated wildlife, including hunting and the rights of farmers to kill animals that interfered with their livestock and property.

Landownership was a continuing problem. In 1961 the Law on Lands and Colonization was passed. A goal was to see that rural people got ownership and to avoid an unfair concentration in the hands of wealthy corporations. It continued the democratic desire to strengthen the yeoman farmer. Yet these farmers were cutting down the virgin forests.

The first nature reserve, located at Cabo Blanco on the Nicoya Peninsula, came from a private initiative lead by foreigners. Olof Wessberg, a Swede, had settled there in 1955 to live an idyllic life in a tropical Eden. But settlers moved in, destroying the forest with swidden (slash-and-burn) agriculture, then selling the exhausted land to cattle ranchers and timber companies. To buy the land Wessberg solicited North American and European environmentalists. Donations to purchase the country's first nature reserve came from the Sierra Club, the Nature Conservancy, Friends of Nature, and the British World League against Vivisection.

The next reserve was sponsored by the government, not private donations. This was at Santa Rosa in the far northwest on the border with Nicaragua. It held historical importance because there in 1856 a Costa Rican brigade defeated an invasion by a North American filibusterer, William Walker, who had grandiose plans to establish his own personal empire in Nicaragua. The land itself was an example of a rare dry forest. The government purchased 300,000 acres to be a national monument in 1966 and later designated it as a national park.[17]

The comprehensive Forest Law of 1969 was developed by experts and top officials. The Minister of Agriculture Guillermo Yglesias assembled a team from government, the university, and groups representing conservationists, stock growers, and timber companies. They hired a Venezuelan forester, Nestor Altuve, to help draft the legislation. Altuve was then working with the UN Food and Agriculture Organization. The international expertise brought to bear was exemplary. The commissioners worried that if the Legislative Assembly did not pass a law soon, deforestation would have gone too far to rein in. The population was growing rapidly, and squatters were taking over land. Only 50% of the forests remained. While public support for the legislation was strong, so was opposition from landowners, ranchers, and loggers. The law finally passed on November 25.

The Forest Law provided that a National Parks Department could be created, but it had little funding and few employees at first. The head was Mario Boza, who had just earned a master's degree from the Inter-American Institute for Cooperation in Agriculture at Turrialba. Part of his studies included a long field trip, including Smokey Mountain National Park in

Tennessee. Boza first turned his attention to Poas Volcano because it was close to the capital of San José and connected by an all-weather highway. Plans were similar to US parks with a visitor's center, nature trails, interpretive signs and access to view the crater. The next year he visited Tortuguero, the site of marine turtle hatching, as a potential park. This was in a remote northeast of the country. His group included the former and future president, José Figueres and his wife Karen Olsen de Figueres (a Danish-American). Boza had a gift for friendship, and Doña Karen adopted national parks as her special mission as First Lady.[18]

The second park created was Santa Rosa in the north, elevated from its status as a monument. Many problems afflicted it. Squatters invaded, loggers cut timber, and nearby ranchers ran their cattle on it. One of the offending ranchers was the agriculture minister himself, and the park service was a branch of the Agriculture Ministry. Fortunately, Doña Karen was able to intervene with her husband.

With funding and staff so scarce, Boza solicited money from abroad. The World Wildlife Fund gave him a check for $5000 for Tortuguero, famous for the sea turtle nesting. He asked the International Union for Conservation of Nature (IUCN) in Switzerland to pay for feasibility studies. In the United States, he secured funding from the Conservation Foundation, the National Geographic Society, the Nature Conservancy, and the Ford Foundation. In 1971 US Peace Corps Volunteers arrived to help staff the Parks Department. Christopher Vaughan, eventually to become a permanent resident, came with the Peace Corps to oppose commercial trade in endangered species. Exporters were shipping dozens, even hundreds, of quetzals, parrots, sloths, ocelots, and green turtles for the black market. To expose these merchants of death, he published color photographs. The British Volunteer Service Organization also sent staff.[19]

Manuel Antonio Park originated from local advocacy. Now the second most visited park, it was established in 1972 after people in the nearby town of Quepos on the Pacific Coast agitated for it. Foreign developers were beginning construction of a big hotel, which offended the citizens, who still revered their radical syndicalist activity in the 1930s, and more recently had elected communists to the Legislative Assembly. Locals were demonstrating against the new hotel, and some had resorted to sabotage. Today, the small park between the beaches and the river is home to sloths, howler monkeys, iguanas, and crocodiles. There are 184 bird species, including toucans, motmots, and parakeets.

In contrast, Corcovado Park on the remote Osa Peninsula in the South had a troubled beginning. The rain forest, extending over 100,000 acres, was unique on the Pacific Coast, with exuberant flora and rare animals. It ranks as one of the most biologically diverse regions on earth. But its valuable timber was becoming possible to reach. Worse yet, gold had been discovered. Settlers had been clearing land for farms and had even done a little mining. To investigate the possibilities, the Parks Department sent Olof Wessberg, the Swedish advocate of the first nature reserve in Cabo Blanco in the North. Tragically, he was assassinated by the guide accompanying him. The park's establishment had the full support of the president, Daniel Oduber, who immediately saw the region's potential to foster tourism. At that time, Costa Rica had not begun its ecotourism industry. It had few foreign visitors and few parks as destinations. The phenomenon grew swiftly.

The Association for the Conservation of Nature (ASCONA) was founded in 1972 in response to the first World Environmental Summit at Stockholm. It began with a full range of activity. It lobbied for parks, urban planning, and watersheds. It opposed pesticides, mining damage, and industrial pollution. In 1983 it opposed the oil pipeline across the isthmus. The committee against the pipeline was able block its construction. The controversy hurt ASCONA; however, many members left and financial support diminished. It remains today much weaker. The Costa Rican Ecology Association (AECO) was founded in 1988 as a broad-based organization for education and lobbying. It is now affiliated with Friends of the Earth.

Like many other developing countries, Costa Rica suffered from the worldwide economic crisis. After 1979 oil prices increased fourfold, sparking a recession, and the republic was borrowing heavily. Its foreign debt was the equivalent to $1500 per person. Inflation rose 10% annually and unemployment doubled. President Rodrigo Carazo suspended payments to the International Monetary Fund, and the IMF retaliated by demanding harsh austerity measures. Domestically, there was little money for parks. The department was reduced to begging from foreign environmental groups.

On the southern border La Amistad International adjoins a park on the Panamanian side. These rugged mountains, extending 200,000 hectares in Costa Rica and a similar area in Panama, have some of the greatest species diversity on the globe. Travel is very difficult due to the steep terrain and high altitudes. Similarly, farming is almost impossible. Indigenous people have hung on there, unlike the rest of the country. The government has established reservations. The concept of the park originated in 1974 with the visit of a UNESCO representative. Eight years passed, however, before it became official.

Santa Rosa Park in the north became embroiled in international affairs in 1983. For many years, the Somoza family, dictators of Nicaragua, had owned a nearby ranch just over the border as a refuge during times when politics became too hot. The last of the family lost power in 1979, forced out by the Sandinista party. The American administration of Ronald Reagan considered the Sandinistas to be pro-Communist, and sponsored guerilla forces, labeled the *contras*, in opposition. They used the old ranch in Costa Rica as an illegal staging area. The US CIA and the Pentagon brought in troops and agents to train the Nicaraguan *contras* and tried to subvert some Costa Rican Civil Guards. They constructed an airfield. The new president, Oscar Arias, denounced the project and closed the airfield. In retaliation, the Americans reduced foreign aid from $180 million to $85 million. In Washington, the scandal became public, and Reagan's top national security officials were forced to resign.

By the end of the 1980s, the park situation stabilized. Many parks and reserves like Areal, Monteverde, and Corcovado had been created, and there was less land remaining for expansion. Tour companies were bringing in North Americans and Europeans in large numbers. President Arias earned the Nobel Peace Prize in 1987 for his work to end civil wars in Nicaragua and El Salvador, improving the country's reputation. Paradoxically, the wars had brought Central America publicity, attracting potential visitors. The Parks Department had wisely directed construction of hotels outside the park boundaries, both protecting nature and giving a boost to local enterprise rather than outside hotel chains. Local entrepreneurs saw the potential for amusements beyond pure nature loving like white-water rafting and zip lines. Moreover, Costa Rica had a long tradition of privately owned nature areas.

Agriculture is the enemy of the environment. Ranchers cut down the forest to pasture beef cattle. The country sells vast quantities of lean, almost-starving cows to Burger King in the United States. Without the forests, peasants who formerly lived using swidden farming, can no longer live there and must leave. Coffee, on the other hand, is a crop that demands intensive labor and has traditionally provided a good living for yeoman farmers. Coffee requires 130 days of work per year for each hectare, while cattle require only six. Thus, the crop provides 20 times the employment per hectare.

Ecotourism is growing, bringing over a million foreign visitors annually who spend over a billion dollars. It earns more than the traditional exports of bananas and coffee combined. Travelers come to the Arenal and Poas volcanos, to the Los Angeles Cloud Forest Reserve, and to beaches like Manuel Antonio Park. Parks like Tartuquero are famous as sites for sea turtles to lay eggs and hatch. A few critics worry that Costa Rica has exhausted its potential for ecotourism. It is being loved to death with too many visitors. Moreover, some tourism is decidedly not ecological. Construction on the Gulf of Papagayo on the Pacific Coast features high-rise hotels, golf courses, and shopping malls.

Costa Rica has been a leader in debt for nature swaps, totaling $125 million. Indeed, in the early days of the concept, nearly three-quarters of the swaps in the world went to this country. Money can come from groups like the Nature Conservancy or WWF or from national governments. In 2007 the Nature Conservancy organized payments totaling $13 million to buy $26 million of government debt, doubling their investment. The private contribution was only $1 million while the US government agreed to pay $12 million under authority of the US Tropical Forest Conversation Act. The funds are going to Corcovado Park and Totuguero Park.[20] Earlier on an experimental basis, Costa Rica was also active after the Kyoto Protocol agreeing to absorb reductions in greenhouse emissions. It signed several deals with the Netherlands. Ultimately, nothing came of this as no structure was ever established under the protocol.

CONCLUSION

Kenya does not have a history of citizen participation like the countries considered so far. Its famous park system came as a legacy of the British colonial government. Today, native Kenyans staff it and support it, but the parks were largely in their present form at the time of independence. Air and water pollution control has not been a priority for ordinary people, who are too concerned with getting jobs and feeding their families. Although Costa Ricans have more citizen participation, much of the early environmental movement owes thanks to foreign residents like Olof Wessberg, Doña Karen, Nestor Altuve, and Peace Corps volunteers. Ticos such as

Mario Boza, who led in the 1950s and 1960, traveled abroad extensively to learn about parks. One instance of popular support was the labor union members who advocated establishing Manuel Antonio Park. The Ticos' devotion to democracy did not translate into environmental activism.

International interest groups like WWF and the IUCN have been active in Kenya. In Costa Rica two key groups are the Association for the Conservation of Nature and the Costa Rican Ecology Association. International groups like Friends of the Earth, the Nature Conservancy, and WWF are active.

Kenyan parties are based on tribes and believe they have more important business than protecting nature. Parties, unfortunately, are sometimes the mechanism for exploiting the parks and reserves via corruption. Parties are also interested in the ownership of land for agriculture and have made it central to the 2007 and 2013 elections. In Costa Rica the two main parties are centrist and support protecting nature.

During the colonial period in Kenya government agencies like the Game Department and the Forest Department established the parks and reserves, and with various reorganizations, continue to maintain them. Today, these natural areas would probably not be doing nearly as well without this bureaucratic presence. Their mission has often put them in conflict with ordinary citizens. In Costa Rica, the Ministry of Agriculture had an early role, but often favored farming and timber over nature. The small National Parks Department was frequently starved for money.

Through the colonial powers, Kenya was a leader in international protection of animals when the British signed a treaty with Italy to prevent smuggling ivory out through Somalia, followed in 1933 by the International Conference on the Preservation of Wildlife (a predecessor of CITES). Today, hosting the headquarters of the UN Environmental Program puts it in a central role. In 1940 Costa Ricans signed the Convention on Nature Protection and Wildlife Preservation in the Western Hemisphere. In 1972 they attended the Stockholm earth summit, and were inspired to establish the Association for Conservation of Nature. The country is active in groups like the International Union for the Conservation of Nature.

Both Kenya and Costa Rica are indebted to others for initiating their parks. For both, the model was the national park movement starting in the United States, Canada, and Australia. The British colonial officials set up Kenya's parks and reserves. Costa Rica depended on the experts like Nestor Altuve from the UN Food and Agriculture Organization and

Christopher Vaughan. Yet one may turn this on its head to note that the British protection of nature in its colony was greater and earlier than at home in the British Isles, and that Costa Rica leads the world in conserving a quarter of its land in parks and reserves.

NOTES

1. Edward O. Wilson, *Biophilia* (Cambridge, Mass.: Harvard UP, 1984).
2. David Gordon, "A History of Kenya," in *Kenya, the Land, the People and the Nation*, ed. Mario Azevedo (Durham, S.C.: Carolina Academic Press, 1993), p. 51.
3. Godfrey Mwakikagile, *Kenya: Identity of a Nation* (Pretoria, South Africa: New Africa Press, 2007), pp. 29–34.
4. Akbarali Thobhani, "Political Developments during the 1990s," in *Modern Kenya*, ed. Mary Ann Watson (Lanham, Md.: University Press of America, 2000), pp. 12–19.
5. Theodore Roosevelt, *African Game Trails* (New York, Scribner, 1920).
6. E. I. Steinhart, "Hunters, Poachers and Gamekeepers," *Journal of African History*, 30 (1989), pp. 248–249.
7. Steinhart, "Hunters, Poachers, and Gamekeepers," p. 249.
8. Steinhart, "Hunters, Poachers, and Gamekeepers," p. 262.
9. Timothy Armstrong, "Wildlife Conservation in Kenya," in *Modern Kenya*, ed. Watson, p. 99.
10. Joy K. Asiema and Francis D. P. Situma, "Indigenous Peoples and the Environment: The Case of the Pastoral Maasai of Kenya," in *Endangered Peoples* (Niwot, Colo.: University Press of Colorado, 1994), pp. 159, 161–163.
11. Martha Honey, *Ecotourism and Sustainable Development*, 2nd ed. (Washington, D.C.: Island Press, 2008), pp. 313–319.
12. Honey, *Ecotourism*, p. 299.
13. UN Environmental Programme, *Kenya: Atlas of our Changing Environment* (Nairobi: UNEP, 2000) p. 143.
14. Esther Duflo, Michael Greenstone, and Rema Hanna, *Indoor Air Pollution, Health and Economic Well-Being* (Cambridge, Mass.: Department of Economics, MIT), February 2008.
15. John A. Booth, *Costa Rica: Quest for Democracy* (Boulder, Colo.: Westview, 1998), p. 39.
16. Sterling Evans, *The Green Republic* (Austin: Univ. of Texas Press, 1999), p. 55.
17. Evans, *The Green Republic*, pp. 63–64.
18. Evans, *The Green Republic*, pp. 73–76.
19. Evans, *The Green Republic*, p. 87.
20. MSNBC, "Costa Rica Gets Largest Debt-for-Nature Swap," Oct. 17, 2007, Web.

8

Russia and Its Neighbors

In contrast to the democracies considered so far, Russia had a Communist government from 1917 to 1991 and many of those patterns linger. Moreover, the Soviet Union imposed its communist system on Eastern Europe after the end of World War II. Czechoslovakia exemplifies the situation there. By the middle of the 20th century, both Russia and Eastern Europe were highly industrialized and suffered extreme air and water pollution.

Russia is a vast land, stretching across Europe and Asia for nearly 7000 kilometers from the Baltic Sea to the Pacific. The land runs from the Arctic south to China, Mongolia, the Black Sea, and Rumania. In size it is twice as big as China or the United States. The original people were Slavs, who lived in the forests in harmony with nature. They farmed, hunted, and trapped, and used the broad rivers for trade. In the ninth century AD the Rus tribe established a government based in Kiev, in present-day Ukraine. The Rus traded furs, honey, and wax with Sweden to the west and with the Byzantine Empire to the south. By the late 10th century, they were a strong military force in the region, and had adopted the Orthodox version of Christianity, converted by missionaries sent from Constantinople (now Istanbul). In 1237 the Mongols invaded from Asia, winning control of Russia for two centuries. To the east, their empire extended to China and Korea.

Russian principalities continued to pay tribute to the Mongols (later called Tatars or Tartars) until 1480, when Ivan the Great won independence for Moscovy. Ruling from the Kremlin, their hilltop fortification, the grand dukes expanded their power. In 1552 his grandson, Ivan the Terrible, won control of the Tatar states of Kazan and Astrakhan, thus becoming an empire. The year 1605 began a Time of Troubles with many rivals claiming the crown, and the Poles invading. In 1612 the Poles were expelled, and Michael Romanov became czar, beginning a dynasty lasting until 1917.

Peter the Great, who reigned from 1689 to 1725, sought to Europeanize Russia. He created a modern army and navy, curbed the power of the nobles, modernized finance and administration, encouraged education, and promoted industry. His masterpiece was to build the entirely new capital on the Gulf of Finland off the Baltic Sea, named for his patron saint, Saint Petersburg. It was constructed in the Western style by architects brought from Italy, France, and the Netherlands. At the same time, Peter continued exploiting the peasants, half of whom were serfs, bound to the land, and little more than slaves. Russia developed a dual society with cities on the European pattern of aristocrats, an educated class who were thoroughly modern, and countryside dwellers tied to the traditional ways.

In the early 19th century, the Romantic Movement swept in from Germany, England, and France. Leaders were Alexander Pushkin and Mikhail Lermontov. Lermontov, who lived in the Caucasus Mountains as a boy and later returned as an army officer, wrote poems glorifying the beauty of the region. During this period, the champions of modernization were countered by Slavophiles who wanted to maintain the nation in its traditional manner. They celebrated the countryside and its wholesome peasants. Westernized elites were limited chiefly to St. Petersburg, Moscow, and a few other places. Lermontov wrote this poem:

> I come out to the path, alone,
> Night and wildness are referred to God,
> Through the mist, the road gleams with stone,
> Stars are speaking in the shining lot.
> There is grave and wonderful in heaven;
> Earth is sleeping in a pale-blue light…

Russia was late to industrialize, hence spared much of the pollution nightmare of the 19th century. It remained largely a rural agricultural society, where peasants lived according to the annual cycle of nature, existing in harmony with it, or at least lacking the capacity to do it much harm. A proto-environmental group was the Society for the Acclimatization of Animals and Plants, which began in 1858. By that time scientists and hunters were voicing alarm about the decline of wildlife. For instance, the auroch was extinct by then, and on the Pacific Coast, the Steller sea cow was hunted to extinction in only 30 years. The government passed a Forest Code in 1888, but it was weak and ineffective. The 1892 hunting law replaced one from a century earlier but was riddled with exemptions. Its goal was more to provide plentiful game for aristocratic hunters than to protect animals. In spite of Russia's late start, by the end of the 19th century, industry was developing rapidly. In terms of manufacturing, it was the fastest-growing country in the world.

The Communists, who won power in October 1917, exalted industry. This was a central tenet of Marxist analysis, for without it there could be no revolution, and no building of socialism. This was both because Marx believed the revolution would occur in an industrial state when the proletariat rose up against the owners, and because the goal of Communism was material well-being. The new regime promoted industrialization ruthlessly. Nature was to be exploited for the benefit of the proletariat. All natural resources and nearly all private property became owned and operated by the state. During the 1920s the government invested in coal mining, steel making, and chemicals. Electric generating plants were built, both hydro and coal, and the grid was extended. Electricity became a symbol of the accomplishments of the revolution. In the 1930s, peasants were forced off their farms, where for generations they had cultivated the land with a respect for the soil, and were herded onto huge collective farms, which depended on chemical fertilizer and heavy machinery, and which eroded the soil. Lenin and Stalin promoted gigantic projects like hydroelectric and irrigation dams that dried up delicate grasslands. Hydroelectric dams on the Volga and Dnieper Rivers built by Gulag prisoners, flooded vast areas and ruined much farmland.

Fortunately for the environment, the most grandiose proposal was never completed. This was a scheme to supposedly change the climate of central Russia by diverting two rivers, the Ob and the Yenesi, which flowed north to the Arctic Ocean to flow south to the Caspian Sea. The purpose was to provide irrigation for agriculture. Additionally, it would have made the Arctic Ocean more salty by reducing the flow of freshwater into the sea. A saltier ocean would not freeze as easily, tipping the balance to an ice free Arctic. Planners believed this would allow ship navigation and permit agriculture farther north.

The dams the Soviets actually built did enough damage. The Aral Sea dried up to a third of its natural size. Fish everywhere died out due to pollution. Rivers and lakes suffered from contamination. The Caspian Sea (actually a freshwater lake) was poisoned by agricultural chemicals and untreated sewage. PCBs and DDT contaminated many rivers. Lake Baikal, the world's deepest and purist freshwater lake, succumbed to pollution after a factory to manufacture cellulose cord for tires was constructed on its shore. Ironically, by the time the factory was completed, the USSR had switched to petroleum-based cord, so the output was never used for tires. Originally, Lake Baikal had been the home to 1,200 unique aquatic species, including the only freshwater seals in the world. Today, many of these species are extinct or endangered.

Marxist ideology optimistically asserted that industry and technology would provide more and more material benefits. Overpopulation and resource depletion were not problems according to Marx. Furthermore, without private ownership and a market system, Communist incentives hurt the environment. Managers were rewarded for their gross output, not profitability or protecting the environment or worker health and safety, or even using energy efficiently. Within the new Soviet Union that replaced the old empire, the core of European Russia continued to exploit the colonial areas like Siberia, the Far East, Kazakhstan, and other republics of central Asia.

The consequence of 70 years of Communist industrialization was an environmental disaster. The air is polluted in nearly all cities and in rural areas near factories and refineries. Toxic metals are dumped into creeks or left exposed in barrels that rusted so the poison leaks into the water table. Dioxin is a threat in Kuban, the lower Volga, the Far East, and the Azov regions. Municipal sewage treatment is often inadequate, and in a few cities, drinking water is unsafe. Male life expectancy has been falling and is now only 59 years. Causes are AIDS, heroin, smoking, alcoholism and suicide. Moreover, infant mortality has been rising, and abortions are common. The result is population decline. The country is projected to decline from the current 143 million to 111 million by 2050, a loss of 32 million people and a decrease of more than 20 percent.

Nuclear electric plants and military facilities present dangers of radiation. In 1957 a nuclear waste storage tank at the Mayak nuclear weapons center exploded. This secret nuclear city is near Chelyabinsk in the Ural Mountains. A radioactive cloud contaminated an area of 20,000 square kilometers. The accident was kept secret for three decades, 11,000 people were evacuated, and the region was permanently placed off limits.

The worst nonmilitary accident was the meltdown at Chernobyl in 1986. Its location was in northern Ukraine near the border with Russia and Belarus. On the night of April 25, Reactor No. 4 was scheduled to be shut down for routine maintenance. A few technicians wanted to perform an unauthorized experiment on how late in the process the turbine could be restarted. They shut off the emergency core cooling system, and when the experiment went awry, further blundered by pulling out the control rods that were supposed to slow down the reaction. Nearly at once the core heated up dramatically. Part of the core "went critical," exploding like an atomic bomb with the force of four tons of TNT. Four seconds later a second explosion, perhaps nuclear or perhaps steam, blasted the thousand-ton concrete roof off the reactor. Radioactive material spewed into the atmosphere. Some drifted west over Sweden and Germany, where monitoring stations detected this mysterious radiation.

The government's immediate reaction followed the old Soviet pattern. This was in spite of the recent reforms at the highest levels. Only a year earlier, Mikhail Gorbachev had taken power in a move toward openness and restructuring. His appointment followed a long period of economic and social decline under Leonid Brezhnev, characterized by stagnation, corruption, and cronyism. On the other hand, this was also a period of diplomatic detente with the West. Brezhnev and President Nixon had signed treaties limiting the use of nuclear weapons, and scientists and experts from the two nations had exchanged visits. By the mid-1980s, the old Communist bosses finally recognized that their system was failing and hoped Gorbachev could salvage it. But for 10 days after the Chernobyl explosion, the Soviet government blacked out news of the accident, in spite of 30 deaths, 238 casualties from radiation, and the evacuation of thousands. Shortwave radio broadcasts from Western Europe had been telling the Soviet citizens of the event for a week.

The secret could no longer be hidden. In a television broadcast, Gorbachev admitted the problem, promised to aid the victims, and pledged to tell the truth. The Chernobyl accident had the effect of unmasking the failings of the old system. The reformers used the incident as a reason to remove many party officials and bureaucrats from their positions. Ordinary citizens came to speak more openly about the dangers of radiation. One consequence was to advance the reform effort. This was not the only case of citizen outrage against environmental danger during the 1980s. People living near the cellulose cord factory on Lake Baikal had voiced their objections, and people living near the Aral Sea had complained about its water being robbed for irrigation. Soviet citizens felt able to object to environmental degradation in a situation when they did not feel safe in objecting to political or social injustice. In 1988 the Socio-Ecological

Union was established as an umbrella for 150 small groups. A few of these had been around since as far back as the 1960s. One, for example, sought to protect historic buildings and paintings. These included sacred icons, hence attracted religious believers. The government was more willing to tolerate dissent on environmental issues than on other ones, because they were not viewed as a direct political threat to the Communist system.

From the Bolshevik Revolution in 1917 until the end of the Soviet Union in 1991, autonomous institutions did not exist as they did in Western nations. A partial exception was the Academy of Sciences, which traced its origins back to 1724, when it was founded under the auspices of Czar Peter the Great. Many early members were immigrant scientists recruited from Western Europe, and they continued their home traditions of pure, rather than applied, science. This independence came to be a hallmark of Russian science. In the eight months of the moderate Kerensky regime after the czar was deposed in February 1917, but before the Bolsheviks took over in October, the interim government created several research institutes, which continued after the communist coup. Once the Communists consolidated their power by 1921, however, they largely coopted the academy, demanding that its members follow the party line. They were not completely successful in this, and the academy remained one of the few places in the Soviet Union where dissenting opinions were occasionally found. The academy excelled in physics, mathematics, and chemistry that supported the military programs in nuclear science, rocketry, and aeronautics. Biology was weak, and ecology was nonexistent.

Besides the Academy of Sciences, the early Soviets tolerated a few other organizations. Because Marxism was supposedly scientific, scientists were among the few people who could criticize it. In 1925 the academy established the Inter-Ministerial Council for Nature Protection, which was to advise on projects. Yet when it objected to elements of the Five Year Plan, Stalin shut it down. Nevertheless, nature lovers were viewed as harmless, and thus tolerated. The All-Russian Society for the Protection of Nature was established in 1924. During the 1930s, the Soviets established nature preserves, yet their purpose was not true protection, but for study as baselines to compare to newly developed industrial areas.[1]

Until Stalin's death in 1953, Soviet scientists had minimal contact with Western science. Even technical publications from the West were censored. The era of Nikita Khrushchev permitted slightly more freedom. At this time the Soviet Union launched the Sputnik satellite, and continued with more triumphs in space, based on its military rockets.

Two scientific disasters—the Chelyabinsk nuclear accident and a rocket explosion—caused some dissent among the scientists.

Government: From soon after the 1917 Revolution until 1991 the Communist Party dominated the Soviet Union. Vladimir Ilyich Lenin soon centralized power with authority vested solely in the party. Other parties and free newspapers were banned. The secret police, the Cheka (later called the KGB), spied on citizens. Courts no longer exercised independent authority. Lenin seized ownership of major industries. The government bureaucracy, supervised in detail by the Communist Party, managed every aspect of the economy and society. This extended to marriage and the family. Control grew tighter after Josef Stalin came to power after Lenin's premature death in 1924. Western critics labeled this totalitarianism, meaning the party and the state sought total control. They equated it to Nazism in Germany and Fascism in Italy. Although the Soviet Union formally had representative bodies like the Congress of People's Deputies, elections were a sham, and only candidates selected by the party were elected. Parallel to the government were Communist Party organs like the Party Congress. Party control was organized from the smallest local level to the USSR level. Any semblance of democracy was phony. In theory the Congress of the People's Deputies elected the Supreme Soviet to govern when it was not in session, and in turn this body elected the Council of Ministers and adopted economic plans and budgets. The parallel, and actually more important, party organ was the Politburo (Political Bureau of the Central Committee of the Communist Party). This was where the real power lay. The party secretary was the ruler.

The USSR was geographically nearly as extensive as the old Empire of the czar, thus including many people were where not ethnically Russian. The largest minority was the Ukrainians, and other major groups were the Turkic in central Asia. Lenin gave all these groups their own geographical regions, establishing republics, or autonomous regions. The largest, Russia, also had republics within itself, known as the Russian Federation. Thus, the name of the overall federation was the Union of Soviet Socialist Republics. Regarding Russia, it was a double federation. The republics were not in fact autonomous, but subject to the rule of the Communist Party, and central control from Moscow.

Besides organizing the USSR along ethnic lines, Lenin had to reconcile Marxist theory to the realities of the revolution. Marx had predicted that the revolution would come in cities as the proletariat rose up against the capitalists. But Russia was more than 80% rural, and the peasants were not industrial workers. Lenin revised Marx to say that the poor peasants, who were the vast majority, were natural allies of the industrial workers, whereas the wealthy peasants were the natural allies of the capitalists. Lenin considered that a major task for the party was to build an alliance between the poor peasants and the industrial workers.

Josef Stalin, who came to power in 1924 after the death of Lenin, was a ruthless dictator. In 1928 he reversed a short experiment in economic flexibility and mandated government control of the economy. Soon he ordered collectivization of agriculture, which proved a disaster. The more prosperous peasants who objected to having their farms seized were exiled or shot. At this time Stalin began the first Five-Year Plan encompassing all industry. By the 1930s he became obsessed with gaining absolute power and began a series of purges. Many of the original Communists were accused of disloyalty, found guilty in show trials, and executed. The next step was to purge army officers who might be disloyal. Those not shot were sent to prison camps in Siberia and remote places, a system known as the gulag. The German invasion in 1941 forced Stalin to moderate his harshest policies. He needed the support of the people and the skills of the army officers. After the defeat of Germany in 1945, Stalin returned to totalitarianism.

After Stalin's death in 1953, power passed to Nikita Khrushchev, who ended the worst abuses but continued strict control of the Communist Party. The economy was run according to Five Year Plans, with emphasis on heavy industries like steel, chemicals, cement, and heavy machinery. These all polluted the air and water. Later Khrushchev tried to provide more consumer goods for the ordinary citizen but was only partially successful. His modest attempts at liberalization threatened the old-line Communists, who forced him from power in 1964. His successor was Leonid Brezhnev, who perpetuated the old policies of strict control by the Party and by the Moscow hierarchy. The consequence was economic stagnation.

This was not a good era for the environment either. Performance continued to be measured by gross productivity, that is, the more tons of steel or numbers of tractors manufactured the better. The efficiency in producing the steel or tractors was not counted. External damage to air or water was not relevant.

By the time of Brezhnev's death from old age in 1982, he was unable to cope and nearly senile. But after brief terms by two other old men, who soon died, even the old-line Communists realized it was time for reform. They put Mikhail Gorbachev in power. Gorbachev advocated moderate steps of openness (*glasnost*) and restructuring (*perestroika*). He believed that limited market freedom and less heavy-handed central planning would bring prosperity and satisfy the people. In fact, he just opened the door to radical changes. A lighter version of Communism would not be enough.

Boris Yeltsin at first supported Gorbachev, coming to Moscow at his request to run the municipal government. They soon quarreled and Yeltsin was removed from the Soviet Union politburo, but he then won the office of president of the Russian Federation. The situation became chaotic, with Yeltsin and those who wanted radical reform on one side and the old-line Communists on the other. Gorbachev was caught in the middle. Yeltsin's solution was to dissolve the Soviet Union, which he did with the cooperation of the 14 other republics, most of which had their own complaints against Gorbachev. The newly independent Russian Federation had democratic features with the popular election of the president and the parliament. The lower chamber was called the Duma and the upper chamber was the Council. The Duma was elected by a combination of direct and proportional voting, and the Council was elected by regional officials. Half-dozen political parties hold seats. The largest is United Russia, followed by the Communists, the Liberal Democrats and A Just Russia. United Russia backs Vladimir Putin faithfully. The Communists are highly nationalistic and anti-Semitic. The so-called Liberal Democratic Party is, in fact, fascist. The A Just Russia Party advocates a welfare state. A small Green Party existed for a few years, but because it could not win elections, in 2008 decided to transform itself into an interest group. The chief executive of the Russian Federation is the president, who in turn appoints a prime minister. Yeltsin served as president until 1999, followed by his protégé, Putin.

Putin served two terms of four years until 2008, when he was required to retire according to the Constitution. He was originally a bureaucrat in the secret police and sought to centralize his power. Russia became less democratic. Putin did not want to give up power, so he manipulated the election of his protégé, Dmitriy Medvedev, who immediately appointed Putin as prime minister, in which capacity he continued to rule much as before. The presidential system of Russia is less like that of the United States, and more like that of France, having both a president and a prime minister. The powers of the president are extensive. Besides appointing the prime minister, the president appoints key members of the cabinet and the heads of seven major regions. He can dissolve parliament. He can propose bills to parliament, veto bills, and issue decrees. The president directs the foreign, defense, and interior ministries and the Federal Security Service (formerly the secret police, the KGB). The prime minister directs the other ministries. Unlike Western democracies, the ministers are not members of parliament but are typically career bureaucrats.

In the 2012 election Putin once more ran for the presidency on the United Russia Party ticket, which he won with 64% of the vote. There were many accusations of fraud, and thousands demonstrated against the election in December. International observers concluded that the voting itself was satisfactory, but that the counting of the votes was not fair in a third of the polling places. Nevertheless, Putin returned to power, and appointed Medvedev prime minister as he had agreed before the election campaign.

Tensions between the central government in Moscow and the regional governments have characterized politics since 1991. In fact there are 89 different regional bodies. The Russian Federation consists of 21 republics, 47 oblasts (provinces), nine krays (territories), ten okrugs (autonomous districts), and two cities (Moscow and St. Petersburg). The 21 republics are based on ethnic groups. Examples are Dagestan and North Ossetia in the Caucasus Mountains. The most troublesome has been Chechnya, which has twice tried to win independence and is now occupied by Russian troops who installed a pro-Moscow leader. (These are not to be confused with the now independent former Soviet republics like Georgia, Armenia, or Azerbaijan.) Russian federalism has been described as asymmetrical because national laws and programs do not necessarily apply equally to all subdivisions. Putin moved to regularize the system by combining the subdivisions into seven new federal districts, over which he appointed the head. Next, he provided that all governors of the subdivisions would be appointed by him.

Environmental laws in the USSR date to the 1960s when many of the 15 constituent republics passed laws. The Russian Republic passed a law stating that "conservation is a major state task and a concern of all people."[2] Specific air pollution regulations were promulgated in 1973 and the Air Quality Control Act passed in 1980. The Sanitary Epidemiology Administration began monitoring air quality in 1955 and in 1978 gained enforcement authority. The 1972 Water Code provided for permits for use and discharge. Laws enacted at the time required planning and protection of the land. The USSR Council of Ministers adopted a resolution to require recycling. The official Soviet standards were strict. For instance, whereas the United States permitted 10 milligrams of carbon monoxide per cubic meter of air, the Soviets permitted only 6 milligrams. These laws, however, were not enforced. In the 1970s the military banned publishing information about the environment, supposedly for security reasons. In 1988 the USSR established the Committee for Environmental Protection Agency (Goskompriroda), later to become the Ministry of the Environment. The constitution adopted in 1993 after the breakup of the Soviet Union provides "Everyone shall have the right to favorable environment, reliable information about its state and for a restitution of damage inflicted on his health and property by ecological transgressions," and "Everyone shall be obliged to preserve nature and the environment, carefully treat the natural wealth."[3]

During this period the Soviet Union claimed to have environmental groups. For example, in 1990 Leningrad (now St. Petersburg) claimed to have 150, but most were small with only a dozen members and focused on a local issue. Many said their chief aims were to educate the public. Mass public demonstrations are another good technique to influence opinion, and perhaps government policy. To an extent these were default roles since they could not undertake activities as in Western countries like lobby legislators, influence bureaucrats, or obtain government reports. Some groups were phony, like the Committee to Save the Volga, which was a front for the ultra-nationalist Pamyat group.[4]

None of the larger political parties are strong advocates of environmental protection, and the one green party has not had much success. The Interregional Green Party began in 1991 as an expansion of a local party in St. Petersburg. It nominated candidates for parliament but never could reach the threshold of 7%.

Environmental issues played a role in the reforms under Gorbachev. Chernobyl was the most dramatic, but with his policy of openness came a stream of revelations about ecological disasters. Censorship was reduced, so newspapers and magazines began to publish data showing the extreme levels of pollution, which in turn fed public outrage. Across the Soviet Union a number of plants were closed and construction projects stopped. One example was the closing of the Baikalsk Pulp and Paper Plant, and another was the abandonment of the proposed Volga–Chograi canal.

Although the Soviet Union did not have autonomous interest groups like Western democracies, nevertheless, a few groups advocated their positions and influenced policy. The opponents of environmental protection were found in the state-owned industries. Most old-fashioned Communists supported the industries. The Marxist goal, after all, was materialism. The few voices in favor of protection came from scientists, journalists, writers, and a few dissidents. Goskompriroda did have an official duty of protection.

Local party officials sometimes sided with the environmentalists such as at Lake Baikal, but more often they were subservient to their Communist Party bosses. Governmental agencies responsible for forests and farmland faced conflicting pressures of exploitation and preservation. A few ecological organizations existed, but they were not fully independent of the government. For instance, the influence of the Socio-Ecological Union on policy was slight. During the 1980s ecological organizations attracted members who actually were more interested in other sorts of reform, such as nationalistic autonomy, rights of prisoners, and nuclear weapons control, because environmental groups were tolerated when other organizations were not. This meant that the groups had a number of members who had only a secondary interest in the environment.

Gorbachev's openness and restructuring outran the original goals he and his fellow reformers anticipated. In 1991 the entire Soviet Union collapsed, to be replaced by 15 independent countries based on the old parts of the USSR federation. In 1922 the Bolsheviks had organized the Union as a successor to the defunct empire. The largest unit by far, in terms of size and population, was Russia. The next largest was Ukraine. The third largest in Europe, Belarus, occupied the land between Russia and Poland. The three Baltic Sea republics of Latvia, Estonia, and Lithuania became independent as well. They had only been incorporated into the Union after the Red Army invasion at the beginning of World War II. These six republics were the most industrial ones. The nine others were underdeveloped regions ranging from Armenia to Kyrgystan. The first six, heavily industrialized and located in Europe, contrasted in their ecological problems with the other nine, with less industry and extending as far east as the border with China.

The Soviet Union's first international treaties affecting the environment addressed nuclear weapons. In 1963 the USSR signed the Test Ban Treaty with the United States and Great Britain. In their propaganda, the Soviets emphasized the importance of ending radioactive fallout from American bomb tests, although their tests actually generated more fallout. They next signed treaties and agreements to restrict the number of weapons and prevent weapons proliferation to other countries. The Soviet Union and the United States were both early proponents of the Law of the Sea Treaty because they wanted to ensure free transit of their navies, but they later took a secondary role in negotiations when its original goals were subordinated to the wishes of the underdeveloped countries. The USSR participated in the International Geophysical Year with a base in Antarctica and signed the Antarctic treaty. It intended to participate in the first Earth Summit in Stockholm, but at the last minute withdrew in protest when East Germany was excluded. In fact, the USSR had an unofficial delegation present, and the director of the conference briefed them almost daily. The Soviets were members of the International Whaling Commission, though they opposed moratorium proposals. In 1976 the USSR proposed a series of Europe-wide conferences emphasizing the dangers of nuclear weapons to the environment. They participated in the UN Environmental Program. In participating in multilateral groups, the Soviet Union tended to bend them to fit its political foreign policy aims.

As part of detente, in 1972 the United States and the Soviet Union signed a treaty on environmental cooperation. American experts visited the USSR, and Soviet experts visited the United States. For instance, a US group went to Lake Baikal. US EPA later expanded on these visits and added conferences. These bilateral efforts were much less subverted toward foreign policy aims than was the case with multilateral efforts. Cooperation inched forward until 1980 when President Jimmy Carter downgraded relations with the Soviets to punish them for invading Afghanistan. Ronald Reagan began his presidency hostile to the USSR, but moderated his stance within a few years, and at a summit meeting in Geneva in 1985, he and Gorbachev agreed to negotiate a treaty on environmental cooperation. Over the next 5 years, with reforms and then with the dissolution of the USSR, the situation became more like normal relations between two countries.

When Russia became independent of the USSR, it revised its environmental laws and agencies. Its 1993 constitution declared that the land and natural resources were to be protected, and that citizens were entitled to information about environmental dangers. The new parliament passed laws to safeguard the land, forests, wildlife, water, and the environment in general. Several interest groups soon came into operation: the Center for Ecological Policy, the Union for Chemical Security, the Center for the Protection of Wild Nature, and affiliates of Greenpeace and WWF. This turned out to be the high point for the movement. In 1994 the government changed the name of the key agency to the Ministry of Environmental Protection and Natural Resources but granted more importance to the resource side. Two years later a further reorganization established the State Committee on Environmental Protection (Goskomekologiya). The Ministry of Natural Resources continued with its responsibilities for resources. Two other ministries are for forests and for health. The

Health Ministry assumed responsibility for the Sanitary Epidemiologi-cal Inspectorate and downgraded its functions. In 2000 the Goskome-kologiya was abolished, and greater emphasis was placed on commercial exploitation of natural resources.

The collapse of the Russian economy after the reforms of Gorbachev and the dissolution of the USSR ironically reduced air and water pollution with the closing of old-fashioned inefficient factories and power plants. After the breakup, its economy contracted by a third or more. Inflation in 1996 was 2,500%, effectively destroying savings. The Russian transition from socialism to a market economy was sudden and brutal. Economic advisors advocated this shock as the most effective way, but the human suffering was great. The crisis came in August 1998 following the Asian financial collapse and the temporary low price for oil (Russia's chief export). Many banks failed. After a change of prime ministers, the government devalued the ruble and stopped payment on bonds worth $40 billion. Amazingly, the economy bounced back, growing at an annual rate of 7%. High prices for its chief exports of oil, natural gas, metals, and timber helped. As of 2010 the GDP was $2.2 trillion according to purchasing power parity, rank-ing seventh in the world. Per capita income was $15,900 per year based on purchasing power parity. (China's was $7,600.) On the positive side, a middle class is emerging, and 80% of businesses are privately owned. On the negative side, poverty is extensive, corruption is endemic, and orga-nized crime permeates society. There is an enormous disparity between rich and poor. A handful of men control the oil business. Corruption adds to the expense of conducting a business.

Some critics maintain that the corruption has overwhelmed the govern-ment, claiming it has been reconstituted as a vast criminal enterprise. It is a money-making apparatus engaged in stealing and extortion. The Federal Security Service exploits the big companies and the local police exploit the small ones. At least during the old days the KGB and the police were sub-servient to the Communist Party. The various agencies are no longer oper-ating as governmental bureaucracies, but as rogues. It is a kleptocracy, meaning a government that steals from its citizens. Putin and the top leaders fear that they can never let go of their control because if they retire, their enemies will go after them for criminal prosecution. All top leaders take elaborate measures for their physical safety. They employ bodyguards and live in secure gated communities. Many own houses in the West and are sending their children there for education and careers. Their fortunes are in Swiss bank accounts. The most rapacious have gotten land and property registered in their names personally instead of for their agencies or companies. This way they can hold it more securely and eventually pass it down to their biological heirs. The critics maintain that political analysis that examines the tensions between the liberal and reactionary forces is naïve. Parliamentary debate in the Duma is a sideshow. The 2011 Arab Spring with democratic demonstrations in Tunis and Cairo terrified the Russian leadership because it showed how ordinary citizens could overthrow a repressive regime.[5]

Civil society refers to the nongovernmental organizations in a society, such as churches, labor unions, clubs, Boy Scouts, interest groups, environmental organizations, and so forth. They are so common in Western democracies that they are often not even mentioned but that is not true for Russia. After 1917 the Communists vigorously stamped out autonomous bodies and replaced them with governmental ones. This was a major aspect of Totalitarianism. The Orthodox Church was nearly eliminated, replaced by official atheism. The Young Pioneers became the only children's group. Environmental groups were not welcomed, although a few appeared in the 1980s. Since 1991 civil society has emerged. The Orthodox Church has reemerged strongly with over half the people saying they adhere to its faith. The Federation of Independent Trade Unions is the successor to the defunct Soviet one, and had been critical of the government on many occasions. Nevertheless, many do not consider it sufficiently independent.

While groups are not strong, a multiplicity exists. The Socio-Ecological Union continues to be the largest with over 250 member groups. Activities include monitoring chemicals and radioactivity, supporting forests and nature reserves and education. Green Cross Russia was founded by Mikhail Gorbachev, himself, after becoming unemployed with the dissolution of the USSR. The All Russia Wild Nature Protection Society offers advice to agencies and local governments. International groups are active, but only a few. The Wildlife Conservation Society, based in New York, runs its Siberian Tiger Project in the Sikhote–Alin Biosphere in the Far East near the border with China and the Pacific Ocean. The Greenpeace effort is not cooperative in this fashion. It criticizes Gazprom, the oil and gas company, for damaging the Arctic in drilling in the Pechora Sea. It accuses the government of opening the Virgin Komi Forests territory, officially protected as a World Natural Heritage Site, to gold mining. In neighboring Ukraine, Greenpeace activists with alpine equipment climbed 10 stories up the European Bank building and unfolded a banner: "The only safe reactor is a closed reactor."

Issues: With the end of the old-style state control of the economy under Gorbachev and continuing with the independence of the Russian Federation under Yeltsin, the economy became chaotic. Many big enterprises were sold cheaply to businessmen who rapidly amassed great wealth, often illegally and in cooperation with criminals. This privatization led to corruption. Many state-owned enterprises were closed because they were inefficient, throwing employees out of work. Much wealth was transferred out of the country to Switzerland or London to hide it. These corrupt businessmen gained the label "oligarchs." Corruption continues to pervade the economy. Even worse, criminality has become enshrined. Critics call it the "mafia state." Citizens who speak out may be beaten and murdered. Victims are political enemies as well as economic rivals.

The gigantic country has extensive reserves of oil, natural gas, coal, and uranium. Russia produces 10 million barrels of oil a day, nearly as much as Saudi Arabia, and exports 7 million barrels a day. It produces 650 billion cubic meters of natural gas a day, and exports 250 billion cubic meters a day. It produces 250 million tons of coal a year, the fifth most in the world. Thirty nuclear reactors produce 15% of its electricity. Although it is the largest country in the world in terms of area, much of it cannot be farmed due to cold temperatures and lack of rainfall. Only 7% is arable. Half the land is covered by forests, and timber is a major industry.

In the 1980s the Soviet Union began building the Baikal–Amur Mainline railway, known as BAM. This was a rail line paralleling the Trans-Siberian railway several hundred kilometers to the north and running from the north end of Lake Baikal to the Pacific Ocean. The reason was fear that the Trans-Siberian line was too close to the border with China and subject to capture in time of war. The BAM was 3,500 kilometers long with nine tunnels, 3134 bridges, and 50 new towns. Conditions in this northern clime are harsh, with permafrost underlying the roadbed for two-thirds of its length. Local civil engineers suggested laying ballast that would freeze to become part of the permafrost after several years. The engineers from Moscow overruled this because it would take too long. They also sited one new town in terrain underlain by ice and in another location disrupted the natural permafrost by digging a new river channel. Other environmental problems occurred. The permanent high pressure center over Siberia exacerbated air pollution from the new towns in Chita. Forests were cut down for the construction, and later the new residents cut fire wood. The builders failed to leave buffers along the rivers. Worst of all, the new railway gave access for commercial logging. These boreal forests take a hundred years to mature. The new towns, rail yards, and factories polluted the rivers.

In recent years Russians have cut large amounts of timber in Siberia for export, chiefly to China and Japan. Furniture made from this wood is exported to the United States. Up to half of the trees are cut illegally, with no attention to whether the forests can sustain the harvesting of these slow-growing forests. Opposition has come from the Bureau for Regional Oriental Campaigns, a nongovernmental organization.

In 1992 at the time the Framework Convention on Climate Change was being negotiated prior to the Rio de Janeiro Earth Summit, Russia (as well as the other former Soviet republics) sat on the sidelines, preoccupied with its radical internal changes. At Rio, Russia officially became one of the Annex I industrial countries, and at Kyoto became one of the Annex B industrial countries. Unintentionally, Russia and Ukraine gained a great benefit because the targets were calibrated according to carbon dioxide emissions as of 1990, and the economic output of the former USSR declined rapidly after that year. The advantage for Russia and Ukraine could not be anticipated at the time because no one predicted that their economies would decline so much. This surplus in quotas, to become known as "hot air," did not help the other 13 republics very much because their level of industrialization was much less.

After President Bush reneged on the Kyoto Protocol in 2001, Russian ratification became crucial, for without it the participating parties would not account for 55% of emissions, the minimum required for it to go into force. Russia produced 17% of the world total. Finally, in 2004 it signed the Kyoto Protocol in return for the promise of the Western Europeans to support its admission to the World Trade Organization. This allowed the protocol to go into effect. The ironic result of this cyclical bargain was nothing. The World Trade Organization did not admit Russia, and the protocol coming into force turned out to be only a formality. Indeed, Russia was not admitted to the WTO for another eight years.

Although the protocol was officially in force, the cooperation of the industrial countries weakened. Even countries like England, Germany, and France, which claimed they would reduce greenhouse gases, did little to meet their goals. Others like Spain and Italy actually increased their emissions. President Medvedev attended the climate summit in Copenhagen in 2009, pledging a cut of 25% compared to the Kyoto Protocol limits based on 1990 emissions. In fact, this was phony because the economic collapse of the 1990s meant Russia was far below the limits.

In 2007 Russia surprised the world by staking a claim to the seabed beneath the Arctic Ocean. Its economic value was its potential for oil, estimated at ten billion tons. A robotic Russian submarine literally planted a flag 4,200 meters under the ocean at the North Pole on an undersea geological formation called the Lomonosov Ridge, claiming it was an extension of the land. Recent warming of the Arctic Ocean due to global warming made exploitation of the region a possibility. Most of the ridge is shallower, about 200 meters deep. The legal basis was slight. The Law of the Sea Treaty, signed by 153 countries, limits such exploitation to 200 miles offshore for an Economic Zone. Russia maintained that this situation was different because the Lomonosov Ridge was geologically part of the mainland. Such disputes are supposed to be decided by the UN Commission on the Limits of the Continental Shelf, a panel of experts established in the Law of the Sea. The United States is the only country that has never ratified this treaty.

Successor Republics: When the Soviet Union collapsed, Ukraine was the second largest of the 15 successor republics in terms of population and industrialization. With 46 million people, its population is about the size of Italy. Its economy was battered, and its GDP fell to less than 40% of the 1991 level in 8 years. Since then it has improved, and the GDP is $305 billion based on purchasing power parity. Its per capita income is $6,700, almost a Third World level. Since 2000 the growth has been up to 7% annually, but now is 4%. Air quality is bad, and with antiquated industry based heavily on coal, Ukraine produces 348 million tons of carbon dioxide a year, making it the 12th worst in the world. It has the highest carbon intensity in the world, that is, the ratio between carbon and the value of the output. The country still suffers from the aftereffects of the Chernobyl accident. It gets a quarter of its electricity from the atom, and until 2000 continued to use Reactor No. 3 at Chernobyl, the sister to Reactor No. 4, the one that melted down. Closing inefficient factories has decreased air pollution, but more automobiles have partially countered that beneficial trend.

Because it is short of all fuels except coal, Ukraine imports much natural gas from Russia, a dependence that has resulted in much controversy. Since 1993 there have been frequent disputes on the quantity and price. The Russian gas exported to Europe goes through Ukrainian pipelines, and the Russians accuse the Ukrainians of stealing large quantities. While the Europeans pay a high price, the Ukrainians were given a large discount as former members of the Soviet Union. Now Russia has grown tired of subsidizing its sister republic, and has raised the price to closer to the market level. Furthermore, it criticizes the Ukrainians for wasting the gas due to inefficient burning. The crisis came to a head in January 2009 when Russia cut off supplies to Ukraine. Understandably, the Ukrainians reduced the amount passed through to the Europeans, who suffered the severe shortage in the middle of winter, causing factories to shut and people to be without heat. Under pressure from the European Union and Russia, Ukraine reluctantly agreed to abide by their contracts for delivery and to pay more (though still a subsidized price).

As a successor to the USSR, Ukraine along with Russia and the other republics became parties to international treaties with the defunct union. These included ones on air, endangered species, hazardous wastes, and ozone layer protection. Some were considered to be transferred directly and others were renegotiated. Those affecting nuclear weapons were by far the most important.

Ukraine renegotiated the Strategic Arms Reduction Treaty and the Nuclear Non-proliferation Treaty. At the time of the breakup, many Soviet missiles were located there, so it briefly possessed the third largest nuclear arsenal in the world. The country decided to renounce these arms and turned them over to Russia for destruction in return for badly needed fuel for its nuclear electric plants. As a successor state, Ukraine continues to be a party to a variety of environmental and other treaties. These include the Framework Convention on Climate Change as well as those on air pollution control, the Antarctic, biodiversity, endangered species, hazardous wastes, Law of the Sea, the ozone layer, and wetlands.

Belarus is the fifth largest of the successor republics, and with 10 million people, its population is about the size of Greece or Belgium. Its economy is battered, with a GDP of only $131 billion a year according to purchasing power parity. Per capita income is $13,600. Like Russia and Ukraine, its economy declined after the breakup of the Soviet Union, but in 1996 it re-imposed old-style government controls and took back ownership of some industries it had privatized. President Alexander Lukashenko, has maintained dictatorial control since 1994. The economy is heavily industrialized, and pollution is extreme. Unlike the other former Soviet republics, Belarus has done little to reform its old-fashioned state-owned industries. The southern part of the country is contaminated with fallout from the Chernobyl accident because its location was only ten miles from the border. Like all of the former USSR, Belarus suffers from water and air pollution. Its soil contains excessive pesticides. The country continued many of the old Soviet laws and added a-half dozen others. Belarus is a party to inter-national environmental treaties. On paper it has a range of environmental laws, requires impact statements for new projects, and has the framework for fees for polluters. Actual implementation is weak, however.

The central Asian republics of Kazakhstan, Uzbekistan, and others have inherited environmental problems from the old Soviet Union, and furthermore have less money to address the problems. One of the most dramatic is the disappearance of the Aral Sea. Back in the 1950s Soviet planners decided to increase production of cotton, in order to have a cash export crop. Irrigation increased and by the 1950s the two main tributary rivers, the Amu Darya and Syr Darya, were diverted. Within a few years the lake level began to drop as millions of hectares came under cultiva-tion. As the sea shrank and became saltier, commercial fishing declined. After 25 years, fishing disappeared, causing the loss of 60,000 jobs. As the lakebed dried up, strong winds caused dust storms. At present the lake is only a quarter as large as before.

Czechoslovakian environmental policies epitomize the political situa-tion in Eastern Europe. Because the country was heavily industrialized, its pollution was great. In many ways it followed the path of the Soviet Union, but because of historic and cultural affinities to Western Europe its course was modified. From 1945 to 1989 the Communist Party and Soviet foreign and military policy dominated. The Soviets, after their vic-tory against the Nazis, used the Red Army to impose control on Poland, East Germany, Czechoslovakia, Hungary, and the Balkans. Communist governments were installed and democratic forms were choked off. The armies of these nations were put under the command of the Soviet Red Army to defend against the West, and their foreign policy was oriented to help the Soviet Union. Their industries were aligned with the USSR. Factories emphasized manufacturing steel, cement, and heavy machinery, and deemphasized consumer products. The fuel was often brown coal, the most polluting form. As the most industrialized country in Eastern Europe, Czechoslovakia bore the brunt.

Prior to World War II, Czechoslovakia had followed a course similar to its Western neighbors. In the early 19th century, the Romantic Movement swept through, glorifying nature and rural life. "Decorative clubs" emerged, dedicated to safeguarding the landscape. Virgin forests were preserved.[6]

People formed tramping clubs to wander in the mountains similar to the *wandervogels* in Germany or the ramblers in Britain. Czechoslovakia at the time was not an independent nation, but part of the Austro-Hungarian Empire, ruled from Vienna. Moreover, historically it was not one but two countries joined by the person of the Emperor. They were similar in language, religion, and traditions but not identical. In 1918 following the defeat of the Austrians in World War I, it became independent in a form combining the Czechs in the west with the Slovaks in the east. Democracy took hold, and for 20 years the new nation enjoyed freedom and relative prosperity due to a modern, industrial economy and a high level of education. It seemed to be a beacon of hope. Unfortunately, in 1938 Adolf Hitler took over the country and mobilized it for the Nazi war machine.

With Hitler's defeat in 1945, the way seemed clear for a return to democracy, but the Red Army that had liberated it stayed in place as an occupying force. Homegrown Communist Party members were placed in influential posts in the reconstituted government, and in 1948 a Communist coup took it over completely. The government appropriated industry. As in the Soviet Union, the party believed in materialism, so raw production was valued more than the environment, or even efficiency. Many factories made weapons and armaments. Clean air and water meant nothing. Politics was completely under the sway of the party. Within a few years, old civic organizations were abolished or reorganized under party dominations. Opponents of the regime were arrested, subjected to show trials, and sent to prison for long sentences. The few nature clubs that still existed disappeared.

In early 1968 Czechoslovakia abruptly tried to break away from the Soviet domination. People were dissatisfied with the sluggish economy and lack of consumer goods. The Party Writers Union called for an end to censorship. A reformer, Alexander Dubcek, was elected to head the Communist Party. He announced an Action Program of freedom of the press, freedom of speech, more consumer goods, limits on the secret police, and better relations with Western countries. It foresaw multiparty government within 10 years. The reforms soon gained the name of the Prague Spring. However, the movement threatened the Soviets. On the night of August 20–21 Soviet troops, joined by allies from Poland, Hungary, and Bulgaria, invaded Czechoslovakia. Dubcek was arrested, and a pro-Soviet government was installed. It was as if the Prague Spring had never happened.

Although political freedom had proved unattainable, in the following years environmentalism provided an alternative. In response to the 1972 Stockholm Conference, people organized a group called Brontosaurus to educate young people about nature and give opportunities for outdoor communal living. It was loosely tied to the official Socialist Youth Union. It grew rapidly and was extremely popular among teenagers. With political repression so heavy, some people joined for an outlet against the government more generally, not just for environmental values. Another group during the 1970s and 1980s was the Ecological Section, originally part of the Academy of Sciences. Members were scientists and experts, numbering as many as 400. A third nature group was Tis, named for the yew tree, which had sent a letter of protest to the country's president in 1971. The group had broadcast a radio program reading extracts from Rachel Carson's book.[7] The government took a benign attitude toward Brontosaurus and other nature groups because they were not overtly anti-regime, cooperated with the Socialist Youth Union, promoted healthy outdoor activities, and discouraged consumerism.

In the late 1980s environmental protest increased. Dirty air and water epitomized the failure of the government and industry. Strip mining of brown coal destroyed the mountains. Acid rain damaged the forests, poorly managed or protected anyway. Untreated sewage flowed into the rivers. Newspapers and magazines pointed to the problems. Group membership was up. The Czech Union for Nature Protection had 26,000 members. Young leaders found links to Western groups like Greenpeace and Friends of the Earth. All across Eastern Europe, reformers ranked the environment alongside human rights, peace, and religious freedom.

During the September and October of 1989, Czechoslovakians closely followed protests in East Germany. As the authority of the East German regime disintegrated, its citizens were allowed to travel to other East Bloc countries, allegedly for "vacations," but in fact as a subterfuge for emigration to the West. Many entered the West German embassy in Prague to apply for visas, until it overflowed. After a few weeks, the Czechs simply put the refugees on trains to the West. Meanwhile, in Berlin, mass protests occurred at the Wall, culminating on the night of November 9, when the government opened the gates so the East Germans could walk out.

Czech events were only a few weeks behind those in Berlin. Environmental grievances were the pretext. Brontosaurus held bigger rallies and sharpened its complaints. On November 11, thousands rallied in Teplice to protest air pollution and two days later thousands rallied in Prague to defend a park. Over the next two weeks the demonstrations became larger and incorporated groups beyond the environmentalists. On the 16th thousands of students rallied in Bratislava, and the next day 15,000 rallied in Prague. They demanded an end to the Communist government. On the 20th the crowd was 200,000 and the next day it was 500,000. The police and the army did not try very hard to repress the demonstrations. On the 28th the regime announced it would resign. The event was called the Velvet Revolution because it was so smooth.

The Communist regimes were collapsing in all of Eastern Europe. The USSR, under the reforms of Mikhail Gorbachev, was loosening its control over its satellites. It was no longer providing military support to the old-line dictators. Mass demonstrations occurred in Poland, Hungary, and East Germany. In all Eastern European countries (save one, Rumania) the revolutions were peaceful. In virtually all of them, environmentalists played a role.

Immediately after the success of the Velvet Revolution, environmentalists enjoyed a period of euphoria. A Green Party appeared. The government established a Ministry of the Environment, and the Ministry promulgated a unified program. It assumed responsibility for land use planning and building codes from the economic ministries. Yet within two years environmental policy took a U-turn. Many progressive features were abandoned. Rather than taking a comprehensive view, the government focused on the minutia of the end of the pipe or the top of the smokestack. The lofty concept of sustainable development disappeared. The Green Party fell apart. Popular support, once seeming to be so strong, disappeared. Analysis of the demise of the "enthusiastic period" concluded that much of the environmental support was really anti-Communism. Furthermore, Czech adherents were sparser than in the West and lacked a background from which to view the broader social aspects. They tended to be engineers and technicians.[8]

More ominously, friction increased between the Czechs and the Slovakians. Soviet domination had kept the two halves united just as the Austrian Empire had prior to 1918. Without an imperial overlord, the country divided. The Czechs had a higher level of income and more ties to the West, and the Slovakians resented this. The forced privatization of industry was not accepted very well in the eastern half. Overall incomes fell and unemployment increased, adding to tensions. In 1992 the two peacefully went their separate ways.

In the ensuing years, Czech environmental movement failed to live up to its initial promise. Although a few citizen groups formed, their membership was small and they had little money. They depended, at least in part, on funding from abroad, which was uncertain and undermined their legitimacy. Groups lacked skills in lobbying. The average citizen was not wealthy and did not have a tradition of citizen action. The Green Party that appeared briefly after the Revolution is now moribund.[9]

CONCLUSION

During the long Communist period, the Soviet Union had almost no citizen participation of any kind because this was a monopoly of the Party. Interestingly, what little participation there was tended to be about the environment. Ordinary people demonstrated for cleaning up Lake Baikal, objected to draining the Aral Sea, or joined the Socio-Ecological Union. The Party considered it a safety valve. Moreover, during the last decade or two of Communist domination, the rigid oppression was loosening a little and consumers were given a few choices. When the end of the USSR came, the trigger was an environmental catastrophe: the 1986 meltdown of the nuclear reactor at Chernobyl. Free elections did not occur until Communist power ended, so this was not a means of participating. Since then there have been multiple elections, although many appear to have been corrupt. They have not been an avenue for expressing popular opinions on the environment.

Interest groups were also suppressed during the Communist era. While the Socio-Ecological Union had the outward form of an interest group, it was not very effective. Although there were many groups, they were small, lacked resources, and could not organize on a national scale. This contrasts with the Soviet satellite of Czechoslovakia where Brontosaurus had many members. Since the fall of the Soviet Union, environmental groups have enjoyed only limited success. With the economic collapse and slow recovery, poor medical care, the rise of organized crime, and Putin's move toward dictatorial control, ordinary people have faced too many more serious problems.

As long as the Communist Party imposed its ideology, manufacturing material goods out ranked pollution control. Today, political parties pay little attention to environmental protection. The biggest, United Russia, claims to favor a market economy, which is not necessarily the best way to protect the environment. Other parties make no claims in their platforms. The tiny Green Party decided not to contest elections any more.

Negotiations with the United States and Britain leading to the 1963 Test Ban Treaty had an environmental dimension. Soviet propaganda had emphasized the dangers of atomic fallout as much as the dangers of thermo-nuclear war. The USSR had cooperated extensively in the International Geophysical Year. Once more scientists were the leaders. As with so many countries, the Stockholm summit initiated concern with environmental protection, yet the Soviet Union's unofficial status hindered it having a full effect. Moreover, as long as the country was not free, it did not really matter what top diplomats and scientists learned at these conferences. In 1992 at the time of the Rio Summit, the former USSR was in such turmoil that it could not be effective, but at the Kyoto conference, it was back in shape and signed. Ratifying the protocol was more complicated, and it did not do so until 2004 after a deal that the quid pro quo would be admission to the WTO.

The Soviet Union came late to many aspects. The Environmental Decade did not penetrate the country the way it did the Western democracies. Nevertheless, the ideas filtered through eventually. Some laws were enacted, but implementation was unenthusiastic. Regrettably from 1945 to the 1980s, the influence of Russia on other countries was harmful as it exported Communist materialism to Eastern Europe and the People's Republic of China. This reversed with the dramatic meltdown of the Chernobyl nuclear reactor. Gorbachev's candid willingness to confront governmental and environmental problems fostered change in Eastern Europe.

NOTES

1. Douglas R. Weiner, *A Little Corner of Freedom: Russian Nature Protection from Stalin to Gorbachev* (Berkeley: Univ. of California Press, 2002).
2. Miron Rezun, *Science, Technology, and Ecopolitics in the USSR* (Westport, Conn.: Praeger, 1996), p. 177.
3. Articles 42 and 58.
4. D. J. Peterson, *Troubled Lands: The Legacy of Soviet Environmental Destruction* (Boulder, Colo.: Westview Press, 1993).
5. Luke Harding, "Mafia State: How One Reporter Became an Enemy of the Brutal New Russia. Review "Fragments of a Defunct State" by Stephen Holmes in the *London Review of Books*, January 5, 2012, pp. 23–25.
6. Fagan, Adam, *Environment and Democracy in the Czech Republic* (Cheltenham, UK: Edward Elgar, 2004), p. 52.
7. Fagan, pp. 60–61.
8. Petr Kehlicka, "The Development of Czech Environmental Policy 1990–1995," *Czech Sociological Review*, 7 (1999): 38–40.
9. Steven M. Davis, "Building a Movement from Scratch: Environmental Groups in the Czech Republic," *Social Science Journal*, 41 (2004): 375–392.

9

China

Environmental policy in China is far different than in Western democracies. Its Communist regime since 1949, its isolation from the West, and its huge population make it unique. Sadly, it is infamous for severe air and water pollution. Its ambitious Three Gorges Dam and South–North water diversion have generated criticism from Europe and America. Its One Child Policy has been condemned. Yet China has not been totally isolated. It has had its own Environmental Decade passing laws to protect the air and water. Three centuries ago Europe eagerly copied its gardens. And, of course, it has many similarities to the communist Soviet Union.

Archaeological evidence demonstrates neolithic settlements along the Yellow River dating to 14,000 years ago. At the Banpo site at Xi'an, villagers were cultivating millet and making pottery 9,000 years ago. Remains of a bronze smelter from 4,000 years ago testify to early mining and refining. Although agriculture and metal working put more pressure on the land than hunting and gathering, the population was small so the damage was slight and localized.

In size, China is comparable to the 48 contiguous United States, extending 5,000 kilometers from central Asia to the Pacific and 3,000 kilometers from Russia and Mongolia to the South China Sea. The country is geographically isolated. On the west, the Himalaya Mountains and high plains and deserts of central Asia form a barrier. The northern boundary with Siberia is cold and sparsely inhabited. Oceans on the east and south protect it from invasion, but also are an avenue for navigation and trade. To the west the Tibetan Plateau is high and dry, marked on the southwest by Zhumulangma Peak, or Mount Everest, as it is known to Westerners. Mountains extend over nearly the entire country, decreasing the land available for farming to only 11% of the total. Nearly all of the population lives in the eastern half of the country, especially along the southeast coast. Much of the soil is loess, making the land there fertile, and it enjoys good rainfall. The northern portion is temperate in climate, and the southern is tropical.

Several large rivers originate on the Tibetan Plateau and flow to the east. The Yellow River, 5,500 kilometers long and named for its yellow suspended sediment, has caused centuries of environmental problems. It is prone to disastrous floods, giving it the sobriquet of China's Sorrow. The flood in 1887 drowned one to two million people and the flood in 1931 drowned one to four million people. No one knows the exact number. The river's last 500 kilometers flow across an extremely flat plain, making it prone to change course, sometimes hundreds of kilometers. To the south of the Yellow River, the Yangtze River flows 6,300 kilometers through narrow gorges and fertile plains to the South China Sea. It is the longest river in Asia, and third longest in the world. In the past, its dangerous rapids made navigation nearly impossible. Still farther south, the Pearl River is 2,200 kilometers long with a volume second only to the Yangtze.

Chinese civilization began along the Yellow River about 4000 years ago. The earliest written records are of the Shang Dynasty of 1700 to 1046 BC, making it more than a millennium younger than Mesopotamia and Egypt. About 1066 BC the Zhou Dynasty arose. For part of this time, the Zhous dominated central China, but at other times, the unity collapsed and the country split into multiple states. Historians label the years 476 to 221 BC as the Warring States Period. All of central China was unified in 221 BC by the king of Qin (pronounced Chin) who proclaimed himself the first emperor. In fact, his reign only lasted 15 years. The following dynasty, the Han, lasted until 220 AD. (It is often compared to the Roman Empire in its time and achievements.) The emperor adopted Confucianism, extended his territory, and fostered science and inventions. The population grew to 60 million due to migration to the south, better strains of rice and irrigation, and adding arable land by terracing and draining wetlands. Adding this land was hard on the natural environment. By this time, the mega-fauna like elephants and rhinoceroses were killed off. Today, a few elephants still exist in the jungles and mountains of the extreme south.

Ancient beliefs and practices both favored nature and exploited it. Daoism, the oldest religion, connected to primitive folk religions in finding peace and oneness with nature. It taught that humans should live simple lives as farmers in the countryside. Spirits and ghosts scattered about need to be propitiated, and certainly not disturbed. Kong Fuzi (Confucius), who lived 551–478 BC, taught mostly about human relationships, such as son to father and subject to emperor, but included admonitions to protect forests and rivers. The focus of Confucianism was agriculture. Farmers should plant and harvest in harmony with nature, and the emperor would mediate, for example, with a spring planting ceremony. Buddhism, which arrived in China from India about the second century AD, is a gentle religion that sees humans and animals as equals. Buddhists believe in reincarnation, so a person may return in his next life as an animal. Most adherents are vegetarians. One feature all religions share is that their temples often preserve nature, especially when sited on a mountain. In a country where farmland is so scarce, the temples are often the only untrammeled places left. For example, Mount Emei in Sichuan covers 12,000 hectares, and has been protected since the 10th century AD.

Some ancient engineering projects, dating even before unification in the Qin Dynasty, affected the environment. In Sichuan the Min River flooded each spring when the snow on the mountains melted. The provincial governor, Li Bing, designed and built a channel to drain off an even flow for the main stem, directing it south to the capital city of Chengdu, and drained the surplus onto farmland in need of irrigation. A small natural island was the diversion point. This required cutting a channel 20 meters wide through solid rock using fire and cold water to crack the solid rock. To divert the flow of the river, workers prepared huge cribs of bamboo and filled them with rocks, then during the dry season dragged them into place in the river. The project, which took 8 years to complete, was an immediate success, guaranteeing a steady flow to the city and adequate irrigation of the fertile plain. Over 2,200 years later, it remains in operation.

Building the Grand Canal began earlier, but took much longer to complete. Eventually, it extended 1,800 kilometers from Hangzhou to Beijing. Its north–south route unified the empire and promoted commerce. Grain could be barged from the south to supply military troops stationed in the north. Construction began in 486 BC and was not completed until about 600 AD. The land is low and level so not many locks were needed. The Grand Canal remains in operation to the present.

Controlling the Yellow River proved an endless task. The volume of water surges in the spring, sweeping away silt from the fertile loess plateau. After leaving the Qingtong Gorge in Gansu, it crosses the flat coastal plain. As the speed of the river decreases, the silt drops out into its own channel, clogging the current and pushing the water over the sides. With each annual flood, the river builds natural dikes that confine it for a while but are breached in the high water, thereby inundating the countryside.

Because of the silt, the riverbed is higher than the surrounding land, so once it floods, it cannot return to its original bed. It has flooded 26 times in the last 2000 years. The middle reaches near Xi'an have been called the cradle of Chinese culture. Since ancient time, the emperor has assumed responsibility for constructing dikes and repairing breeches, a nearly impossible job.

Another environmental feature dating to ancient time is the Chinese garden. These originated in the Shang Dynasty, 1766–1027 BC, and continued nearly to the present day. Often known as scholars' gardens, they are small, naturalistic, and artificial. The "scholars" were frequently government officials, who had earned their positions by passing rigorous examinations, so they were powerful and wealthy. Their gardens, which adjoined their homes, served as a place for relaxation, reading, and writing. Each would asymmetrically combine plants, rocks, and water. Plants were symbols: bamboo was strong but resilient, pine represented longevity, and the lotus meant purity with a white flower nourished by muck at the bottom of the pond. The flowering plum represented renewal and strength, and peonies represented wealth. When accounts of the Chinese garden reached England and France in 1692 and 1749, many Europeans promptly adopted the form in contrast to their existing formal, symmetrical gardens. These gardens are an early example of the international transmission of environmental ideas.

The ancient Imperial management of rivers attracted the attention of an early theorist of comparative government. In 1926 Karl Wittfogel published his first major analysis of China, concluding that the Empire's control over water had given it a particular form of government characterized by strong central authority, a powerful bureaucracy, and forced labor, labeled a hydraulic empire.[1] He noted similar examples of what he called Oriental Despotism in ancient Egypt, Mesopotamia, and India.

Unlike India, China successfully resisted European colonization, at least for about 300 years. Since the days of the Roman Empire, a trickle of contact was maintained through central Asia over the Silk Road. Marco Polo had taken this route east in 1271. Although the European Age of Discovery is the great historical event of the modern era, it almost happened the other way around. In 1405 the Chinese launched their own age of discovery. The Ming Emperor sponsored a series of seven armadas that sailed throughout the Indian Ocean. From their home port of Nanjing, these treasure ships visited as far as India, Arabia, and East Africa. The admiral was Zheng He, a Muslim eunuch from western China. He commanded a fleet of two to three hundred ships. In tonnage, the ships were several times bigger than anything built in Europe at the time. Besides trade goods, the expeditions brought back animals like zebras, giraffes, and ostriches, some dead and some alive. Then a new emperor came to the throne and abruptly ordered an end to the exploration.

Soon after the discovery of America, Portuguese and Spanish ships ventured to Chinese ports by sea from Goa and Malacca or the Philippines. Jorge Alvares landed in the Pearl River estuary in 1513. Being forbidden from entering the cities, the Portuguese established a settlement at Macao. After many decades, Jesuit missionaries, led by Matteo Ricci, were permitted to come to Beijing, where they introduced western astronomy and science. A few Jesuits served as advisors to the emperor but wider contact was sparse. The Chinese considered themselves culturally and economically superior, hence saw no benefits from contact and trade. Their name for their country, Zhong Guo, is usually translated as the Middle Kingdom, but perhaps better as the Central Kingdom because it considered itself to be the center of the world.

Population began to grow at about this time. Demographers estimate that in the Han Dynasty in the year 2 AD the population was about 60 million and fluctuated at this level and lower until about 1600 AD. It then began to grow greatly to about 430 million in the middle of the 19th century. In spite of wars, rebellions, floods, and bad government over the next century, the population increased by another 100 million.[2] This put severe pressure on the land.

By 1842 Chinese ability to keep out the Europeans was weakening. By this time, the Portuguese were weaker as a world power, and the English were much stronger. Trade was at a low volume because the Chinese did not want European products, finding them inferior to their own manufacturers. Silver was the only commodity they would accept. Trade of any sort was highly restricted. This changed in 1773 when the British began to smuggle opium into China. The emperor had long proclaimed opium illegal, but the British persisted. When in 1839 the Imperial government tried to arrest British and other European traders in Guangzhou (Canton), the Royal Navy attacked. The old-fashioned Chinese junks and cannons were no match, and they were soon defeated. The Treaty of Nanjing of 1842 forced China to pay an indemnity, allowed the British to establish trading facilities in four ports, and ceded Hong Kong Island. Two years later France and the United States forced similar treaties on the Empire. These are still referred to as the Unequal Treaties. In the Second Opium

War, a combined British–French force again defeated the Imperial forces and exacted further privileges. The British and their allies marched into Beijing, destroying the Emperor's Summer Palace. Europeans and Americans, and later Russians and Japanese, got the right to trade in many ports (some a thousand miles inland on rivers), to travel anywhere, to send missionaries, to receive more indemnities, and to have their own legal courts and autonomous sections of cities where Chinese law did not apply.

At the same time, 1850 to 1864, a major rebellion devastated the south. A radical religious reformer, Hong Xiuquan, had a vision of being taken up to heaven where he met with God, who told him he was the younger brother of Jesus Christ. Hong returned to earth to preach his version of Christianity. He raised a big army and defeated the Imperial army for many years. He established the Taiping Heavenly Kingdom, with a capital at Nanjing, and controlling a population of 30 million people. During the civil war, up to 100 million died, and the countryside was devastated.

The 19th century ended with the Europeans and Japanese scrambling for concessions in commerce. In 1895 Japan defeated China to gain possession of Taiwan and Korea. In 1900 eight nations joined for a military expedition to Beijing, known in the West as the Boxer Rebellion. This was one more embarrassment for the Qing (Ching) Dynasty (in power since 1644 when its ancestors seized the government with Manchu troops from Manchuria). Chinese attempts at reform failed. A movement known as "Self Strengthening" advocated Western education, public schools, civil service improvements, modernizing the army and navy, and sound finances. It opposed corruption, nepotism, and inertia. Elected local assemblies and eventual parliamentary government were goals. In 1898 the young Emperor Kuang-hsü appointed a reform prime minister and began to issue modernizing decrees. This lasted only a hundred days, however, before reactionary elements, led by the Dowager Empress Cixi, carried out a coup d'etat, and imprisoned Kuang-hsu for the rest of his life. In the very last years before her death in 1908, however, Cixi reversed course and implemented some of the reforms she had opposed. In 1909 under the last emperor, Pu Yi, a boy only three years old, provincial assemblies were established, and the following year a national assembly was held. This came too late to save the empire, however.

On October 10, 1911—Double Ten Day—a revolution overthrew the ancient empire, establishing a republic. The imperial government dissolved with little resistance. The civil government was corrupt. Taxes were increasing. Crime was rampant. The army was weak, and many junior officers sympathized with reform. The ordinary people were impoverished due to population growth and lack of industrial development. The power of foreign governments brought shame on China. The Imperial dynasty lost the support of local and provincial leaders.

Although the revolution had many leaders in different parts of the country, Sun Yat Sen was the best known and became the first president of the republic. Born to peasant stock in a village near Guangzhou, Sun's early education was in the traditional Confucian style. When he was thirteen years old, his parents sent him to Hawaii to live with his brother who was in business there. Sun received an American education and became a Christian. Later he went to British Hong Kong to study medicine and moved to Portuguese Macau to practice as a physician. There he joined a secret revolutionary group. Sun lived in Japan for 10 years and traveled throughout the United States, England, and Europe, promoting the revolutionary movement and raising money from Chinese living overseas. In London, he was kidnapped by thugs from the Chinese embassy and held for 12 days until rescued. The widely reported scandal made him the most famous Chinese revolutionary in the world. When the revolution occurred on October 10, Sun, who was in the United States, learned of it from a newspaper article. He returned to China and was elected president of the new republic, taking office on January 1.

While the provisional Republican government controlled the south, the north was under the sway of General Yuan Shih-k'ai. In its last days, the Manchu Dynasty had appointed General Yuan to fight the revolutionaries, but he had turned sides to cooperate with them. His army controlled Beijing and the north. The provisional government in the south believed the only way to unify the country was to elect Yuan president, which it did. At first this expediency succeeded, but Yuan did not truly adhere to Republican values, and in 1915, declared himself emperor. Opposition was immediate and Yuan backed away from implementing a monarchy, until overtaken by death in 1916. His early death left a power vacuum, with no central authority. The entire country entered a period of civil war among different governments, often headed by military generals, known as warlords.

In the south, Sun Yat Sen returned to power as the head of a military government in Guangzhou; then in 1919, he was elected president of the Guomindang, the nationalist political party that was the force behind the republic, although it did not control all the country. Sun encouraged modernization. He promoted railroads to improve commerce, reduce poverty, and tie the country together. He advocated building a hydroelectric dam at the Three Gorges of the Yangtze River to generate power, control floods, and improve navigation, a project revived in 1992 and only completed in 2006. In the early 1920s, the Soviet Communists, newly in power in Russia, sent political and military advisors to help the Guomindang Party, and Sun accepted local communists into the party. Unfortunately, he fell victim to liver cancer and died in 1925.

In 1921 53 men met in the French Concession of Shanghai to found the Chinese Communist Party. They chose the quarter under French admin-istration to avoid Guomindang police and spies. They were inspired by the example of Russia where the Communists had gained power four years earlier. The Comintern (Communist International organization) sent a Dutch party member to assist. Closer to home, an inspiration was the May 4th Movement, named for student riots on that date in 1919. The unrest came when word was received that the World War I victors meeting in Paris had transferred occupation of the city of Qingdao from Germany to Japan rather than repatriating it to China. This reward for colonialism outraged the students. One of the founders of the Communist Party in Shanghai was a young librarian from Beijing, Mao Zedong.

The Communist Party had a hard time. In 1923 it merged with the Guomindang, but 4 years later the Nationalist Party, now under the leadership of General Chiang Kai-shek, turned on the Communists and murdered many of them. The party retreated from its bases in the south in 1934 to begin its Long March of a thousand kilometers, eventually reach-ing Yan'an in central China. During this period, Mao Zedong emerged as the clear leader. This was an era of constant low-grade warfare as Chiang sought to consolidate control, fighting both the Communists and several warlords. The condition of the average peasant was no better than it had been for centuries. In 1931 the Yellow, Yangtze, and Huai rivers all flooded after heavy rainfall. The estimates of deaths ranged from 1.3 to 4 million, and many more were stranded. Cholera and typhus spread.

Worse was yet to come. In 1931 Japan invaded and soon conquered Manchuria, in the northeast. The Japanese had turned to outright military aggression, as more effective than the older quest for commercial privi-leges. In previous years, the Japanese had invested in the region building railroads, mines, and factories. In fact, industrialization was more suc-cessful there than in the rest of China. Moreover, the region appeared ripe for settlement from the overpopulated Japanese Home Islands.

In 1937 the Japanese extended their aggression against the rest of China. It wanted the oil and minerals and was soon to invade Malaya, the Philippines, and Vietnam for its Greater East Asia Co-Prosperity Sphere. By now it had clear models of militarism in Europe with Nazi Germany and Fascist Italy. The Japanese easily conquered Beijing. When they moved south to Shanghai, the Guomindang army was stronger, and resisted for 3 months. The next target 250 kilometers upstream was Nanjing, which they attacked on December 13. The Japanese decided to set an example to show that resistance was futile by killing and raping indiscriminately. The Chinese estimate 300,000 were murdered in 6 weeks in this Rape of Nanjing. The Nationalist army was unable to defend the city, and withdrew to Wuhan, and eventually up stream to Chongqing where its remote and mountainous site put it beyond reach except for occasional air bombardment. The strategy of the Nationalists was to offer minimal resistance in order to preserve their army and keep the Communists at bay. Help from the Americans was almost impossible because the Japanese controlled the sea and occupied Vietnam and Burma to the south. High mountains cut off access from British India. The Nationalists were on their own, and Chiang Kai-shek correctly predicted that after the war was over, the civil war would resume.

Unlike the Nationalists, the Communists, who were centered in Yun'an, aggressively fought the Japanese invaders. Much of their resistance took the form of guerilla attacks behind Japanese lines. The only factor China had in its favor was its immense size in area and population. The Japanese army simply did not have the manpower to occupy most of the country. At its maximum extent, the Japanese only occupied about a quarter of the country, mostly along the east coast. On June 9, 1938, in a desperate attempt to slow down the invasion, the Nationalists blew up the levees on the Yellow River. The river was close to the peak of its annual flood and swept over 20,000 square kilometers of the plain. Close to a million Chinese peasants died or starved, and 12 million were made homeless. The Japanese were slowed but not stopped.

Once Japan surrendered in 1945 after the Americans dropped atomic bombs on Hiroshima and Nagasaki, the Chinese Civil War resumed immediately. At first the Nationalists had the advantage of more men and equipment, launching an attack with 1.6 million soldiers. Yet within a year, the tide shifted so the Communists had two million soldiers. They controlled a third of the population and won favor by seizing land to give to poor peasants. By the end of 1948, they controlled almost all of the

North, and turned their troops toward the South. In April they crossed the Yangtze River and took the Nationalist capital of Nanjing. The Nationalists retreated first to Guangzhou, which they held until October then to the island of Taiwan in December. Meanwhile, in Beijing on October 1, Mao Zedong proclaimed the People's Republic.

Mao moved to consolidate power, putting the battle-tested Communist cadres (party bureaucrats) into positions of authority. He enlisted the aid of the other big Communist country, the USSR, signing a treaty of friendship and cooperation. The Soviets sent thousands of engineers and agricultural experts. They gave some money, and built many factories and steel mills. Meanwhile, in neighboring Korea, the North had invaded the South in June 1950. (Korea had been occupied by the Japanese since 1910, and at the end of World War II the Soviets accepted the Japanese surrender in the north and the Americans accepted it in the south. The Soviets soon imposed a Communist government in the north.) However, by October the United Nations troops had reversed its early defeats and had advanced nearly to Korea's northern border with China. (Nearly all the UN troops were American.) The Chinese feared the UN forces would cross into China; therefore, they intervened with thousands of their own troops. Meanwhile, on China's west, the Communists invaded Tibet, which has been effectively independent since the fall of the Empire in 1911.

At home, the Communists at first were moderate, but within a year began a domestic campaign against their enemies, attacking landlords, business owners, foreigners, and Christian missionaries. Their land seizures dated back to the 1930s in Yun'an, but now the process intensified. Peasants were organized into collective farms and later into communes of five thousand families. Machinery was owned in common, and villages had quotas of grain to meet. Landlords and wealthy peasants were put on trial and beaten and humiliated. A million landlords were executed, and others were sent to "reeducation camps." Mao next began the Three Anti and the Five Anti campaigns. The first targeted unreliable government officials, and the second targeted businessmen and industry owners. These policies of land reform and eliminating private ownership and the bourgeoisie copied the Soviet Union policies of the 1930s. Millions of people were victimized. At their trials, they had to publicly confess and engage in "self-criticism."

In 1953 China launched its first Five-Year Plan, modeled after the Soviet plans. Its twin goals were to increase industry and to collectivize agriculture. Within a few years, 90% of the peasants were in communes.

The People's Republic built thousands of steel mills, cement plants, oil refineries, and chemical factories. Coal production more than doubled. The government constructed hundreds of electric generating plants, almost all coal fired. All this was hard on the environment, with no laws against air and water pollution.

In 1958 Mao Zedong decided that the first Five-Year Plan was not moving China ahead fast enough and that the people were capable of much more. The second Five-Year Plan was known as the Great Leap Forward. Life in the countryside was even more regimented. Twelve families formed a work group, and 12 work groups formed a brigade. Party officials supervised everything. The peasants ate in village mess halls. Their young children and elderly parents were put in day care so all adults and older children could work in the fields. Propaganda played from morning to night on loud speakers. The peasants attended party-run meetings. Quotas for wheat and rice were raised. For a while, the peasants could lie about their success in production, but eventually they were discovered. A famous project was to smelt iron in backyard furnaces in the villages. At the high point, there were 600,000 of them. However, it soon became apparent that the quality of the iron was low, and they burned valuable trees for fuel. Industrial output of regular steel mills and factories for heavy machinery was of low quality also. During the first year, rainfall was abundant, but the following 2 years were dry, so crops failed. Food was scarce, and people went hungry. As many as 20 million people starved to death. To make matters worse, the Soviet Union quarreled with China, and withdrew its thousands of engineers and experts.

One of the stranger features of the Great Leap Forward was the Kill a Sparrow Campaign, which Mao personally instigated. The concern was that sparrows ate grain, so fewer sparrows would mean more grain. People were instructed to kill the birds with sticks and slingshots and to bang on pots and pans so the sparrows would fly away or die from exhaustion. They were to hunt for nests and squash the eggs or kill the fledglings. The campaign was successful in that it killed almost all the sparrows in China, but since they eat insects, it allowed mosquitoes to multiply. Only many years later did the sparrow population recover.

With the obvious failure of the Great Leap Forward, Mao stepped down as head of the state, although he kept his more important position as head of the Communist Party. His replacements leading the government on a day-to-day basis, such as Deng Xiaoping, followed a moderate course. Peasant brigades got more autonomy, and factory managers could determine production.

By 1966 Mao began to reassert his authority. He worried that the Party had lost its old zeal. He sought to restore ideological purity, revolutionary fervor, and the class struggle. To counter the unenthusiastic Party, Mao found two allies: students and the army. The students, mostly in high school but some in universities, formed units called the Red Guards. Millions joined. The Red Guards marched and demonstrated. They were personally loyal to Mao Zedong, often reciting from the government-distributed "Little Red Book," the *Quotations of Chairman Mao*. They physically attacked the police and sometimes other Red Guards units. Tens of thousands would assemble in Tiananmen Square in the heart of Beijing to chant slogans and hear Mao address them. Soon even Mao realized they were becoming uncontrollable.

Mao's other ally was the People's Liberation Army. He had personally led the army since the days of the Long March, through the Civil War and the War against Japanese Aggression, and finally to victory over the Nationalists. With the breakdown of social order due to the collapse of the Communist Party and the rampages of the Red Guards, the army was the only force for stability. It both restrained the radicals and cooperated with them in Revolutionary Committees that filled in for the vanished Communist officials. Because the Red Guards were so numerous and violent, Mao and the Army decided to send them to the countryside, where they would be out of the way, and perhaps learn old-fashioned virtues from the peasants. This was not voluntary. In many cases, schools and universities were closed. Half a generation of young people were denied education.

By 1969 the pendulum began to swing back toward the center. Leaders such as Deng Xiaoping and Zhou Enlai (Mao's longtime prime minister) moved toward moderate policies. All sectors of the economy were to be modernized. The 1973 National Party Congress voted to confirm this. Two years later, Zhou Enlai spoke to the People's Congress to announce the Four Modernizations for the four sectors of agriculture, industry, defense, and science and technology. The year 1976 brought the deaths of both Zhou Enlai and Mao Zedong. China was headed on a new course.

Government: Upon winning power in 1949, Mao Zedong established a totalitarian government under the control of the Communist Party. The structure was dual: both party and government existed at all levels, though the party always dominated. His model was the Soviet Union. Authority extended into every aspect of life. The state owned all industry and businesses. Everyone was assigned a work unit, which also controlled housing, food, marriage, family planning, education, and so forth. In the countryside, farms were collectivized. Privately owned land was seized, and the former landlords were often shot. Their children had the lowest priority for food and education. While these policies were a product of the Communist Party, they echoed thousands of years of authoritarian government under the empire and contained elements of Confucian beliefs.

The geographic boundaries of the People's Republic were close to those of the old empire. In 1945 Manchuria was returned from Japanese control. The People's Liberation Army chased the Nationalists out of the south by early 1950. Later in that year, the Army conquered Tibet, effectively independent since the 1911 Revolution. Outer Mongolia had been lost to the Republic in 1921 and was officially an independent country, but in fact it was a satellite under the domination of the Soviet Union. The only other territory lost was Taiwan, to which the Nationalist government and army retreated in 1949. The People's Republic continues to maintain that this island of 23 million people is an integral province. Perhaps the biggest difference by 1949 was the nearly complete end to the foreign treaty ports. The British, French, Russians, Portuguese, Americans, and the Japanese no longer controlled territory in the major cities. The only exceptions were Hong Kong and Macao.

The population, about 400 million in 1949 and 1.3 billion today, is homogeneous in ethnicity. About 92% are Han, that is, racially Chinese, and speak one of the dialects of the Chinese language. About 4% are also racially similar, but speak different languages and have different cultures, and another 4% appear racially different, and do not speak Chinese as their native tongue. Tibetans and Uighurs are examples. These 8% are referred to as "minorities" or "nationalities," and may have distinctive citizenship status. Many of the minorities live in the south along the border with Vietnam, Laos, and Myanmar. Uighurs are a Turkic people living in the northwestern province of Xinjiang and are Muslim. There are only eight million Uighurs and five million Tibetans. In both Xinjiang and Tibet, government has encouraged immigration of Hans, so they now constitute about half the population, an item of resentment. The homelands of many other minorities, however, are not geographically remote but are scattered all over China.

As a Communist country, adherence to the doctrines of Karl Marx was paramount. In its earliest days, the party believed that, as Marx had predicted, a revolution had to take place in a city by industrial workers. This was hard to do in a country at least 90% rural. In 1927 the party promoted riots in Shanghai by workers, who briefly established a commune. This failed and was quickly put down by the Republican forces. Soon after that the Nationalists in Guangzhou turned on their Communist members, whom they had encouraged to join only a few years before. Thereafter, the Communists redirected their efforts and their ideology toward the peasants. While living in Yan'an after the Long March, Mao devoted much study and writing to reconciling this rural basis with the words of Karl Marx.

The People's Republic is, in theory, a unitary government, not a federation. Authority is supposed to come directly from Beijing. There are 22 provinces, five autonomous regions, and four municipalities. Provinces may be as large as Guangdong, with 95 million people. Sichuan in the southwest has 87 million people. In turn, the provinces are divided into counties. Beijing and Shanghai are independent municipalities. Hong Kong and Macao became Special Administrative Regions after their return from Britain and Portugal. Although the country is supposedly unitary, in fact the various provinces and municipalities can often act autonomously. Some have described the system as decaying centralism. On the other hand, the so-called Autonomous Regions like Tibet and Xinjiang are not really autonomous. Because of fear of ethnic independence movements, they are strictly governed by Beijing.

In the early days of the People's Republic, and again toward the end of the Cultural Revolution, the People's Liberation Army was supreme. Mao was the Army commander from the time of the Long March until his death, and his successor, Deng Xiaoping, was a commanding general. More recently control has shifted to civilians and to those with backgrounds in engineering. While the Army has 2½ million troops, its power is less than its size would suggest. The technocrats in Beijing work very hard to neutralize its power. For example, the commander of one military base is not permitted to simply telephone or visit the commander of a neighboring base. They must communicate through Beijing. This restriction is to prevent the two of them from plotting against the government. On a different dimension, cooperation between major state-owned enterprises is not always encouraged so, for example, provinces compete in manufacturing automobiles.

The People's Republic of China has many of the outward forms of democratic government copied from the West. The national level has a legislature called the People's Congress that meets annually in the Great Hall of the People on Tiananmen Square in Beijing. It has nearly 3000 members supposedly elected to represent all parts of China. In addition there is a People's Consultative Conference representing various groups and is sometimes compared to a senate. These two bodies meet for only 2 weeks a year. The official role of the Congress and the Consultative Conference is to pass legislation. In fact, all members of both chambers are under the thumb of the Communist Party. This includes a handful of representatives of eight tiny non-Communist political parties. Occasionally, however, some independence sifts through, and on several occasions this has been on environmental legislation. When in 1991 the People's Congress was asked to authorize the Three Gorges Dam, 174 voted against and 664 abstained,[3] marking the greatest opposition ever encountered in the People's Congress.

President Xi Jinping, who is the head of state, is elected by the National People's Congress to a 5-year term. The congress also appoints the State Council that is chaired by Premier Li Keqiang, appointed in 2013. The State Council oversees both the central government agencies (the executive branch), and the 22 provinces. Its membership overlaps with the Communist Party Central Committee.

The top party organ is the Politburo Standing Committee, consisting of nine members selected from the Party Central Committee of 24 members. In turn, they are appointed by the Party National Congress. While in theory the People's Congress appoints the president and the State Council, in fact they are named by the Politburo, that is, by the party. Thus, there is a dual structure with a governmental National Congress and a Party National Congress. The Central Military Commission is another top-level body. Since the time of Mao, control of the People's Liberation Army through this commission has been crucial. One might say it is even more important now that the top figures are no longer army generals like Mao and Deng. The dual party and governmental structure is found in each province and down to the county level. At no level are there free elections as in the West.

The concept of law is not the same as in the West. Until recent decades, the People's Republic tended not to have laws in the Western style. Instead, it relied on broad principles and policies. Even today, laws tend to be highly general, with vague and hortatory language. Implementation is a difficult problem. Decisions were based on policies, often unwritten, of the government and of the Communist Party. In 1999 the People's Congress amended the constitution to provide that laws would be taken more seriously. The PRC has courts that superficially seem like those of Western countries. There are trial courts, appellate courts, and the Supreme People's Court. However, courts still are weak because rule of law is not adhered to fully, courts are not staffed adequately, lawyers are few and ineffective, and corruption continues. When the National People's Congress passes legislation, it does not have the same status as a law passed by a Western parliament. An administrative agency prepares a draft bill and the People's Congress discusses it in committees and a plenary session, then votes to pass it. The result, however, is not a law but a detailed set of suggestions that the agency uses in promulgating its own regulations.

The Chinese constitution has been more changeable than that of a Western country. The country has had five different ones from 1949 to 1982, and amendments are easy to enact. The first one was modeled on the Soviet Constitution of 1936. The present constitution, that of 1982, is less ideological than earlier ones. For example, the 1975 constitution proclaimed that "State officials must diligently study Marxism, Leninism, and Mao Zedong thought." While the 1982 version still reveres ideology, it relaxes aspects of state ownership. It has been amended four times to reflect economic changes.

Environmental protection is officially part of the Constitution. Chapter 1, Article 26, provides that "The state protects and improves the living environment and the ecological environment, and prevents and controls pollution and other public hazards." In 1979 the People's National Congress, enacted the Law on Environmental Protection, which provided a framework. Like other countries around the world, China passed a series of environmental laws, although its Environmental Decade was the 1980s instead of the 1970s. Laws against air and water pollution were enacted in 1984 and 1987. It passed laws protecting forests, grasslands, wild animals, and soil. The Environmental Impact Assessment Law was passed in 2003.

The 1979 Environmental Law authorized an administrative organization to draft and implement rules and to plan for the future. This was the National Environmental Protection Agency, which was responsible for formulating nationwide guidelines and standards, preparing plans, coordinating with environmental offices in other ministries, and investigating severe pollution incidents. In 1998 it was upgraded to the level of a full ministry: SEPA. The People's Congress has an Environment and Resources Protection Committee to support the legislative aspects. In the executive branch, the State Environmental Protection Administration is supposed to coordinate government wide steps to protect the environment. Subjects include general principles, connections to economic development, and prompting local governments and enterprises to conform to the standards, education and research.

China has virtually no independent interest groups as are so prominent in Western democracies. In recent years the government has changed its prohibition of such groups, as an attempt to gain acceptance in the rest of the world for membership in the World Trade Organization in the skeptical opinion of some. The oldest, Friends of Nature, dates only to 1994, when it was founded by Liang Congjie. Like all so-called nongovernmental organizations, it must be sponsored by a government agency, in this case the Ministry of Civil Affairs. These are called government-organized nongovernmental organizations—GONGOs. Unlike early environmental groups in the Soviet Union and Eastern Europe, however, so far Friends of Nature has not gained a rush of members who utilize it as a way to express opposition to the Communist government. It concentrates on innocuous activities like protecting endangered species such as the snub-nosed monkey and the Tibetan antelope. Through education it tries to encourage a "green culture" of recycling and energy conservation. Global Village Beijing focuses on the urban environment. Founded in 1996 by Liao Xiaoyi, the group eschews political activism. It has produced television programs, promotes recycling, and runs a model community. When the government declined to register it, Liao registered it as a business.

Some NGOs have thin support. For example, the International Fund for China's Environment seems to exist solely as a conduit for American grants. It lists its functions as promoting new technologies as well as education and cooperation. Its small staff shares its offices with an investment consulting company. Unlike most NGOs, it has branches, in this case in Shanghai, Yunnan, Shenzhen, Wuhan, and Tianjin, as well as Washington, DC. Funds have come from the US Department of State and EPA, the Ford Foundation, and private companies. It is sponsored by a Chinese government agency.

Chinese affiliates of international groups barely exist. One exception is WWF, which began a program in 1980 to protect the giant pandas, now the official symbol of the parent organization. For the first 15 years, it did not have an office in the PRC. Staff was located first in Switzerland and later in Hong Kong. However, in 1995 it was allowed to establish a local office. Its governmental sponsor is the Forestry Ministry. Now it has a bustling office of 30 staff located next to the Imperial Palace in Beijing. It also has a branch office located in Chengdu to be close to the Panda Breeding Center and the Wolong Panda Reserve in Sichuan. This is a rare exception to the PRC policy of not permitting branches or affiliates. In addition WWF has projects on other rare animals, forests, and the Yangtze

River. Another exception is the Nature Conservancy, which maintains its national headquarters in Kunming, the capital of Yunnan Province, rather than Beijing. In 2007 it helped establish Pudacuo National Park in Yunnan, the first national park in the PRC. The Nature Conservancy foresees this as a way to introduce professional park management and promote nature education.

Other international groups have had little success in penetrating the People's Republic. Greenpeace established an office in Hong Kong in 1997. Although the former British colony reverted to Chinese control that year, it is a Special Administrative Region, hence retains some democratic features. Greenpeace engaged in the activism for which its parent organization is famous. It opposed the city's new airport and a golf course. From its Hong Kong base it opposed the Daya Bay nuclear plant in nearby Guangzhou on the mainland, but did not operate from Guangzhou itself. Recently, it established a small office in Beijing, but this branch will not engage in direct action. "Friends of the Earth (HK)" claims not to be affiliated with Friends of the Earth International, and the parent organization does not list the Hong Kong group as an affiliate.

Although the number of NGOs is small and their membership is sparse, they are growing. Guobin Yang found that in 1994 there were only five environmental groups, but that in 2002 there were 71. He notes that the groups avoid confrontation and promote education through public lectures, field trips, and newsletters. They are skilled in using the rhetoric and commitments of the government and the Party to promote their side of the argument. They use the regime's own words as a weapon of protest and resistance. Official goals of "sustainable development" and the "harmonious society" lend themselves to this. In addition the environmental groups are now calling for legal action as Chinese society becomes more attuned to citizen rights. Environmental groups have found support from the media: television and newspapers. The Internet has been a new resource.[4]

Because of its deliberate isolation beginning in 1949 and continuing for the next two decades, the People's Republic lacked many of the international connections deriving from diplomatic treaties that brought nonindustrial countries into the environmental age. Then in 1971, Mao began to seek international connections. In October the PRC successfully campaigned to get the Chinese seat in the United Nations transferred from the Nationalist Republic of China government in Taiwan. In February 1972 President Richard Nixon made his famous visit to Beijing. Both countries saw this as a way to counter the Soviet Union. To the surprise of many, the PRC participated in the 1972 Stockholm environmental summit. This was an aberration because China really did not have much interest in nature, and was doing so to counter the Soviets and to denounce US nuclear weapons. While most countries around the world were weaving a tighter net of environmental exchange and cooperation during the 1970s, China did little.

China signed the Convention on International Trade in Endangered Species of Wild Fauna and Flora (CITES) in 1981. This international treaty of nearly 180 countries restricts trade to protect endangered animals and plants. Its biggest success has been the control of the ivory trade that has achieved protection for African and Indian elephants. For China two animals have been contentious: tigers and rhinos. Traditional folk medicine attributes healing properties to nearly every part of the tiger: bones, teeth, whiskers, eyes, and the penis. Taken in wine, pills, balms and powders, the potions relieve rheumatism, arthritis, malaria, burns, pain, aging, and impotency. To supply these demands, there are 5000 tigers in captivity being raised for their body parts. Other members of CITES, particularly India, object because supplying some tiger parts encourages the demand for more. It maintains that this leads to shooting wild tigers in India that are then exported to China. Officially, China banned trade in tiger parts in 1993, but other countries believed this was not effective. Rhino are similarly endangered. Many believe that powder made from the horn can treat fevers, convulsions, and delirium. At present only 5000 to 7000 rhinos survive in the wild in Africa and Asia. None have lived in China since ancient times. Traditional medicine is not confined to the countryside or to the uneducated. Hundreds of millions use it. Physicians have modern hospitals in all cities. They advocate holistic treatment of the patient with plants like ginseng and techniques of massage and acupuncture. Recently, the national association of traditional physicians has voted to not use extracts from tigers, rhinos, and other endangered species.

Over the past two millennia, China has had a number of capital cities. They display clear evidence of orderly planning. Orientation toward the cardinal points of the compass is standard. Important buildings face south, the most auspicious direction. Xi'an, for example, is laid out as a square with its stone walls and streets oriented north–south and east–west, and a bell tower at the center. Beijing centers on the Imperial Palace, known as the Forbidden City because the public was forbidden to enter. Within the palace proper, a series of buildings, such as the Hall of Supreme Harmony and the Hall of Heavenly Purity, all face south toward Tiananmen Square. Next to the northern wall is a traditional scholar's garden. To the west is Beihai Park, 70 hectares of gardens with several artificial lakes, originally reserved for the Imperial Court. Temples and pavilions date to the Ming Dynasty and earlier. Farther away, one finds the Temple of Heaven and the Temple of the Earth. Chinese urban planners were able to enforce the orderly arrangement over many centuries. Even during the riots and chaos of the Cultural Revolution, Communist leaders protected the Imperial Palace.

Economic Reforms: At the Party Congress in December 1978, Deng Xiaoping announced economic reforms. Farmers could now sell their surplus crops, foreign trade would be encouraged, many businesses could sell on the open market, and towns and villages could operate businesses enterprises. Collective farms and communes nearly disappeared. Employment in Townships and Villages Enterprises (TVEs) grew from 28 million in 1978 to a peak of 135 million in 1996. On the negative side, they tended to produce much air and water pollution. Big state-owned enterprises (SOEs) were not privatized but could enjoy more management autonomy and could keep their profits (although now subject to taxation). These were often steel mills, cement plants, and oil refineries that generated much pollution, and because they were only partially subject to the price system had less incentive to economize by burning less coal.

The result of these economic reforms was spectacular. Since 1978 the national rate of economic growth has been 9% or 10% year after year. The GDP is $10 trillion, third highest in the world after the European Union and the United States. Per capita income is $7600. For three decades after 1949, Mao had tried to make China self-sufficient, minimizing imports. The PRC was isolated economically as well as politically. However, after 1978 this was reversed. Imports were seen as a source of profit, investment, and new technology. The government established Special Economic Zones to foster foreign trade. The SEZs enjoyed tax incentives and more autonomy for international trade. They relied on investment from overseas, and their products were chiefly for export. They were to be guided by market forces, not central planning. At first there were 4 SEZs, but the number has increased to 20. The first ones were in the southeast near Hong Kong and Taiwan and sparked a boom, which continues to the present. Cities in the interior did not prosper as much.

Some observers expected that the economic freedom would lead to political freedom. In 1979 a few protesters, mostly students, had written criticisms on posters that they pasted on a wall in Beijing, soon getting the nickname of "Democracy Wall." Posters written in big characters, so they could be easily read, were about the only way to publicize ideas because censorship restricted newspapers and magazines. Moreover, paper, printing presses, and mimeograph machines were not available without government permission. The first wall was on Xidan Street downtown, and soon posters appeared on other walls in Beijing and in Shanghai, Guangzhou, Wuhan, Hangzhou, and Qingdao. However, Deng Xiaoping and the top leadership did not want reform to get away from their control and soon clamped down on them. Many protesters were arrested and imprisoned. Although suppressed, by 1986 more calls for democracy came. News was filtering in of anti-Communist protest in Poland. Factory workers were inspired by news of the Solidarity Union there.

Discontent flared again in April 1989 with the death of Hu Yaobang, a high-ranking party official who had supported economic and political reform. A hundred thousand people gathered in Tiananmen Square to honor him. Instead of dispersing after his funeral, they lingered to demonstrate for reform, camping out in makeshift shelters. Leaders of the crowd gave speeches denouncing oppression and urging economic and democratic freedom. They sang patriotic songs and tried to present petitions to officials. On May 27 they erected a 10-meter-tall statue of the Goddess of Democracy, assembled of foam and papier-mâché, being a near-replica of the Statue of Liberty in New York. Dozens of protesters engaged in hunger strikes. Over a period of 5 weeks the demonstrations continued. Thousands of students marched to the square from their campuses, ordinary citizens joined, and the crowd spread onto nearby streets. Estimates were as high a one million. Protests occurred in Shanghai, Xi'an, Guangzhou, Chengdu, and elsewhere. All this worried Deng and the party leaders. Several times they sent police to disperse the crowd, but those forays were not successful. Finally, on the night of June 3–4, they mobilized the army. Infantry and tanks attacked the demonstrators, killing eight hundred (and perhaps more), and chasing away the rest. Leaders of the demonstration were arrested and imprisoned.

The crackdown proved successful for Deng for no more political protests occurred. In the following years, the economy prospered and the public seemed to lose its desire for democracy. The GDP continued to grow at an average of 9% percent annually. Economists estimate that 300 million Chinese moved from poverty to middle-class status. Deng often spoke of the slogan "Socialism with Chinese Characteristics" (in other words, a touch of capitalism). Already old by then, Deng eased into retirement, living to the age of 92.

His successor, Jiang Zemin, was an electrical engineer and, having been born in 1926, did not share the revolutionary and military background of Mao, Zhou Enlai, and Deng. From engineering jobs, he soon moved into party affairs. Like Mao and Deng as the paramount leader, he simultaneously held the three key positions of general secretary of the Communist Party, president of the PRC, and chairman of the central military commission. Jiang presided over a period of rapid economic growth and little controversy. He did not permit political liberalization. His premier was Zhu Rongji, trained as an electrical engineer, and a party cadre.

Jiang's successor, Hu Jiabao, spent his entire career in the party. Like Jiang (and Zhu), he was an engineer, and like Jiang simultaneously held the three key positions of general secretary of the Communist Party, president of the PRC, and chairman of the central military commission. As a young man, he worked on the Liujiania Dam on the Yellow River. Later he served as party and government leader of the Tibet Autonomous Region. Again like Jiang, he presided over a period of rapid economic growth and little controversy. He often advocated a "Harmonious Society." The term is intentionally vague, but at least does not mean conflict and violence.

His premier was Wen Jiabao, who trained as an engineer and geologist. Like Jiang and Hu, he has a long career as a party cadre. Like Hu, Wen supported economic growth, but occasionally tempered it with concerns about social welfare. A narrow reading of the constitution gives the day-to-day management of the government to the premier, but since the president is also the secretary general of the party, the premier does as he says.

A new leader, Xi Jinping, succeeded Hu as general secretary and president in 2013. Xi was educated as a chemical engineer, following the technical background typical of Chinese leaders. His father was an early leader of the Communist Party but was purged in the Cultural Revolution. The son also suffered and was sent to the countryside in 1969 as a teenager. He survived and soon began a career in the Communist Party serving in Shaanxi, Hebei, Fujian, and Zhejiang provinces and in Shanghai, areas of rapid economic growth. He is known for his opposition to corruption.

Rivers: The Three Gorges Dam has been the most contentious environmental issue in China. It is the largest in the world measured by generating capacity. Advocated as early as 1916 by Sun Yat-sen and again by Mao in the 1950s, it dams the Yangtze River to impound nearly 40 cubic kilometers of water. It was an example of the gigantism of hydroelectric projects of the 1920s and 1930s found in the United States, the Soviet Union, Italy, and elsewhere. In 1992 the hundreds of abstentions and negative votes in the National People's Congress was unprecedented. The World Bank would not support it due to its environmental damage and poor cost-benefit ratio.

Located in Hubei Province as the Yangtze River comes out of the mountains onto the plain west of Wuhan, the dam is 185 meters high and 2.3 kilometers across, and its reservoir extends upstream 660 kilometers to Chongqing. Its electric generating capacity will eventually reach 22.5 gigawatts. The dam aids navigation and control floods. Its cost is $30 billion. At present its capacity exceeds the electricity demand in the region, and the distribution system is inadequate. Environmental damage is extensive. Prior to the dam, the scenery was spectacular as the huge river rushed through the narrow gorge for hundreds of kilometers. Spring floods poured torrents into the river, causing it to rise greatly and flow dangerously fast. High mountains line both sides. Numerous tributaries flow in from even narrower gorges. Monkeys and mountain goats can be spotted on the cliffs. The dam has displaced 1.3 million people in 13 cities and 140 towns. It has submerged ancient temples and archaeological sites. Silt filling the reservoir behind the dam threatens to diminish its holding capacity and change the river downstream. Warmer water temperatures endanger fish. The weight of the water threatens earthquakes.

Until the 1950s, boats could only sail upstream against the fast current by being pulled by human labor hauling towropes. Teams of dozens and even hundreds of men would strain against the lines with all their might, bending in their harnesses nearly to the ground along narrow footpaths chipped into the rocks along the gorges. Their subhuman labor symbolized all the poverty and depravity of ancient China. Peasants were desperate to earn a few coins. The naked laborers were whipped, while drums beat to keep them pulling in rhythm. Each man wore a special harness that revealed to the overseer whenever he was not pulling his weight. Sailing boats downstream was less laborious but more dangerous. Treacherous currents and hidden rocks often capsized boats or ripped holes in their hulls. In recent years stronger marine engines eliminated the need for human labor, and dynamite has blasted away most underwater rocks.

Upstream, where the Yangtze is known as the Jinsha River, China plans to build 12 more dams. The upper reaches of the Jinsha are particularly desirable for hydroelectricity because the river falls steeply, nearly 3 meters per kilometer. In these remote mountains, the gorges are deeper and more numerous than the Three Gorges. In the Tiger Leaping Gorge, steep cliffs rise 2000 meters on each side. Collectively, the dams would generate 60 gigawatts of electricity, control floods, and reduce siltation downstream. However, they would also destroy the natural flow through the canyons and endanger species like the 7-meter-long paddlefish. The national Ministry of the Environment ordered some construction to stop, but the builders have only partially complied.

The Jinsha makes up part of the Three Parallel Rivers National Park in the mountains of Yunnan Province in southwest China bordering the Tibet Plateau. It is a World Heritage Site certified by the United Nations Educational, Scientific and Cultural Organization (UNESCO). In this location, the upper reaches of three of the great rivers of Asia—the Jinsha (Yangtze), Lancang (Mekong), and Nu (Salween)—run parallel, north to south, through steep gorges and are bordered by glaciated peaks more than 6000 meters high. The site boasts great biodiversity. The Mekong flows into the South China Sea in Vietnam, and the Salween flows into the Indian Ocean in Myanmar.

The Nu River Project, a series of 13 dams, which the government announced in 2003, generated public opposition unique in China. The environmentalist Yu Xiaogang had created the Green Watershed organization after an earlier dam project disturbed the people and ecology of the region. An early tipoff to problems came during the creation of the UNESCO world heritage designation. Chinese officials insisted that the protection should not include the famous Tiger Leaping narrows and further insisted that the protection did not extend below 2000 meters in elevation, in other words protecting only the mountaintops. The UN experts soon learned the reason was to construct dams.[5]

Yu gained favorable publicity from national news organizations, lobbied in Beijing, and brought local people into the process. Most residents are members of the Lisu and Nu minorities. He found support from the State Environmental Protection Administration (SEPA, now renamed the Ministry of Environmental Protection) to oppose National Development and Reform Commission (NDRC, formerly known as the State Planning Commission). Besides concerns with nature, Yu pointed to corruption and the failure to resettle people who lost their homes and farms. Another NGO was Green Earth Volunteers, founded by Wang Yongchen, a woman journalist. Although the PRC does not allow NGOs to have branches, there are many NGOs. Were they to affiliate nationwide like the Sierra Club or Friends of the Earth do in democracies, their coordinated power would be great. Yu, Wang, and others got the attention of Premier Wen Jiabao, who stopped the project first by demanding a comprehensive impact study and then directly suspending the project.[6] However, the forces in favor of the dams appear to be evading the ban by proceeding with construction with one of the dams just upstream of the Nu Prefecture capital of Liuku.

The South-North Water Transfer Project affects many rivers. Its scale is massive, comparable to the Three Gorges Project. Its total cost is estimated at $60 billion. Water will be transferred from the south, which has adequate supplies, to the north, which does not. The idea is attributed to Mao in the 1950s. (Mao gets credit for many good ideas.) In fact, there are three routes, quite independent of each other. In the east, water from the Yangtze will be pumped north in the Grand Canal to a tunnel under the Yellow River, whence it will flow by gravity to Tianjin. Work is nearing completion. Heavy pollution has been a problem because, of course, Tianjin does not want dirty water. The central route transfers water from the Han River north via canals and a tunnel under the Yellow River, whence to Beijing. Work began in 2004 and completion is projected for 2014. Industry and agriculture in Yunnan will have to reduce consumption to provide enough water. Engineers worry that the diversion from the Han River, amounting to a third of its volume, will concentrate the pollution. A remedy may be to divert water from the Three Gorges reservoir. A further problem is that the central route requires resettling 300,000 people. The western route, still in the planning stages, would divert water from the headwaters of the Yangtze to the headwaters of the Yellow River, greatly augmenting the volume, and then at a point downstream, shunt it off to Beijing. Sending water across the Qinghai and Yunnan plateaus and mountains would require expensive tunnels and dams. Even more speculative proposals are to divert water from the headwaters of the Nu River. Nothing has been done on these western routes. Environmentalists object to all three routes in part because the Beijing is not doing much to conserve water. Simply repairing leaks would be the first step.

Although flooding has been a problem since ancient times, cutting down forests upstream makes it worse. In 1998 the Yangtze flooded, leaving 4000 people dead, 150 million homeless, and 13 million houses destroyed. The Yellow and Songhua rivers flooded that same year. Deforestation appeared to be the cause. Top leaders became alarmed. The premier, Zhu Rongji, noted the irony of efforts during the 1950s to harvest trees and the disastrous consequences. The Great Leap Forward was especially destructive to the forests. Zhu Rongji immediately banned cutting most forests and began a program to plant saplings. The government also campaigned against illegal cutting. In addition, the ongoing construction of the Three Gorges dam was seen as a way to control future flooding.

Water pollution is a major problem. Shanghai citizens were shocked recently to find hundreds of dead pigs floating in the Huangpu River. Soon the total reached 16,000. The carcasses had been dumped upstream in the Jiaxing area of Zhejiang province. Evidently, unscrupulous farmers had discarded them because police had started cracking down on the illicit sale of pork products made from diseased pigs who had died.

Statistics demonstrate the larger problem. One report lists 436 of the country's 532 rivers as polluted. The danger is greatest in the north where the climate is arid, hence water volume is low. The contamination comes from industrial waste, chemical fertilizers, and raw sewage. Around 90% of household sewage and a third of industrial wastewater is discharged without treatment. Nearly 80% of the cities have no sewage treatment plants. Pollution of the rivers makes it hard to obtain drinking water. Moreover, wells as a source of drinking water face the problem that 90% of the groundwater is contaminated. Municipalities have tried to provide sewage treatment by requiring that newly constructed buildings have treatment facilities, but this leads to multiple, small, inefficient plants.

Like any other industrial country, most pollution in China is chronic; that is, every day a small (or not so small) amount of fertilizer, chemicals, and household waste flows onto a river or lake. However, other times the pollution comes from a dramatic accident, when a large amount escapes. China is particularly prone to this. One study estimates that it suffers a water emergency every two or three days. (In comparison a Western country might suffer a few a year.) In November 2005 at a plant of the Jilin Petrochemical Corporation in China's northern Jilin Province exploded, resulting in a hundred tons of benzene, aniline, and nitrobenzene flowing into the Songhua River. Downstream it flowed into the Amur River in Russia. In December 2009, 150,000 liters of diesel fuel spilled from a China National Petroleum Corporation pipeline in Shaanxi province, some two-thirds of which flowed into the Wei and Chishui rivers, tributaries of the Yellow River. In July 2001 tributaries of the Huai River overflowed their banks due to heavy rains, picking up 150 billion liters of severely polluted water. Downstream the river was filled with toxic chemicals, sewage and garbage. The contamination endangered 150 million people.[7]

China's biggest river, the Yangtze, is polluted with 40 million tons of industrial and sewage waste. Half of China's 20,000 petrochemical factories lie on its banks. About 40% of all wastewater flows into the river; only 20% is treated beforehand. Fish catches are only 100,000 tons compared to 400,000 tons in the 1950s. More than 600 kilometers of its length and almost 30% of its major tributaries are severely contaminated.

Lake Tai is the third largest freshwater lake in China. Located near Shanghai, it is bordered by the smaller cities of Suzhou, Wuxi, and Yixing that rely on it for drinking water. Nearly 3000 factories producing paper, film, and dyes surround the lake. Nearby farms contribute phosphates. Ironically, Yixing was designated as a "Model City for Environmental Protection." In 2007 an algae bloom of pond scum turned the lake fluorescent green and generated a horrible smell. Its water became unsafe for drinking or bathing.

Throughout China, protecting water from pollution forces SEPA (now the Ministry of Environmental Protection) to balance pressure from industry and municipalities against a few small citizen groups. Pressure to build dams likewise comes from industry and government bodies like the China Power Investment Corporation and the Huadian Corporation. The forces on the side of industry are powerful. Many are big State Owned Enterprises that continue to enjoy government and Party support even after the economic reforms of the past three decades. Other major polluters are the TVEs that also continue to enjoy government and Party support.

Air pollution is the worst in the world. According to a World Bank study, 16 of the 20 worst cities in the world are in China. Air quality in Beijing is 16 times worse than in New York. Airports sometimes have to shut down because of poor visibility. City dwellers virtually never see blue sky. Weather forecasts have a special term for fairly clear days: "White clouds." Yet on such a day in the countryside or even in the suburbs the sky will be blue. At the time of the 2008 Olympics, the Beijing municipal government launched a campaign to minimize the pollution. The athletes needed to breathe, and visitors should not have a bad impression. For several weeks cement, steel, and electric generating plants were shut. Driving was severely limited. For 16 days the air improved. Beijing, however, suffers from a number of natural disadvantages. The region is arid, and dust from the deserts to the west and north blows into the city.

The greatest source of air pollution, however, is the coal that is burned by industry and households. Seventy percent of the country's total energy comes from high-sulfur coal. Most electric generating plants (even new ones) are not efficient, hence, consume more coal than would be the case in advanced countries. Much comes from small mines that do not wash the coal before sending it to the cities for burning. Rapid economic growth leads to extensive construction of buildings and factories, hence the demand for cement is high, and making cement pollutes the air a great deal. The fuel is coal, not burned very efficiently, plus the limestone raw material creates dust that enters the atmosphere. Steel manufacturing pollutes greatly. Building construction and automobiles take a lot of steel. Since the days of Mao, steel has been a favorite of the party, being a symbol of industrialization. This is one more way that the PRC imitated the Soviet Union. At least half of Chinese households use coal briquettes for cooking and heating.

Even though China has vast coal reserves, the country imports more than 200 million metric tons, out of total consumption of 3.2 billion tons. The reason is that foreign coal is cheaper. Most coal comes from Australia and South Africa, but to meet the increasing demand, imports will come from the United States and Columbia. Chinese coal mines are notoriously dangerous. About 6000 miners are killed each year. Several factors contribute to this. First is that only 10% of the operations are strip mining, which is much safer than underground mining. Second is that many mines are small, often owned by TVEs, that are inherently more dangerous. Third is that that safety is poor in many industries, not just mining. Finally, it is financially expedient to neglect safety. Miners earn as little as $150 a month, and the compensation paid to a family in the case of a death ranges from a few hundred dollars to $2,400.[6]

Besides local pollution, coal creates acid rain that travels long distances. Sulfur dioxide from burning coal floats up in the atmosphere where it combines with oxygen to form an acid. Nitrogen oxides from petroleum similarly form acid. This falls out in rain or snow. In cities, the acid leaches away on stone buildings. Damage is worst in the south. Some acid goes high in the atmosphere where it is carried across the sea to fall on Korea and Japan. In addition, low-level pollution of soot, dust, and sulfur also blows over to Korea and Japan.

Automobiles and trucks have become a major source of air pollution. A generation ago, there were scarcely any motor vehicles. The cities were famous for thousands upon thousands of bicycles. There are many buses, usually jammed with riders. Only a few cities have subway trains. Today, there are 170 million motor vehicles, three quarters of them privately owned. Annual production of automobiles is 18 million, surpassing the United States. The People's Republic enacted its first emissions controls on automobiles in 2000 and has raised them several times since. The autos demand a lot of petroleum. China has limited domestic oil reserves, which means it will need to increase imports. Now over half of it is imported, mostly from the Middle East. The PRC is lining up new supplies from Russia, Kazakhstan, and Sudan.

The government has been building modern, long-distance expressways only since 1989. At that time, there were only 147 kilometers in the entire country. As of 2010, there were 74,000 kilometers. Obviously, these highways encourage automobiles and trucks, which increase pollution. Moreover, the expressways dump the traffic onto city streets that are already congested. Virtually, every city has bumper-to-bumper traffic crawling along at every hour of the day.

The Ministry of Railways runs a rail system totaling 86,000 kilometers. It operates 36,000 trains a day. This is the major means of intercity transportation, and helps the environment by avoiding highway travel. In 2007 the government began high-speed rail operations. These sleek trains of eight cars run at 200 kilometers an hour on existing lines. Potentially they will go 350 kilometers an hour on special lines. The government claims credit for this rail initiative as a means of reducing global warming. An even more innovative technology is the Maglev train from downtown Shanghai to the airport. The trains travel 30 kilometers in 7 minutes, with a top speed of 430 kilometers an hour. The cars are suspended without wheels by magnetism.

Global Warming: In 2005 China surpassed the United States to become the world's largest emitter of greenhouse gases, but details are elusive because China has kept its statistics secret since 2002. Under the Kyoto Protocol, it has no obligation to limit its emissions because it is considered an underdeveloped country, therefore exempted. China got this privileged status for the first time at the 1988 World Conference on the Changing Atmosphere in Toronto that set forth the initial ideas about how to control global warming, then had it reinforced in the Rio Earth Summit in 1992 when it was not listed as an industrial country subject to control, and had it confirmed at Kyoto in 1997. In addition to China, more than 130 developing countries are exempt. Moreover, they are supposedly entitled to financial aid to help them reduce their emissions, another concept first proposed at Toronto, and confirmed at Kyoto. In contrast to China, they emit far lower amounts of greenhouse gases. Their combined total is only about 23% of the world total, less than either China or the United States.

In preparation for the Earth Summit in Rio, China sought a leadership role among the underdeveloped countries. At a meeting of Third World environmental ministers that it hosted in Beijing, it promoted a unified stance. The ministers called for international cooperation but insisted on the right of the developing countries to industrialize and the need for money from the First World. China participated in the preliminary negotiations for the eventual Framework Convention held at the UN headquarters in New York in the months preceding the Rio Summit. Its spokesmen argued that it would be unfair to impose restrictions on China, when Western countries had been polluting the atmosphere for more than a century, and China had only recently become a significant offender. "It's not good enough to calculate total emissions of a year, but for the last 200 years. ... If you calculate the emissions for 200 years, China's concentration is very small."[8] Chinese Premier Li Ping traveled to Rio de Janeiro, where he stressed the right and need of the underdeveloped countries to pursue economic growth. With the exception of the United States, nearly all the industrial countries were eager to exempt the Third World, and to promise them money.

In preparation for the Kyoto Conference, China cooperated with the Group of 77, the block of 77 developing countries. Although the concept of these countries being exempt from limits was proposed in Toronto and affirmed in Rio and in annual negotiations, the PRC wanted to be sure that is was reaffirmed at Kyoto. While the Rio Convention had given many privileges to underdeveloped countries, these were not necessarily blanket exemptions and indeed could be interpreted as providing several categories of graduated responsibility. The Chinese goal at Kyoto was to ensure total exemption from emissions limits and to garner foreign aid funds.

Premier Li Peng argued that restrictions on developing nations would be unfair because the industrial countries had had more than a century during which they had built up the carbon dioxide in the atmosphere. "Those who are overweight need to be on a diet, while those who are undernourished need more nutrition," Li said.[10] The head of the Chinese delegation, Chen Yaobang, told the convention that his country could not undertake emissions limitations until it reached the level of a medium-developed country, estimated to take 50 years. He criticized the industrial countries for failing to meet their emissions targets and for shirking their responsibilities by means of carbon trading and joint implementation. By the end of the conference, China had gotten its way. The developing countries, including China, were still exempt and still entitled to financial aid.

The Chinese government asserts that it is greatly improving its energy efficiency, using less fuel to produce the same output. The Chinese Energy Research Institute claimed energy use was increasing only half as fast as the total economy. It further pointed out that the country consumed only one-tenth as much per capita as the United States. Yet analysis by the

International Energy Agency refuted these optimistic claims, arguing that Chinese statistics were inaccurate. A further justification has been that hydro projects like the Three Gorges dam have no emissions. Pointing to per capita emissions is a common argument visitors hear.

The consensus (at least of the Europeans) in favor of the Kyoto Protocol eroded in the decade after Kyoto. In the United States, President Bush frequently denounced the Chinese exemption. The Europeans were not so outspoken but grew less enthusiastic about the protocol as its burdens became more apparent. Furthermore, during this period the Chinese economy grew rapidly and so did its level of greenhouse gas emissions. It burgeoned from a moderate emitter in 1988 at the time of the Toronto conference to the biggest emitter. At the annual conference of the parties at Copenhagen in 2009, China took an active role in removing specific targets and accused the United States, Germany, and the industrial countries of bullying the developing countries. Most observers considered it was China that tried to domineer the session. The motive appeared to be that the PRC feared that within a few years it would be considered ripe for limits. The top leaders of the world were at Copenhagen: President Obama, Chancellor Angela Merkel of Germany, President Nicolas Sarkozy of France, and Prime Minister Gordon Brown of the United Kingdom. Premier Wen Jiabao led the Chinese delegation. As negotiations got more difficult, Wen Jiabao refused to participate and withdrew to his hotel room. The conference ended in disarray.

Birth Control: China is well aware that its huge population figures are bad. This is not just an environmental concern but also an economic one. Since the Communists came to power in 1949, their policies have shifted several times. At first, Mao Zedong favored a large population. The Communists had needed manpower for their army and still feared a counterattack by the Nationalists. The decade of warfare with the Japanese was fresh on their minds. In 1952, the country was short of food, with many dying. Mao rejected the idea that the cause was too many people. He wrote that:

> It is a good thing that China has a large population. Even if China's population multiplies many times, she is fully capable of finding a solution: the solution is production. The absurd argument of western bourgeois economists, like Malthus, that increase of population cannot keep pace with increase in production was not only thoroughly refuted in theory by Marxists long ago, but has also been completely exploded by the realities in the Soviet Union and the Liberated areas of China after their revolutions.[10]

This policy shifted in 1955 when the Communist Party announced that "reproduction be appropriately restricted." The purposes were to improve maternal health and provide for education. The effort was ineffective because of lack of contraceptives and squeamishness of the party cadres to discuss sexual behavior. As the Communists consolidated power, however, population control seemed a more appropriate function of the government. Over a million people were resettled in Inner Mongolia and the northern and western frontiers in order both to strengthen their defense against the Soviet Union and to relieve crowding in the east. The growth of the cities was getting out of control. In 3 years, 840,000 people moved into Shanghai. In 1957 Mao Zedong announced a 10-year program for family planning.[11] Almost at once, the policy got lost with Mao's Great Leap Forward. According to official propaganda, agricultural and industrial productivity would solve the problem of poverty. At the same time, China still felt threatened militarily. The Soviets withdrew their friendship and ended economic aid. Tibet began an armed revolt, border warfare began with India, and the Nationalists seemed to threaten an invasion. The Chinese leaders feared that the United States and the Soviet Union would begin a suicidal nuclear war. A larger population seemed to offer at least some protection.

By 1963 the birth control program was back on track. The Great Leap Forward proved a great disaster, an estimated 30 million died, and the military threats passed. Food was scarce, and deaths exceeded births in at least one year. From 1966 to 1969, China suffered another convulsion of Communist direction with its Cultural Revolution. Mao Zedong decided that the country had lost its Marxist zeal and had fallen into bourgeois error. One remedy was to order professional cadres from the cities to move to rural areas where they could be reeducated. This was also a way to remove Red Guards, often out of control, from the cities. Millions were sent to the countryside. Part of the rejection of urban expertise was to create thousands of "barefoot doctors," who were supposed to care for the medical ailments in spite of having few professional qualifications. While overall the Cultural Revolution was another disaster, it did expose the urban experts to the poverty and backwardness of the countryside. Moreover, the barefoot doctors were ideal for the low-level medical functions of running a birth control program.

China's return to normalcy after the Cultural Revolution saw renewed concern about population size. It no longer seemed so vulnerable militarily, and its growth rate was an astounding 2.5% a year. The Fourth

Five-Year Plan called for an urban growth rate of 1% by 1975. The Fifth Five Year Plan continued the 1% rate and projected a reduction to 0.5% by 1985, and a zero rate by the end of the century. The methods were to be delayed marriages, greater space between children, and fewer children overall. Its slogan was "One is good, two is all right and three is too many." Contraceptives were now to be distributed free, and women could get free hospital care for abortions, IUD insertions, and sterilizations. Propaganda attacked the Confucian beliefs about fertility, including the preference for sons.[13]

By the end of the 1970s, the policy was working. The birthrate had declined from 34 per thousand to 18 per thousand.[13] However, this was not enough. Because of the baby boom of the 1950s, more young women were of childbearing age. The total numbers were going up sharply. The only solution was one-child families. This required both positive and negative incentives. First, a couple who wanted to have a child needed to get permission. The rewards for complying were a monthly subsidy, priority in housing, free medical care, maternity leave, exemption from tuition, and additional vacation. Those who did not register their marriages or had a baby without permission, or had too many babies did not get these benefits and had to pay a fine.

The one-child policy was unpopular, particularly in rural areas. Parents wanted more than one, and they especially wanted sons. For a peasant, a son has a duty to care for his old parents, whereas a daughter does not. The country did not have old-age pensions or health insurance. One consequence of the one-child policy was, of course, abortion, but when that did not occur, another option was to kill the unwanted babies. A second or third child might be smothered at birth or drowned in a pond. In cities, obstetricians would give the mother an injection that would cause a stillbirth. Hospitals were penalized if unauthorized babies were born. Because of the desire to have sons, parents might kill their baby daughters. This is, however, against the official government policy.[14] Because the government will make an exception and permit a second birth when the first child is deformed, some parents maimed their daughters. The only child, the product of this policy, ended up smothered in attention from by his parents and grandparents. If he were a boy, he gained the nickname of the Little Emperor. More sympathetic observers concluded these only children were thriving from the love of their families.

In recent years, the government has eased its program slightly in response to domestic and foreign opposition. A few localities, mostly rural, have permitted a second child, but this did not have the official sanction of Beijing. Couples having a second baby have to pay a fine, but some places the cost is not high, so they are willing to pay. Because parents have tested the sex of their fetuses in the uterus with ultrasound or chromosome tests in order to ensure a boy, that practice has been made illegal. Ethnic minorities, who comprise 8% of the population, are not supposed to be subject to the limits on the numbers of children. But in fact, the government often demands that they use IUDs and abortions. In answer to foreign criticism, the government has soft-pedaled its programs, denying that quotas are rigid or that women are forced to abort or be sterilized. Few critics accept these protestations. The Tenth Five-Year Plan, which was forced to revise the population projection upward to 1.33 billion as of 2005, reiterated the one-child policy. Popular discontent surfaced. In 2007, 3000 people rioted in Guangxi Province. Then in 2010, Shanghai announced it would tolerate a second child in some cases. Everyone waited for the Beijing government to crack down, but this did not happen. Observers speculated that the top leaders were becoming worried about the graying of the population. There would not be enough young workers to support the old retired people.

Recent Trends: Popular demonstrations against environmental accidents have occurred rarely. In Chengdu in 2008, 200 people marched to protest a petrochemical plant. The police did not intervene. In Haining in 2011, a 4-day protest of 500 against a solar panel factory was not so peaceful, when riot police fired tear gas and clubbed the people. Protesters had invaded the factory and overturned vehicles. The toxic effluents poisoned fish, and the factory had been ordered to clean up months before, but had not done so. A few months later in Haimen in Guangdong province people demonstrated against construction of a coal-fired electric generating plant that was one more case of polluting the air and water and seizing land illegally. Echoing scenes from the Cultural Revolution two arrested protesters were put on television to confess. One prisoner said, "It was wrong to surround the government and block the highway." The other said, "I did not know the law."[15] Other times the environmental demonstrations have succeeded. In 2011 in Dalian tens of thousands of citizens rallied against a paraxylene plant, and the city government promised to halt operation. Four years earlier demonstrations against a similar paraxylene plant in Fujian province had also halted operation.[16]

Analysts use the term "mass incident" as a neutral description for the phenomenon. Yu Jianrong of the Chinese Academy of Social Sciences has counted over 87,000 per year. Most are small, but occasionally more than a thousand people demonstrate. Only a few are environmental. Many stem from police brutality. Yu points to encroachment of the interests of rising middle class in the name of economic development projects as the cause. Land grabs and corruption are typical targets. He believes the mass incidents have gained publicity and support due to easier communications with the Internet.[17] His numbers show a 10-fold increase in the past decade. Evidence of ordinary people joining environmental protests as a safe means of opposing the government, as in Russia and Eastern Europe, seems slight.

Extreme air pollution in Beijing in January 2013 attracted global attention. The Air Quality Index hit 755. A reading above 100 is considered "unhealthy for sensitive groups" and anything above 400 is rated "hazardous" for everyone. The index does not even go above 500 normally.[19] The municipality ordered factories closed and automobiles off the road, but it was not enough. Other cities in the north faced similar pollution. Top party officials could not ignore the crisis. A common explanation of Chinese politics is that the middle class will accept bad government, corruption, and secrecy as long as the prosperity continues; the economic boom has lasted three decades. But this was too much. Tens of thousands complained on the Internet and Twitter. A few newspapers even wrote editorials criticizing the party. In response, Xi Jinping, who became party general secretary two months before, allowed the state news media to run in-depth reports on the air pollution crisis.[19]

CONCLUSION

Participation by ordinary citizens is slight in China. Voting is not a means since there are no free elections. Public marches and rallies are extremely rare and small, and few are to protect the environment. The exceptions are only a handful: 200 people marched in Chengdu, 500 protested in Haining, and a few thousand demonstrated in Dalian. Protesting against seizing land and houses for real estate development is much more common.

Interest groups are numerous but small, and the prohibition on branches and the requirement for government sponsorship greatly limits their strength. They do not influence legislation and policy the way groups in the West do. At some future time, their multitude may enable them to burst forth. International groups like WWF and the Nature Conservancy are present, but likewise they are restricted by the requirements for government sponsorship and the prohibition of branches.

Because the Communist Party runs everything, its ideology of materialism continues to dominate. Only a few cracks have appeared in the monolith as top leaders have acknowledged the popular concern with air pollution or dirty water.

The extreme authoritarianism of the government means the official legislature, the People's Congress, rubber stamps the direction of the party. Yet environmental issues have been one of the rare areas where dissent breaks forth, such as the vote on the Three Gorges Dam. Since the 1980s the People's Congress has enacted laws and constitutional provisions giving the formal forms of protection. The creation of the Ministry of Environmental Protection and its predecessor agencies has created a bureaucracy that pushes that direction. On the other hand, the continued power of State Owned Enterprises frequently overrules protection in individual cases.

After 1949 the People's Republic was diplomatically isolated for two or three decades. Although it did attend the Stockholm Summit, the conference did not become an avenue to bring in environmental ideas the way it was for other developing countries. Leading up to the 1992 Framework Convention on Climate Change, China suddenly became engaged, coordinating closely with the Group of 77 developing countries to advocate that they should not be subject to restrictions on greenhouse gas emissions. Their arguments that they did not emit much, and that they deserved time to catch up with the industrial countries, seemed more disingenuous with each passing year as Chinese economic growth and gas emissions grew. In 2006 the People's Republic surpassed the United States in carbon dioxide emissions. Nevertheless, the industrial countries acquiesced and did not impose quotas on China, yet its claim for privilege became meaningless as the entire Kyoto program dissolved around that time.

Although the impact of the environmental movement was slow and fitful, China did absorb some ideas. It put provisions in its constitution and laws and established agencies. More recently, ordinary citizens have become aware of programs in other countries as they confront contaminated rivers and dirty air. One of the most notable gifts from China to the world dates back centuries as the Europeans imitated the scholar's garden. More recently, China assumed strong leadership of the Group of 77 on the issue of global warming.

NOTES

1. Karl Wittfogel, 1926, Das erwachende China: Ein Abriss der Geschichte der gegenwartigen Probleme Chinas. He is best known in English for *Oriental Despotism* 1957.
2. Vaclav Smil, *China's Environmental Crisis* (Armonk, N.Y.: M. E. Sharpe, 1993), pp. 15, 17.
3. Gorlid Heggelund, *Environment and Resettlement Politics in China: The Three Gorges Project* (Aldershop, U.K.: Ashgate, 2004), p. 32.
4. Guobin Yang, "Environmental NGOs and Institutional Dynamics in China," *China Quarterly*, 2005, No. 181, pp. 46–66.
5. Andrew C. Mertha, *China's Water Warriors: Citizen Action and Policy Change* (Ithaca, N.Y.: Cornell UP, 2008), p. 116.
6. Mertha, *China's Water Warriors*, p. 122.
7. Elizabeth C. Economy, *The River Runs Black* (Ithaca, N.Y.: Cornell UP, 2004), pp. 1–8.
8. Sheryl Wu Dunn, "The Road to Rio," *New York Times*, May 25, 1992.
9. Asher Bolande, "China," Agence France Presse, November 27, 1997.
10. Quoted in Penny Kane, *The Second Billion: Population and Family Planning in China* (Ringwood, Victoria, Australia: Penguin Books, 1987), p. 58.
11. Kane, *The Second Billion*, p. 70.
12. Kane, *The Second Billion*, pp. 78–79.
13. Kane, *The Second Billion*, pp. 86–87.
14. John S. Aird, *Slaughter of the Innocents: Coercive Birth Control in China* (Washington, D.C.: AEI Press, 1990), pp. 93–94.
15. "Teargas Fired at Chinese Protesters in Haimen," *Guardian*, UK, Dec. 23, 2011.
16. Sui-Lee Wee, "China Says It Will Shut Plant as Thousands Protest," *Reuters*, August 14, 2011.
17. Justine Zheng Ren, "Mass Incidents in China" *East Asia Forum*, July 13, 2011.
18. T. P., "Beijing's Air Pollution Blackest Day," *The Economist*, Jan. 14, 2013.
19. Edward Wong, "In China, Widening Discontent among the Communist Party Faithful," *New York Times*, Jan. 19, 2013.

Index